Heaton Village, seen from Heaton Reservoir on 3 May 1958.   (Copyright: author)

HEATON

the best place of all

A history of Heaton in Bradford Dale

by

John Stanley King

Published by:
Bradford Arts, Museums and Libraries
Central Library
Prince's Way
BRADFORD
West Yorkshire
BD1 1NN

ISBN: 0 907734 59 6

Printed by:
The Amadeus Press, Cleckheaton
Graphic Layout:
Highlight Type Bureau Ltd., Bradford

"I have considered the days of old
and the years that are past."
                    (Psalm 77, v.5)

" . . . though for no other cause,
yet for this, that posterity may know
we have not loosely through silence
permitted things to pass away."
                    (George G. Hopkinson,
                        "Heaton Review," 1934)

Let us pay a tribute to Heaton, before memories fade or interest wanes.
Let us recall and record the tranquil days of the old village life –
    dusty highways and crooked snickets,
    plain cottages, trim terraces and sumptuous villas,
    clatter of early-morning clogs and clank of milk-pails,
    daily doings of housewives at coal-oven or mangle,
    long hours of Double Summer Time,
    lamplighters on their rounds,
    leisurely dialect of village folk and chatter of children at play,
    lowing of beasts in the slaughterhouse as well as the call of cuckoos,
    rumble of tramcars and distant shriek of railway trains,
    clip-clop of horses drawing carts and carriages,
    quiet religious life – and homely taverns,
    sights, scents and sounds of hayfields and pastures,
    murmur of becks in the deep woods,
    contrasts of frugality and opulence, parsimony and generosity,
    brown stone roofs and white hawthorn blossom,
    click of handloom and swish of scouring-stone,
    thoughtful men and women who have patiently gleaned old
    memories of bygone days and kept them for future generations.

Contents

	Author's Foreword	7
Chapter 1	Old Law	11
Chapter 2	Feudal Folk	15
Chapter 3	Reformation	27
Chapter 4	Civil War, Restoration and Toleration	39
Chapter 5	Land Tax	46
Chapter 6	Heaton on the Hill	47
Chapter 7	Turnpikes	55
Chapter 8	The Squire	60
Chapter 9	Inclosure	64
Chapter 10	Rural Heyday	68
Chapter 11	Census, Taxes and War	72
Chapter 12	Life at the Hall	76
Chapter 13	Industry and Welfare	86
Chapter 14	1851 Census	94
Chapter 15	Crime and Constables	98
Chapter 16	The Age of Improvement	109
Chapter 17	Boardroom and Borough	119
Chapter 18	Characters and Pranksters	144
Chapter 19	Desirable Suburb	151
Chapter 20	A Changing World	163
Chapter 21	A New Identity	178
Appendix 1	Heaton Speech	182
Appendix 2	The Origin of Heaton Place Names	185
Appendix 3	Sources Consulted	190

Author's Foreword

I acknowledge with immense gratitude the help and encouragement I have received for more than half a century in my pursuit of Heaton's history.

Particular thanks are due to my childhood friend Brian Whitaker, son of the Baptist minister, who in 1944 first alerted me to the existence of local history; to my mother, Mrs F. L. King (1902-1994) for her long memory and invaluable experience of Heaton matters; Messrs. Arnold Pickles and F. Denis Richardson for their keen observations of Heaton life; the Rt. Hon. the Earl of Rosse for the generous use of his archives and kind hospitality at Birr Castle; Messrs. Greaves, Hutchinson and Messrs. Vint, Hill and Killick, solicitors; Messrs. Wheater Smith, A. T. Smith and Redford, land agents and surveyors; Mrs. Vera Scott, Messrs. Norman Stewart, Ted Greenwood, Arthur Bulcock, Kenneth Rook and Wilfred Robertshaw, M.A., Alderman Horace Hird, F.S.A., Bradford Libraries, Bradford Industrial Museum, Bradford Corporation and Bradford Metropolitan Council, West Yorkshire Archives at Bradford, Huddersfield and Wakefield, the "Telegraph and Argus" and "Keighley News", St. Barnabas' Church, Heaton Baptist Church, "The Parish Chest" by W. E. Tate and that great company of people – "Heaton fowk" – to whom this book is gratefully dedicated.

I owe a great debt to Mr. and Mrs. W. E. Wakefield for their word processing skills and to Messrs. John Triffitt and Bob Duckett of Bradford Libraries for accepting and publishing this book.

It needs to be stressed that the term "Heaton" as used in this book relates exclusively to the historic township which led a separate existence until its absorption into Bradford in 1882, rather than to the present-day Heaton Ward which has somewhat different boundaries, and only minimally to the vague "Heaton" of newspaper reports and estate agents' advertisements.

John Stanley King,

Heaton, September, 2000.

Heaton Village seen from North Hall (at the top of present day Roydscliffe Road) on 2 October, 1965.   *(Copyright: author)*

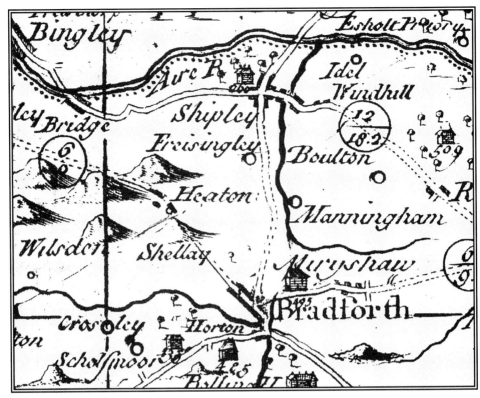

Warburton's 1720 map.

Bowen's 1750 map.

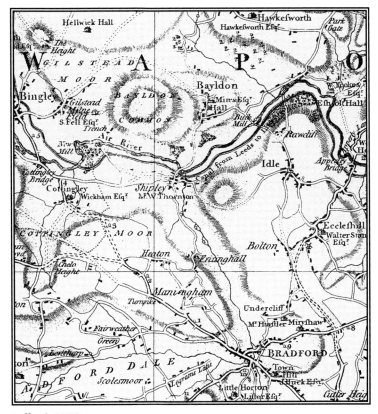

Jeffrey's 1775 map.

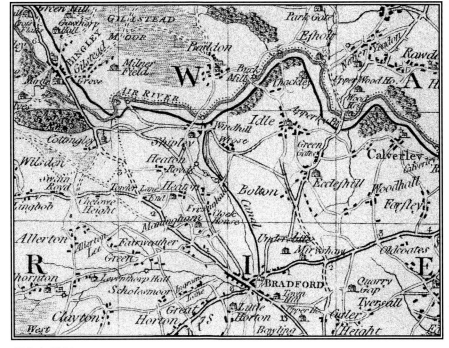

Tuke's 1816 map.

Chapter 1   –   Old Law

"When all ye fowk are as owd as me
Ah'm pretty sure that you'll agree
If ther's one thing that maks it hard to dee
It's thowts o'leaving Heaton."

(Arnold Pickles, 1934)

"Heaton should be a happy place,
seeing that it contains both Paradise and Eden."

(William Cudworth, 1876)

"Aloft on a hilltop by Bradford's fair dale,
Caressed by the breezes and swept by the gale,
Stands Heaton's high township, renowned far and wide,
Where true Yorkshire ladies and menfolk abide."

(Author, 1990)

What is this corner of Yorkshire that can inspire such expressions of affection? Is it a spectacularly picturesque and world-famous village, the birthplace of renowned men and women, and does its fame attract ardent pilgrims from all parts of the world?

Hardly. As one of the many suburbs of the modern Metropolitan City of Bradford, it is traversed daily by hordes of uncaring commuters who, hastening to workplace, home or distant motorways, sweep by with scarcely a glance. But often, to those who know it, it becomes a treasured gathering of homely dwellings, populous housing estates, rustling woodlands, busy streets and rural vistas - thronging schools as well as tinkling becks. It casts an indefinable spell, never wholly to be shaken off.

The pre-history of Heaton will always remain debatable, and must be deduced from trends and events involving a much wider area as well as from the scanty archaeological remains that have survived the pick, the plough and two centuries of intensive stone-quarrying. Long-forgotten tribes, bands of warriors and wandering family groups in search of a permanent abode must have passed this way. Wolves, wild boars, fierce cats and other less imaginable creatures will have haunted the primaeval woodlands, which once mantled the landscape, but they left no trace.

At one period ice covered the hills and dales up to a height of 1,000 feet, so that even the highest point of Heaton township was concealed beneath a glacier. With the gradual warming of the climate the Aire glacier retreated to the valley and rainfall created lakes which overflowed across the hilltops. In this way overflow channels were carved out between "Lake Cottingley" and "Lake Bradford" by way of the Northcliffe Woods, Chellow Dene, Noon Nick, Miles Rough and Duck Syke ravines.

Early inhabitants of the island of Britain tended to shun low-lying areas where their modest settlements could be overwhelmed by sudden floods or hostile warriors. Heaton and Chellow on their elevated hilltops may have attracted settlers who believed that safety and survival depended upon isolation and extensive views of an unfriendly terrain.

Thus it was that the highest summit in Heaton township, Old Law Field at Chellow Heights, was the scene of the only significant archaeological discovery in the area. When preliminary excavations for the Chellow Heights water filtration plant were being carried out in June, 1921, a mound known since the Boer war as Spion Kop yielded a few bones and pottery fragments which were set aside by an observant quarryman. On examination Dr. Hambley Rowe found that there were three cremation urns and a food cup, the urns being about 10 to 14 inches high. Sir Arthur Keith analysed the bones as those of a young girl who had lived in the mid - Bronze Age, about 1500 - 1000 BC, when her sorrowing family laid the remains to rest at the nearest point to the windswept heavens.

Pre-history ended in A.D.71 when the Romans occupied the North at the invitation of Cartimandua, Queen of the Brigantian tribe of Celts who had settled in the area. Within a few generations a network of military roads linked headquarters, camps and villas constructed by the invaders, the most famous local example being the Roman highway from Manchester to Ilkley which strode across Harden Moor.

Did a Roman road pass through Heaton? Archaeologists have traced parts of a road from Ribchester (Lancashire) in the Ribble Valley, through the Aire Valley to Elslack near Skipton and thence towards Pontefract by way of the western edge of Airedale to Keighley, Long Lee, Harden, Lee Lane, Noon Nick, Heaton High Moor, Toller Lane, Whetley Causeway, Wakefield Road, Tong Street, Westgate Hill Street and Drighlington.

The road was depicted on all maps prior to Teesdale (1828); fragments indicated its width as 17'0", and parts fell into disuse when turnpikes were established. As late as 1876 the Harden section was remembered as having been a packhorse route, but the theory of its Roman origins were reinforced by excavations carried out by Bradford Grammar School in 1975..

Supporting evidence in the form of coins has been unearthed near the supposed Heaton section of the road. A tetradrachma of the Emperor Diocletian (284-305) was dug up in Highfield Crescent in 1948, while in 1978 the garden of 26, Duchy Avenue, yielded a "third brass" of the Emperor Valens (364-378); the Emperor's head is shown on one side and the figure of Victory on the other - unfortunately victory eluded Valens at Adrianople when he was trapped and burnt to death by the Goths. Frizinghall, too, had a Roman visitor: a denarius of Elagobalus (218-222) was found in Park Grove on August 9th, 1911.

Also, the significant name of "Street Close" was applied to a small pasture alongside Toller Lane, although the land could not have acquired its name until a thousand years after the measured tramp of soldiers' feet and the distant blare of trumpets had faded into the twilight of Imperial Rome.

Urgently summoned to defend their embattled homeland, the final departure of the Roman armies around 410 A.D. left Britain unguarded against marauding Picts and Scots, and the way lay open for the westward expansion of English settlers imported from North-West Europe by the later Caesars to guard the east coast - the " Saxon shore". Gradually the Angles and their close cousins the Frisians absorbed the resident British tribes or caused them to flee beyond the Pennines to the Lakeland fells, so that after the year 616 English-speaking families and groups were free to advance up the Aire Valley. Their arrival was gradual and, regrettably, unchronicled, but some assumptions are possible. Although an Anglo-Saxon cemetery has been discovered at Addingham, Anglo-Saxon literature records no Yorkshire town or village west of Ripon or Leeds, and the only safe conclusion to be drawn is that if early settlements existed in the Pennine foothills, their inhabitants did nothing to attract historical notice.

Some of the settlers must have turned aside into the valley later known as "Bradford Dale" where, on the banks of the rushing "broc" they set up their homes. Linguistic evidence suggests that their earliest settlements may have been established by the followers and family of Maena at Maena-inga-ham and by a group of their Frisian relations at Frisa-inga-halh and Frisa-inga-ley.

Later, perhaps feeling a need for protection against marauders sweeping down from the surrounding heights, they set up an outpost just below the brow of the nearest hilltop, which they naturally named Heah-tun, the high farmstead. A more adventurous settler named Ceol built a home adjoining the old Neolithic burial mound, which thus became known as Ceoles-hlaw and which provided wide views over the wild moors and thickly-wooded dales.

Other "tuns" - Bodeltun, Alretun, Thorentun, Claitun and Hortun - soon extended in a southwesterly arc across the high ground, while in the broader reaches of the dale where the "broc" could usually be crossed in safety, dwellings grew up "aet bradum forde". All these settlements, which subsequently developed into mediaeval townships or hamlets, were set at a respectable distance from each other, with sufficient land for agriculture and grazing, and all had plentiful sources of timber and water.

Slowly the hand of man began to transform the landscape. The ancient woodlands yielded to the axe as men struggled to hew clearings or "royds" for their ploughlands and pastures. Domestic animals gradually superseded the dangerous boars and wolves which had lurked in the forests, and eventually it was safe to loose swine in the wooded ravine adjoining Chellow. There they could root in peace for nuts and delicacies without spoiling the hard-won meadows. The very name of Chellow Dene recalls the days when the pig - the most valuable animal in the rural economy of England - was a regular occupant of that peaceful glade.

In the ninth and tenth centuries Danish warriors from the east and Norse Vikings from the west seized control of Northumbria; in Bradford dale the swirls and eddies of their violent conflicts can be deduced from faint traces of Scandinavian influence on local placenames such as Gaisby and Leaventhorpe and, in Heaton, the substitution of "Birks" and "Kirk" for the older forms, "birch" and "church". The Danes and Norsemen, like their English kinsmen, were basically farmers who, when not "away at the wars", wrested a precarious living from the unwilling soil.

Self sufficient with their pastures and ploughlands, the moorland flocks and herds watched over by cowherd, shepherd and goose-girl, pigs in the thicket guarded by the swineherd and yoked oxen in the furrows urged on by the ploughman, the wattle-hutted farmsteads supervised by the "gerefa" and his "hlaford" lived out an obscure and unchronicled existence until the conquest of England by William, Duke of Normandy, in October, 1066.

GLOSSARY

Anglo-Saxon "straet", Latin "strata". Mediaeval Toller Lane qualified as "the King's highstreet" or highway.

Broc (Anglo-Saxon) - brook, later superseded in Bradford Dale by the Scandinavian "beck".

Maena-inga-ham (Manningham) - the settlement of the family and followers of Maena.

Frisinga-halh and Frisinga-ley (Frizinghall and Frizingley) - the settlement and meadow of the family and followers of the (unnamed) Frisian."Frising" was pronounced to rhyme with "fizzing"; "Frizingley", likewise Frizington in Cumberland, has always been spoken of as though it were spelt "Frizzingley", whereas the modern pronunciation of "Fryzinghall" probably dates from the 1870s when newcomers ("off-comed `uns") settled in the area in large numbers and imposed their own version of the ancient name.

Heah-tun (Anglo-Saxon, the high town) – the original pronunciation of "Hee–a-ton" survived until the death in 1968 of Ted Greenwood of Parkside Farm.

Bodeltun (pr. Botheltoon) – Bolton, the "bothy" (hutted) town.

Alretun (A!lerton) – the town among the alders, and Torentun (Thornton) among the thorn trees.

Claitun (Clayton) the town on the clay soil.

Hortun (Horton) – apparently the "filthy town".

Aet bradum forde (Bradford) – the place at the broad ford.

Royd (Anglo-Saxon rod, pronounced by Yorkshiremen as "roa-id" in the same way that "coat" became "coa-it".)

Dene (Anglo-Saxon denu), a narrow valley.

Northumbria (Anglo-Saxon Northanhymbrelond), the land north of the Humber.

Gerefa (Anglo-Saxon) – modern English "reeve", locally "grave", German "graf".

Hlaford (Anglo-Saxon), lord, literally "loaf-giver" or benefactor.

Ceoles-hlaw (Chellow) – Anglo-Saxon for "a low hill" (c.f., The Lawe at South Shields and the Sidlaws in Angus-shire). The name "Old Law Field" was recorded as late as the reign of James I, and is identifiable with the later Birks Close.

Chapter 2 — Feudal Folk

The Domesday Book, compiled with remorseless thoroughness twenty years after the Norman Conquest, reveals that by the reign of King Edward the Confessor (1042 – 1066) the mighty Northumbrian shire of York with its three Ridings extending from sea to sea had developed into an organised territory divided into landed estates which comprised towns, villages, hamlets, farmlands, waste and woods. The status of Chellow and its neighbours was briefly revealed in the pages of Domesday: -

"MANOR   In Bodeltone Archil had four carucates of land for geld, where there may be two ploughs. Ilbert has it, and it is waste. In King Edward's time it was worth ten shillings. To this manor belongs this land: Celeslau, Alretone, Torentone, Claitone, Wibetese (Wibsey). Together, for purposes of geld, ten carucates of land where there may be six ploughs. It is waste. In King Edward's time it was worth forty shillings."

Shaped like a horse-shoe, the Bolton estate, called a "manor" by the Normans but probably a "lordship" by Archil the Englishman, was so elongated that it crossed the Bradford Beck twice as it undulated over hill and dale from the edge of Eccleshill Moor to the head of the Spen valley. Heaton and Frizinghall must have formed part of the estate, otherwise Bolton would have been physically separated from Chellow and the more southerly settlements; presumably they were mere hamlets dependent on Chellow, a role destined to be reversed in later centuries.

The straggling Bolton estate could not have been managed as one unit, and had therefore

Part of Chellow Grange – a collection of buildings of various dates erected on the site of the ancient settlement listed in the Domesday book of 1086 and photographed by the author on 19 July 1972.

been subdivided into convenient agricultural and administrative areas or "townships" based on the principal farms. The area centred upon the Chellow farmstead extended from the Chellow valley west of the farmstead to the bottom of the dale at Frizinghall where the Bolton "home farm" began. None of these settlements contained permanent buildings; all comprised huts, "booths" and "shielings" which were easily constructed and just as easily destroyed if the wattle or thatch caught fire.

As stated above, Archil had previously owned four carucates or ploughlands in Bolton and a total of ten in the other five settlements, possibly two in each. A carucate - a Norman-French word derived from the Latin "caruca", a plough - denoted as much land as a plough could till in a season, and presumably Chellow, Heaton and Frizinghall contained between 100 and 200 acres of arable land in addition to pasture, wood and the moorland wastes.

The stark discrepancy between the taxable (geld) value of the ploughlands before the Conquest and their description as worthless waste twenty years later is explained by the appalling "Harrying of the North" in 1069, the year in which William the Conqueror learned that Northern armies had gathered in York to shake off his rule, and would oppose him if he came North.

Nevertheless come North he did, crushing the rising with systematic and ruthless efficiency. York and its minster were sacked and plundered, and the pages of Domesday bear a silent but eloquent testimony to the devastation that followed. William remained six months in the North while his army ranged far and wide, from south to north, apparently in two detachments returning via Craven and the lands beyond the Pennines, pausing only to push up the side valleys to burn dwellings and crops and put the inhabitants to the sword. Much of this dark work took place in the depths of winter. Chroniclers avowed (with some exaggeration, one assumes) that every man and boy in Yorkshire was slain, and Simeon of Durham wrote that the survivors had to subsist on rats and other vermin. Herr Hitler would have approved, but King Herod was merciful in comparison.

Whether Archil, the English lord, perished in the slaughter is not known, but his lands were seized and presented by William to his close colleague Ilbert de Lacy of Lassi in Calvados, Brittany, whose new feudal barony or "honour" based on Pontefract was so large that it filled seven pages of Domesday.

When Ilbert took possession or "seisin" of his landed booty he carefully parcelled it out among trusted tenants by the process of subinfeudation, i.e., a chain of allegiances binding tenant, sub-tenant, villein and serf to himself as the Chief Lord of the Honour, with a specific obligation to provide or pay for the services of a stated number of "knights" (Anglo Saxon cniht, an armed and mounted soldier) in time of need. The cost of maintaining the "knights" had to be spread over a number of manors which were then valued as being worth (for instance) "one quarter of a Knight's Fee."

Much of Ilbert's new fief was worthless and desolate; the bright pastures and hard-won ploughlands had reverted to waste. Nevertheless human life began to creep back from the woods and wildernesses to which it had fled. The few survivors must have been sufficiently acquainted with the area to recall the names of the settlement and the size and value of their farmlands "on the day that King Edward was alive and dead."

Chellow, Heaton and Frizinghall arose from the ashes, separated now from Bolton not only by "the water that runneth by Bradford" but also by a new boundary dividing the large parish of Bradford from that of Calverley. The organised structure of the hamlets and their ability to pay dues to the lord had been destroyed and would have to be rebuilt as the humble churls and cottars began to scratch a living with plough and ox, axe and spade, scythe and flail.

The first post-Conquest lord of Chellow, Heaton and Frizinghall appears to have been Asolf (Aswulf ?), possibly an Englishman whom Ilbert de Lacy had cause to trust, and who was succeeded by his son Peter and grandson Adam. The latter, usually known as Adam of (de) Birkin by reason of his residence at Birkin near Selby, was born about 1141 and died in 1207, leaving four sons and a daughter by his second wife Maud de Chaux.

Early records of the de Lacies' Honour of Pontefract include a list of their chief tenants in the reign of King Stephen (1135-1154). Adam of Birkin owed fealty in respect of his manors at Birkin, Farborne, Havercroft and Stainborough in the plain of the Ouse, Lepton, Mirfield, Shitlington, Shepley and Shelley south of the Calder, and "Frisinghall et Heaton". Thus the two last-named hamlets entered the pages of recorded history within seventy years of Domesday.

No mention was made of Chellow, for which a similar fealty should have been due. The explanation may have lain in an unrecorded lease of the timber, mineral and grazing rights in Chellow to Rievaulx Abbey which was subsequently converted into a formal grant by Adam when he came of age in 1166.

By the terms of the grant the monks were entitled to "... all the dead wood (timber) and minerals in Harden, Shipley, Heaton and Chellow", together with the exclusive right to smelt and forge the iron ore and transport it by means of "their horse-loads and carts, and to pasture four horses, eight oxen, ten cows, a bull, calves up to the age of a year, twenty pigs and forty goats" wherever the flocks and herds of Adam and his tenants usually pastured, i.e., on the common.

The aim of this apparently pious gift was the hoped-for future well-being of the souls of Adam and his family, but the monks of Rievaulx were probably quick to discover that the ironworking rights were of little value, as they were not heard of again. A reference to cinderhills at Sandy Lane more than four

Grant of mineral and grazing rights to Rievaulx Abbey by Adam of Birkin in 1166. On lines 5 and 6 can be seen the Latinised forms of local placenames – Hageltona, Scippeleia, Hetona and Chelleslaua, i.e. Harden, Shipley, Heaton and Chellow.

centuries later may have been a late echo of the monks' attempts at iron-smelting in Chellow, while the "iron stream" which issues from an adit in Roydscliffe Wood and gives the "Red Beck" its name may also be a relic of monkish labours, but dates of up to five centuries later are equally possible.

Adam's successor was his son John of Birkin, who died in 1227, when the manors passed briefly to John's son Thomas (died 1230) and then to his daughter Isabella, wife of Robert of Everingham near Market Weighton. As required by feudal custom Isabella had to pay a "fine" or tax of 200 marks for licence to take seisin or possession of her late brother's lands in Yorkshire. Evidently she and her husband believed, like Adam, that they could secure their spiritual future by means of earthly gifts, as they gave the manor of Chellow to Selby Abbey in 1245.

Commenting on this apparently munificent gift John James described Chellow as "one of the chilliest and bleakest spots in this parish, lying on the side of a high and exposed copped hill." He added dryly, "I apprehend that the number of masses which were said or sung for this barren gift would be scanty." Centuries later and for purely secular reasons the local quarrymen often complained that Chellow was "a coat colder than Heaton," as the Chellow quarries were always the first to become "frozzen aht" in frosty weather.

The ink was barely dry on the deed of gift when Robert of Everingham passed away - a timely gift, one might say - but the grant was confirmed by his widow and her feudal superior, John, Earl of Lincoln, lord of the honour of Pontefract, who, had he wished, could have quashed the transaction, as gifts to the Church deprived him of death duties and other incomes.

From that date the two manors of Chellow and Heaton-with-Frizinghall were separate entities. Lack of well-defined boundaries led to persistent disputes that were complicated by the purchase of a moiety (portion) of Chellow by the lord of Heaton in 1620.

On taking possession of his new "grange" or outlying estate at Chellow, the Abbot of Selby appointed a steward to supervise its administration, and his recently-acquired rights were soon challenged. A few years after Isabella's death in 1252 a writ of Quo Warranto was served on him to prove by what right he claimed free warren at Chellow, and a deed dated 1251/2 was produced as proof. Then in 1288 unknown persons pulled down the farmhouse and carried away the building materials, a calamity that cost the Abbey's coffers £10.

Subsequently, in 1370, the Abbot took action against the townsfolk of Allerton who, he alleged, had felled some of his timber at "Chelleslawe" and hunted his hares, rabbits, pheasants and partridges. Poaching in the local woods persisted until they became public property in the 19th and 20th centuries. Fleeting reference to a family resident at Chellow in the 14th century can be found in local records, i.e. Cecily of Chellow in 1338 and Henry of Chellow in 1362, while Gilbert of Chellow was referred to in the Poll Tax of 1379, but the name was not recorded after about 1430, when surnames first made their appearance.

Within the extensive land-holdings of the Birkin/ Everingham families there may have been an arrangement whereby small estates were parcelled out for the support of individual members without strict regard for the right of primogeniture. Thus on the death of Isabella in 1252 the manor of Heaton reverted to her old great-uncle Thomas of Leedes, whilst an unspecified acreage of land at Frizinghall passed to her son Robert of Everingham. On January 9th, 1288, a few months after Robert's death, an inquest was held at York by Thomas of Normanville, when John Scott of Calverley, Walter of Hawksworth, William of Bolling and others testified to the value of the Knight's Fees and advowsons held by Robert. They duly declared Robert's heir, Roger of Northalle, to be the new owner of half a Knight's Fee by knight service in "Heton, Fresinghale, Armeley and Shepeker" whose value was £20 a year. As late as 1505 Sir John Everingham was still paying feudal relief to Pontefract on the land at Frizinghall.

In the early Middle Ages a form of civil administration separate from and independent of the manorial system was arising. The vast moorland parishes of the North had been found too unwieldy and cumbersome for everyday purposes, and most of them were therefore subdivided into townships whose boundaries often but not always coincided with those of the manors. Chellow, Heaton and Frizinghall were deemed to constitute the Township of Heaton, one of twelve such subdivisions of Bradford parish.

A township comprised a "town" and the area on which it depended for its subsistence. Once a year the chief inhabitants (i.e., those who paid taxes) convened a Town's Meeting (popularly but inaccurately known as the "vestry") for the purpose of appointing a few officers to represent them in the world outside. Tithes and taxes had to be collected and arrangements for baptisms, weddings and funerals at the distant parish church had to be made.

Understandably, therefore, the earliest-known appointment made by Town's Meetings was that of Churchwarden, who was joined in later years by the Constable (1285), Highway Surveyor (1555), Overseer of the Poor (1601), Pinder and Byelawman (bellman). All these worthies were unpaid amateurs, often reluctant, who bore for a twelvemonth the burden of keeping the King's Peace, issuing summonses, executing warrants, making proclamations and collecting monies due to the Wapontake, Shire and Church.

The Shire's influence over law and order had been diminished during the Barons' Wars, when the Lacies had taken the opportunity of enriching themselves at the expense of the Crown. It was commonly reported that they "used liberties otherwise than they ought to do, had appropriated lands and rights of neighbouring lords, taken tolls of things bought and sold outside Bradford market place, of both sellers and buyers, which sellers and buyers they had also oppressed and amerced (fined), and in addition had done many things there contrary to ancient usage."

In 1277, probably on the orders of King Edward I, the local Agbrigg and Morley Wapontake Court had instituted an inquiry to ascertain how certain Crown rights had passed into the hands of Edmund de Lacy, who had died in 1258. The Court jurors had a clear recollection of the events: in a judgement, whose mediaeval Latin title has been quaintly translated as, "Concerning those who have Ancient Suits," they declared "... that the townships of Clayton, Thorneton, Allerton and Heton were formerly taxable to our sovereign Lord the King, but were appropriated to the Liberty of Lord Edmund de Lacy by John of Hoderode, late steward of the said Edmund, which practice has been maintained up to the present day by Henry de Lacy, Earl of Lincoln."

In other words, the four townships had previously enjoyed independent status under the Sheriff's Tourn and Wapontake Court. However, John de Hoderode had used his master's power to compel them to subject themselves to the Bradford Court Leet, Tourn and View of Frankpledge, a feudal body which performed shrieval duties, ostensibly in the name of the King, but siphoned off the profits of fines to the steward. As the illicit arrangement was allowed to continue, it can be assumed that the "profits of court" were thenceforth shared with the Crown. This was the origin of the custom whereby until 1926 the townships (not the manors) owed "suit and service" to "the Court Leet of our Sovereign Lord the King" held at Bradford, and were obliged to seek its approval of township officers elected by the Town's Meeting. Ultimately the only township in Bradford parish that escaped this unwelcome intrusion was Shipley, which maintained direct dealings with the Honour of Pontefract court until the reign of Queen Victoria.

Until late mediaeval times the "open field" system of agriculture prevailed in Heaton and Frizinghall, although not at Chellow where the "Grange" was maintained by Selby Abbey as an individual farmstead surrounded by an irregular patchwork of "closes" or inclosures from the moor.

A full mile eastward at Heaton, a system of village life was slowly beginning to develop, regulated by the seasons, the climate and the varied endeavours of the manorial tenants and freeholders. The "town", i.e., the village centre, though it scarcely merited such a title before 1780, was confined to a rectangle bounded by the Town Street, the Back Lane and the site of present-day Quarry Street and the "King's Arms" - this probably represented the site of the original Anglo-Saxon defensive settlement. In full view was Bradford dale with its vistas of dark woods and scattered settlements. A few spirals of distant wood-smoke marked the huddled hutments of Manningham, Bolton and Shipley.

Closer at hand, descending on all sides from Heaton's hilltop - the Cnoc - lay the common fields, woods, copses and moors. Shaggy cattle, geese and sheep wandered over the common, carefully excluded from the cultivated areas by hawthorn tangles and vigilant eyes.

Assuming that Heaton's open fields were three in number, as they are known to have been in neighbouring Manningham, it seems likely that they comprised Emm Field, Cold Hill and Northsides. Each field bore barley, oats or rye for two successive years and lay fallow the third year.

Each house (and thus its tenant) was allotted a number of strips of land in each field; these were known as "lands" in the arable fields and "doles" in the meadows. Divided by turf "balks" or quickthorn hedges, the strips were in theory a furlong (furrow-long) in length, but in practice varied considerably. The cattle grazed on the pastures and the moor until harvest, after which they were turned onto the arable fields to feed on the stubble.

As the centuries passed and the population slowly increased, additional open fields were carved out of the common - Lillands (Leylands), Well Springs, Ashwell and, ultimately, the great West Field beyond Toller Lane. Many place-names which survived until modern times recalled their ancient origins as doles, lands, acres or rows in mediaeval fields - Jole Dole, Hiver Dole, Maylands ("mare lands"), Rows, Ross (or Rost - "horse"?) Rows, Half Acres etc. Odd corners in the fields were termed "nooks", e.g. Pyke Nook at Chellow, or "butts", e.g. Butts Dike west of Heaton "town", where the archers doubtless practised their skills when the day's work was done.

At the foot of the hill, among fertile meadows watered by small sykes tumbling down to the Bradford Beck, lay the pleasant hamlet of Frizinghall. The original settlement was probably in the area of present-day Swan Hill and Buxton (anciently Buckstall) Lane, safely above the level of the floodwaters, which sometimes filled the dale bottom. The Frizinghall pastures and ploughlands - Sough Field, Harry Royds and the larger Smithy Field - were separated from Heaton's fields by the High and Low Greens.

Lower still, at the eastern tip of the township, the manorial corn mill bestrode one of the channels of the meandering Bradford Beck. In later centuries the Beck was straightened and concentrated into one channel, leaving on the new eastern bank an isolated enclave of Heaton known as Lower Smithy Field. The mill played an important role in the life of the township and manor, as the lord of the manor of Heaton (- cum- Frizinghall) had provided it, and his tenants were under feudal obligation to have their corn ground there. Part of the

A view of Dumb Mill prior to rebuilding in 1911. The cottages on the left are part of the old corn mill and the taller buildings and chimney were erected by Benjamin Wood.

(Photo: Messrs. G.A. White, courtesy Mr H. Ambler)

grain was retained by the miller as his "toll and mulcture", which paid his wages and the upkeep of the mill. Traditionally, millers were suspected of withholding an unfair proportion of the grain brought for milling; a mediaeval riddle asked, "What is the boldest thing in the world?", to which the answer was, " A miller's shirt because it clasps a thief by the throat!"

Before the advent of street drainage and public sewers in modern times, the volume of water carried by the Beck and its tributaries was considerably greater than at the present day, but the flow was seasonal, and as Mr. Edward Bolling later discovered, it dwindled to a trickle when mills higher upstream impounded it in order to keep their own water wheels turning. Heaton's cornmill was therefore at the mercy of its neighbours, not least the confusingly-named "Frizinghall Mill" in the adjacent Bolton township, and from time to time the yeomen farmers had no choice but to cart their grain elsewhere, to Leaventhorpe Mill or even further afield. Its very name - Dumb Mill - was a silent testimony to the long periods when it stood empty and untenanted.

What is probably the earliest reference to the mill occurs in the Court Leet rolls for "the Feast of St. Wilfred" in 1354 when

"Adam of Fresynghale came here into Court and agreed to pay a toll of 3s 9d to the lord (of Bradford) for permission to carry fifteen pairs of millstones through the lordship."

The surviving Court Leet records provide fragmentary glimpses of life in the Plantagenet period. In 1339, "in the twelfth year of the reign of King Edward the third after the conquest... at the Court of our Sovereign Lady Philippa, Queen of England, holden at Bradford," Adam of Heton was named as a surety. Five years later the Court ordered that the goods of Richard de Hilton of Heton should be distrained for unpaid tolls, and each township was reminded to make an annual election of an Aletaster who would present his findings at the Court. Bread and leather were similarly subjected to scrutiny as a precaution against short measure and bad workmanship.

In 1350 Robert of Frysynghale was named as one of twelve plaintiffs in a lawsuit, and Thomas of Chellowe was admitted and enrolled as a tenant within the Bradford manor.

Other Heaton men made brief appearances in 1355, when John of Bakshelf was punished for false accusations of trespass against Adam son of Michael of Heton and Adam Dixon of Hilton, and Thomas Harper of Baksholfker and Hetonker (possibly Carr Syke) was found guilty of having falsely accused Adam son of Richard of Hilton (presumably the aforementioned Adam Dixon) and Adam son of Michael of Heton of the theft of wood. Four years later Adam son of Michael was a plaintiff in a lawsuit against John of Chellow, and in 1360 he appeared with his servant John in a further suit. Perhaps the servant was the John Childe of Heton who in 1360 appeared as plaintiff in a case of assault, only to find himself condemned as the guilty party! The name Child(e), signifying "the youngest," was to feature in Heaton records for more than six centuries.

At Martinmas, 1361, Henry of "Chelleslowe" was fined at the Leet for a minor offence while simultaneously the Constable of Heaton was assuring the Court that all was well within his township. A year later, "Heton, Stanbyry, Manyngham and Wik" all declared that they had nothing to report, and Thomas of Chellowe was appointed Bailiff of Bradford manor. The last reference to Heaton in the Leet rolls for a whole generation occurred in 1363, when Adam Fidcock of Heton ungallantly laid a formal complaint against Alice, the widow of Roger.

In a world where people rarely travelled beyond their everyday horizon, distant echoes of national events were of small importance when compared with the slow, unchanging cycle of the seasons - ploughing, sowing, growing, mowing, reaping, stacking, threshing and grinding, calving, weaning and slaughter, birth, life and death.

The daily diet was based on oatmeal, with meat or freshwater fish and eels only on special occasions. Home comforts were minimal - families slept on straw with a log as pillow; clothes and tools were home-made, and the smoke from the wood or peat fire had to make its escape through a hole in the thatch. Nothing was wasted: dung of man and beast manured the fields while urine was carefully collected as a means of "finishing" the home-woven cloth. The nreturn of spring and the balmy days of summer were gladly welcomed by the weatherbeaten field labourers chilled by frosts and lashed by wind-blown rain from the higher Pennines.

If winters were long and summers wet, and if plague or cattle murrain swept over the land, there was no remedy. Although the wooded, varied landscape patterned with meadows, furrows, grazing herds and sparkling becks was undoubtedly beautiful, those who beheld it were more preoccupied with the challenges of daily bread, growing families, illnesses, tithes for the church and services, dues or boon days for the lord of the manor.

The nature and extent of the lord's feudal dues in Heaton are unchronicled, although in most manors tenants were obliged to devote a few days each year to the tilling and manuring of his demesne or "home farm," attend his Court Baron, use his mill and occasionally present a "boon hen" for his table. In return, the lord or his steward would provide a feast; the twice-yearly Rent Dinner held regularly until 1911 was probably the direct descendant of the feudal feastings. Eventually the inefficient and grudgingly performed boon days were commuted for a cash payment, especially when the feudal system began to wane.

Indeed the system received a mortal blow when the horror of the Black Death swept pitilessly across the country; whole villages perished, and only six miles distant from Heaton, the township of Shelf was officially declared "dead." Presumably Heaton did not escape, and how many of its townsfolk survived will never be known; all that is certain is that no one handed down their story. But the ensuing shortage of labour destroyed the old concept of villeinry and serfdom; thenceforth the labourer was worthy of his hire.

A rare glimpse of pageantry and colour was seen from time to time when the great John of Gaunt, Duke of Lancaster(1340-1399) travelled between his castles at Pontefract and Clitheroe. The Honour of Pontefract had long been Duchy of Lancaster property, and it was a great occasion when the royal Duke, Shakespeare's "time-honoured Lancaster," and fourth son of King Edward III, attended the customary hornblowing ceremony in Bradford market place before riding westwards, presumably by way of Toller Lane and Chellow Heights, to Colne and Ightengill, Lancashire.

Throughout history the boundaries between manors, townships, cities, counties and states have been a source of contention if they are not clearly defined by natural features such as rivers or streams which are too large to be surreptitiously diverted. When lords beat their bounds and clergymen perambulated their parishes they pointedly recited those portions of Scripture which foretold Divine displeasure upon those who "removed their neighbour's bounds".

Heaton and its neighbours were no strangers to these disputes. The curious and illogical Heaton/Shipley boundary suggests that Shipley was the more determined township of the two, as Shipley Fields protruded south of the Red Beck which formed the dividing-line higher upstream, whilst at the head of Roydscliffe Wood the portion of "Six Days Only" nearest to Heaton has always formed part of Shipley.

The Court Leet took the opportunity of a disagreement with Allerton in 1686 to order,

> "That if the Inhabitants of Heaton do claime the parcell of common from Swaineroid bottom along down by Sinderhill and so near Standing Stone within the jurisdiction of this Court, that then the Overseers for the Highwayes or (the) Inhabitants of Heaton do sufficiently repaire the highwaye down the same before the first of December next, upon paine of £5."

As the townsfolk considered the Cottingley Beck to be their boundary at that point, they accepted liability for the "highwaye", which was often known as "Small Tail Road" on account of the tail-shaped "parcell of common" between the highway and the beck from "Swaineroid bottom" to the point where the beck crossed the road by means of a ford (and later, a bridge). The "Standing Stone" would be either a boundary stone or a marker to guide travellers when the highway was obliterated by snow, as it constituted the way from Bingley to Halifax for those desirous of making such a journey.

The grant of a substantial landholding in Manningham to one John Northrop by John of Gaunt obliged the Duke to define the Heaton/Manningham boundary, a task which was carried out some time before 1377. Beginning at the lower end of Chellow Dene, the boundary was deemed to run "to the height where the rainwater divides, and upon the east to one small brook called Shaw Syke to the water which runneth from Bradford". The Anglican parishes of Heaton still use the same boundaries, seven centuries later.

'The place where Heaven Water divides', the watershed and boundary dividing Manningham (i.e. Daisy Hill and Hazlehurst) from Heaton. Chellow Heights waterworks buildings stand on the summit, with Chellow Grange and part of the Haworth Road estate below.   *(Copyright: author)*

The Poll Tax of 1379 levied by King Richard II to finance the upkeep of his French possessions provides the first of a long line of lists of inhabitants and property values:-

> "HETON IN BRADFORTHDALE.
>
> Alice of Birchew, Alice and John of Chellow, John Couper, Adam and Emma of Halton, Richard of Heton, John Kirkeman, Cecily widow of Richard, Thomas of the Rodes, Robert and William of the Scholes, Robert Smyth and his wife Alice Smyth, John of Stainland, John son of Thomas, John servant of Thomas.   Total 4d each: 5s 8d.
>
> Heton is included in Bradforth."

The seventeen taxpayers thus listed were the principal residents: others paid less and some nothing. The place-names are of interest. While the location of Birchew is doubtful, Halton may denote Harden and Stainland the present-day Calderdale village. The "scholes" (Old Norse, skali, huts) wherein Robert and William dwelt were no doubt on the edge of the moor, and the placename itself vanished when the huts decayed, but the "Rodes" which Thomas, his son John and their servant inhabited were Heaton Royds, a delightful hamlet which has thus been in continuous occupation for over six centuries.

Alice and John were presumably the tenants of Chellow "Grange", and Richard the foremost Heaton resident. John Kirkeman and John Couper may have been the founders of local families, as their relatives achieved brief fame in the Court Leet rolls a generation later:

> "October 23rd, 1410: William Kyrkeman is elected to the office of Constable of Heton this year and sworn in " - as was William Couper a year later.

However, William Kyrkeman together with William son of William Capp and John son of John Hunsflete were summonsed for being common players of dice and knucklebones only three years later.

A Yorkshireman's hearty disregard of rules and regulations was revealed at the Leet on May 2nd, 1414: –

> "They (the jurors) say that the Constable of Heton took by way of distraint for payment of taxes to our Sovereign Lord the King, one cow belonging to John Bentley of Heton, and impounded the said cow in the common pinfold there, whereupon the said John on the Sunday before the feast of the Apostles Philip and James broke into the said pinfold and took and carried away the said cow which had been impounded there for the tax due to our Sovereign Lord the King, in contempt of our said Sovereign Lord, wherefore it is ordered that he be attached (i.e. summonsed)."

Until at least the 17th century the pinfold (or pound for stray animals) was located at the foot of Leylands (Lillands) Lane, but by Queen Victoria's time it occupied the present-day car park of the "Hare and Hounds."

The existence of another essential feature of mediaeval life – the public stocks – was revealed at the Leet when, following a neglect of duty on the part of Clayton township, the jury warned on May 4th, 1412, that they and "all other townships within this Leet shall sufficiently cause their stocks to be kept in repair, on pain of 6s 8d each township." Where Heaton's stocks stood and when they fell into disuse is unknown; all that can be stated with any confidence is that generations of miscreants were obliged to sit in them for a specified period, enduring either brazenly or shamefacedly the jibes and jeers of their neighbours, who were allowed to pelt them with over-ripe fruit or vegetables but no hard substances!

An obscure reference to property transactions in Heaton is found in the Feet of Fines Rolls for Michaelmas law term, 1492, when the plaintiffs were Richard Straytebarrell, clerk, Robert Crosseby, chaplain, and Thomas Thornton, with Roger and Isobel Thornton and Robert and Joan Braythwayte as defendants. The property comprised "a moiety of two messuages, with the appurtenances and lands thereto attached, at Fresyngehowe near Heton in Bradfortdale in the parish of Bradforth." The identity of the participants is unknown, but they bore solid northern names!

On the death of William of Leedes in 1430 the manor of Heaton had passed to his sister Emma, Lady Hussey, wife of Sir John Hussey. Widowed soon afterwards, Emma re-married to Sir Geoffrey Pigott of Clotherham near Ripon, and their son Ralph gave Heaton and other portions of his inheritance to his son Sir Geoffrey Pigott in 1437. By his wife Margaret of Sewerby, Sir Geoffrey had two sons, Ralph and Thomas. The elder, later Sir Ralph, married Joan, daughter of Sir Richard Strangeways of Harsley Castle, North Riding. At the time of his death on August 9th, 1503, Sir Ralph was one of the wealthiest of Yorkshire knights, with landed possessions in more than sixty Yorkshire towns and townships from Ripon to the east coast, including "North Hall near Leeds, Great Oakwell, Gomersall and little Gomersall, Heckmondwike, Birstall, Birkenshaw, Heaton near Bradford, Frisinghall near Bradford," etc.

Sir Ralph's niece Jane ultimately inherited the lands at Heaton, Frizinghall, North Hall and around Gomersal. She married Sir Giles Hussey of Caythorpe near Sleaford, son of John, Lord Hussey, whose family was influential in southern Lincolnshire.

For a generation or two a branch of the Leaventhorpe family of Thornton township dwelt in Heaton. In his will dated May 3rd, 1426, Jefferey Leaventhorpe of Bradforthdale awarded one mark (6s 8d) to his relative Thomas for his services as executor. Then on October 31st, 1481, the Abbot of Selby leased to Nicholas Leaventhorpe " the village of

Chelleslawe otherwise the site of their manor of Chellow" for a term of fifty years beginning at the Feast of St. Martin in Winter, and at a yearly rent of 40 shillings. The tenant undertook to maintain the buildings in good order with timber from the woods, and to keep the Nether Dene in sound condition. In return the Abbot was to provide the tenant with clothing (livery) similar to that given to the stewards of the other Abbey manors, and would permit him to cut branches for winter fuel. Nicholas was in fact an influential man in Bradford dale, being lord of Horton as well as "farmer" of the revenues of the manor of Bradford.

In 1492 the lease of Chellow was assigned for a sixty-year term to Robert Ryshworth of Pontefract, who sub-let the tenancy to Tristram Bolling, formerly of Bolling Hall in Bowling township. On his death ten years later, Tristram was succeeded in the tenancy by his son Edward Bolling, who subsequently bought the lease from Mr. Ryshworth in 1515,

Mr. Bolling proved to be the last of the long line of Abbey tenants or stewards, as the fundamental disagreement between the Pope and King Henry VIII caused the latter to revoke the acceptance of papal authority which King Oswy had decreed eight centuries earlier. Selby Abbey was dissolved in 1539 and its properties vested in the Crown. In worldly terms the effect on Chellow was small, as crops still had to be garnered and rents paid, and on the death of Edward Bolling in 1543 the lease passed to his son, another Tristram.

The Lay Subsidy of November 11th, 1545 provided a living link between the Heaton of Henry VIII and the village of modern times.

HETON

Robt. Cravyn	in bon	iiij li	iiij d
Ricus Baildon	in terr'	xl s	iiij d
Thoms Roids	in bon	iiij li	iiij d
Jacob hillyngworth	in bon	xl s	ij d
Robt. migley	in terr'	xx s	ij d
Ricus Cappes	in bon	xx s	j d
georg Cappes	in bon	xx s	j d
Jacob Cappes	in bon	xx s	j d
Thoms Joiett	in bon	xx s	j d
Elizabeth garth	in bon	xx s	j d
			Sma xxjd

The left-hand column of figures denotes the value of the named person's estate in goods (in bon) or in land (in terr'), while the right-hand column represents the sum due at a rate of 1d (one penny) in the £ for goods and 2d in the £ for land. The total collected in Heaton (sma = summary) was therefore 21d (1s 9d), and £22-15-4d for the whole of the wapontake (of Morley).

Behind their dog-Latin disguises, the ten taxpayers were Robert Craven, Richard Baildon, Thomas Rhodes, James Illingworth, Robert Midgley, Richard, George and James Cappes, Thomas Jowett and Elizabeth Garth - the leading inhabitants whose families played a prominent part in Heaton life generation after generation, some of them until modern times. The Cravens were the principal Frizinghall family; the Rhodes clan derived their name from Heaton Rhodes or Royds where they were still living two centuries later; Capps and Midgley were small landowners in Heaton until the eighteenth century and the Illingworths were more usually associated with Manningham. But the Jowetts, later of Clock House and Chellow, are remembered as Heaton landowners until as recently as 1947, and it was the Garths who later built Garth House, and thus bequeathed their name to Garth Barn Close in the heart of Heaton Village.

The Subsidy provides useful comparisons between the various townships in Bradford parish:-

Bradford 76 taxpayers, Haworth 74, Horton 44, Allerton 42, Thornton 22, Manningham 18, North Bierley 17, Clayton 16, Bowling 12, Heaton 10 and Shipley 9. Obviously the humbler folk paid no tax.

Other family names which became familiar in Heaton in later centuries were listed elsewhere in the West Riding i.e.,

Broadley (Southowram), Crabtree (Langfield, Allerton and Thornton), Field (Elland), Firth (Barkisland, Ryshworth, Marsden, Quarmby, Fixby and Rastrick), Gaukroger (Hartshead), Greenwood (Langfield, Wadsworth, Northowram and Rastrick), Marvell (Tong), Murgatroyd (Warley), Sowden (Allerton) and Stead (Bradford and North Bierley).

On the death of Henry VIII in 1547 the Reformation gathered pace rapidly despite a brief but violent check during the brief reign of his daughter Mary (1553-8). When Heaton folk made their Sabbath journey down Emm Lane and over the Kirk Steelhole to Bradford Parish Church they found the services being preached in their own language for the first time. Suspicion of new ways and new thinking aroused some passive resistance which lingered for years until the stirring tidings of the Spanish Armada - that mighty victory "whereby the whole fleete of Spayne was defeated and dis-comfited" - caused the flares on Reevy Beacon to arouse patriotic spirits on Heaton's hilltop. Thereafter Protestantism took such a hold on popular imagination that the more austere Puritan version of the reformed doctrines began to encroach on official Anglican practice, especially in areas such as Bradford dale where the influence of nobility and gentry was scarcely felt.

At the same time the dark old mediaeval superstitions and fears of witchcraft were slowly ebbing as enlightenment dawned. Nevertheless remote villages and the lonely haunts of the moors continued to harbour strange, half-believed tales of baleful apparitions - boggarts (spectres), guytrashes (great black dogs with saucerlike eyes), hobs (helpful hobgoblins) and barguests (bier ghosts) which might harass or "flay" (frighten) the unwary, especially after dark. In his youth the author expressed eagerness to glimpse a ghost said to haunt a certain Lincolnshire dyke. Whimsically confident that such an encounter would produce bodily as well as mental shock, his Lincolnshire host replied briefly but earthily. "Nay", he said, "You'd be to cleean!" (i.e., "you would need a thorough wash afterwards!")

Ironically, the site of St. Barnabas' Church may once have been considered haunted. Generally known as the Half Acres - denoting a series of half-acre strips when Emm Field was an open field - its name appeared in early deeds as "Hovacres" or "Hob acres". Reputedly friendly, shy beings who willingly milked cattle or cleaned houses in return for simple payments in kind, the hobs of Hob Acre might have provided a voluntary caretaking service had St. Barnabas' been erected in mediaeval rather than Victorian times!

Until the advent of trade, the Highways of Heaton were of little consequence, most being little more than tracks to the fields. Now that feudal superiors no longer made stately progresses from place to place, the only regular users of the muddy, rutted paths were beasts of burden, cattle on their way to mistal or market and townsmen and women going about their daily tasks.

Frizinghall and Heaton were linked by the steep, winding track known as Emm Lane in its upper reaches and Heaton Lane lower down, where it was joined by a more businesslike lane solemnly known as "The King's Highway from Bradford to Otley" by way of Shipley. In Frizinghall a farm track known as Buckstalls Lane led to Mosscroft Farm (later Firth Carr), and from the lower end of Heaton paths such as Ashwell Lane and Whiteley Lane led past the fields. At Chellow Dene a precipitous path known as "Heton Sty"(Anglo-Saxon stig, a path) pointed towards Allerton. West of Heaton "town" a rutted track "down the Cliffe" wound its way through the steep descent of Royds Cliffe Woods to Heaton Royds where it opened out on to the common, while a branch connected with Toller Lane for access to Chellow. A deed of 1655 described "Old Manningham" (Daisy Hill) as "lying on both sides of the way leading from Bradford to Haworth", thus indicating that Smith Lane, Manningham, and Heights Lane, Heaton, were alternatives to Toller Lane as shown on a Manningham map of 1613. From "Chellow houses" a track usually known as "Dead Lane" crossed the edge of the common to a gnarled guidepost, which pointed the way to Keighley down the old "Roman road".

The upkeep of public paths and thoroughfares was the responsibility of landowners and their tenants, and predictably little work was carried out without prompting from the courts. In consequence of the 1555 Highways Act the Town's Meeting began to elect a Surveyor of the Highways, who, like the other "town's officers" was a local man – blacksmith, yeoman farmer or the like – unpaid and inexperienced, on whom fell the task of "viewing" the highways thrice yearly and attempting to ensure that "statute labour" was performed as the law prescribed. The statute in question obliged owners of ploughs and oxen as well as able-bodied householders, cottagers and labourers to perform a few days' unpaid labour every year, but the Surveyor was rarely in a position to impose his will on men who, after all, were his own neighbours and relatives. The comfortable theory that the highways would improve of their own accord if allowed to do so, found little favour with travellers who occasionally "presented" him before the Leet (and later the magistrates) for neglect.

On the death of her first husband, Sir Giles Hussey, the lady of the manor, Jane Hussey, nee Pigott, remarried to another Lincolnshire man, Thomas Folkingham, to whom his wife's inheritance was formally confirmed in 1565; he was thenceforth known as "of North Hall". Evidently an acquisitive and arbitrary man, Thomas Folkingham aroused the wrath of the freeholders of Heaton by wholesale inclosures from the Common, which culminated in an inquiry by the Council of the North on May 8th "in the reigns of Philip and Mary the fourth and fifth" (1558). At the request of Robert Craven and Robert Midgley (two of the principal freeholders named in the 1545 Lay Subsidy) and others, ten questions in the language of Shakespeare and the first Book of Common Prayer were put to "divers witnesses sworne by the Quene's Majestie's counsell".

"FIRST, whether do you knowe the Comon or More called Heaton More now in Variance, and if ye do, how many years have ye knowne the same?

2, ITEM, whether do ye knowe any of the meares or bounds of the northe parte of the said More, and what is the names of the said Boundes?

3, ITEM, whether do ye knowe the Bounders of the weste parte of the said More, and what is theyr names?

4, ITEM, whether do ye knowe the Bounders of the Southe parte of the Moore called Heaton Moore, yea or no, and What be the names of the Bounders?

5, ITEM, whether do ye knowe the Bounders of the Easte parte of the said Moore, and what be theyre names?

6, ITEM, howe many Acres doth the said More contayne . . . and how and by what meanes do ye knowe the nombers of the said Acres?

7, ITEM, whether did the Defendant inclose the cheife wateringe-places belonginge to the said Waste and Comon, yea or no?

8, ITEM, whether the Comon High-Waies and Streetes belonginge to the said towne of Heaton were inclosed and stopt by the said nowe Inclosure, which Strete and High Waie hathe bene ever Occupied by all the Kinge and Quene's liege people as one High Waye for Carts and Wayns, and all other manner of Carriage to the Kynge and Quene's Townes and Marketts, yea or no?

9, ITEM, whether coulde the Compleynants be forced to dryve theyr Cattell the space of one mile to the residue of the More if the Defendant had inclosed the nowe inclosure, yea or nay?

10, ITEM, did ye ever knowe the said Compleynants or any of theyr

Anncestors have used to be stynted or rated with theyr Cattels, or dryven or ympounded any tyme heretofore of the said More . . . tyme out of Remembrance of men, yea or no?"

To these leading questions virtually identical testimonies were given by the witnesses, William Allerton of Allerton, aged 67, John Midgley of Thornton, 54, Henry Aikeroide of Wilsden, 54, William Boythe (i.e., Booth) of Shipley, clothier, 70, Roger Apleyeard of Allerton, 40, and George Gargrave of Bolton, 68. On the north side of the moor, they said, "the Heremite Hole, the Deade Waye and the sett or standinge Stone" constituted the "bounds", whilst "Salterclough, Dean clough, Hew cloughe and the grene Welles" marked the western limits. The southern "bounders" were Hazillhurst dyke and Heaton Fielde nooke", whilst "Heaton towne and th'olde Springe" comprised the eastern "meares".

The witnesses also testified that "twyce synce Christmas last past" John Midgley had been employed by the "compleynants" to measure the moor, "which by his measuringe ... it did appeare to be about Fourteene score Acres". The lord, "Thomas Fawkeingham, Esquire, "they alleged,

"... hath inclosed all the chief Wateringe-places belonginge to the said Comon, So that in Summer season there is no Water to be gotten on the said More but in the said place inclosed, beside the builde of Bushes and a Cloughe which the said Defendant hathe also inclosed, and lefte no Builde for Cattell depasturinge the said More."

In addition Mr. Folkingham had,

"... enclosed up all the High-Wayes which were belonginge to the said towne of Heaton, Which was ever occupied with Carts and Carriages, So that at the West ende of the Towne no man could passe or repasse with Carts and Carriages to the Markette townes or any other parte on that syde, but were dryven to goe a longe myle and more aboute ... by reason of high dyke and hedge... but one Tyme a gappe was made in the Hedge....

... nor could the Compleynants dryve their Cattell to the More, but were compelled to dryve them almost a myle about to the residue of the said Comon."

As for the stinting of livestock on the Common, they were adamant that they had...

"... sene the said More occupied by the said Compleynants and theyr Anncestors, and neyther theyr cattle were rated, stynted, dryven or impounded of the said More, nor any other man's Cattle adjoyninge the said More were impounded, but suffered to enter Comon upon the said More...."

Not all the above claims should be accepted at face value, particularly those which relate to stinting, as one of the prime functions of the Heaton Court Baron was to ensure that the common was not overstocked; hence (in later years at least) all tenants who by virtue of their freehold or copyhold tenure from the Manor were entitled to pasture their beasts on the common were usually allotted a specific "stint" or quota, infringements of which were duly noted by the manor bailiff.

Although the verdict of the "Quene's counsell" is not known, Thomas Folkingham's flagrant trespass was obviously not allowed to continue; nevertheless only a few years later, in 1564, William Dixon of Heaton Royds was obliged to file a Bill in the Duchy of Lancaster Court against the lord and other freeholders who had allegedly inclosed other parts of the common. In 1566 the Court duly ordered that the disputed lands be laid open and enjoyed in common as formerly.

Thomas Folkingham's wife Jane represented the thirteenth generation of descent from Asolf, the lord of Chellow and Heaton in 1166, but like many other Lincolnshiremen her husband had unwisely implicated himself in the failed Rising of the North in 1569, and although he was eventually pardoned by Queen Elizabeth in 1572, he and his wife had found it necessary to sell their Oakwell, Gomersal, Heckmondwike, Birstall and Heaton manors in 1568 to Henry Batt of Haley Hill, Halifax.

Henry Batt, keeper of the manor courts of Sir Henry Savile of Thornhill near Dewsbury, had married into the influential Waterhouse family of Halifax. No less unscrupulous than Thomas Folkingham, he has been described as "a lawyer by profession and a rogue by instinct." At various times he had been accused of the theft of documents and goods from the Vicar of Halifax, the appropriation of £100 entrusted to him for the building of a school, and, even more flamboyantly, the sale of the largest bell from Birstall parish church and the theft of the vicarage from the vicar! No doubt the remaining bells rang a merry peal at the news of his death in 1572. It was left to his son John Batt to pay a large fine, build the school and make amends.

On July 31st, 1575, Mr. Batt, "of Birstall, gentleman," entered into a lease to Thomas Grenegate, husbandman, of Heaton, of the messuage (dwellinghouse) in which Thomas dwelt. The lease included an obligation, probably traditional, for the repair of the corn-mill dam with timber from Heaton Woods, and was made for a term of 14 years beginning March 20th, 1582. The rent was to be 8s per annum, payable on "the feaste of Penticost and Seynt Martyn in wynter by even porcions, and one henne yearlie at the feaste of Seynt Thomas th'Appostill."

Thomas Greengate undertook to maintain his house in good order and to keep in repair,

> "... suche part of the Milne Damme called Frisynghall Milne Damme accordinge as the said Thomas and the other (i.e., previous) tenantes of the said premises have been accustomed to do ... and shalle lead tymbre nedefull for the said reparacions, such as he, the said John Batte shall have growinge within the lordshippe of Heaton onlie excepted, which tymbre (except latte and borde) the said John Batte covenanteth and graunteth to assign and appoynt within the lordshippe of Heaton upon reasonable request."

In addition, the tenant agreed to,

> "... well and sufficiently save and keep the great wood and other woods now growing and that shall hereafter grow upon the said land, from waste and destruction",

although Mr. Batt as lord of the manor was entitled to "fell and carry away all or any of the said wood at his pleasure". In return for these important obligations, Thomas Greengate was authorised to

> "... intake, plowe and sowe any parte of the common or moore of Heaton afforesaid for three croppes together, or more if the tenantes and other the inhabitantes of the said townshippe can and will agree to the same,"

which they probably did not!

The perennial problem of poverty and pauperism inspired Parliament in 1572 to create in each township the office of Overseer of the Poor, whose task was to collect alms and use them for the provision of work for "rogues and vagabonds." It would appear that Heaton and Clayton may have objected to the imposition of the Act upon them, on the grounds that their sparse populations could not afford the expense which it incurred. The outcome was that they were amalgamated as a joint township in 1573. The partners were ill-matched from the outset, being physically separated from each other by the township of Allerton. Nevertheless the new joint arrangements came into being in October, 1573, when Edward Bolling, Thomas Roides and Richard Cappes of Heaton and John Midgeleye, Robert Hayneworthe and Humphrey Kellett of Clayton informed the Leet that their respective Town's Meetings had elected George Roides and Thomas Greengate (see above) as Constable and Deputy Constable of "Heaton et Clayton". The term "Heaton - cum - Clayton" came into being in 1576 and was then used for the duration of the "marriage".

At a later date better arrangements for the supervision and relief of paupers were provided by the Poor Relief Act of 1601 which made the useful distinction between "sturdy beggars", i.e., those who could work but would not, and "impotent poor", i.e., those who were incapable of labour through old age or infirmity. The legislation specified for each township one Overseer and an assistant who were to find work for the able and relief in the form of clothing, meals, tools etc. for the infirm, the expense being met by a Poor Rate laid (levied) on occupiers of land, houses, mines and woods and owners of tithes. The population of Heaton at this period was under 500.

Barnard's Survey of the Liberty of the Duke of Lancaster (i.e., the Queen) compiled in 1577 listed the "hamlet" of "Heton - cum - Frizinghall" as one of nine townships in Bradford parish owing indirect feudal dues to Pontefract, and added briefly that ...

> "Lady Margaret Leedes formerly held two carucates in Heton, previously Roger of Leedes as appears by record; afterwards Jane Pigott (late Lady Hussey), now Henry Bat, in which village he claims to have the manor by reason of the land aforesaid."

Henry Bat(t) had in fact died five years previously, and his demesne evidently comprised up to 200 acres of land.

In addition to owning the fishing rights in the short section of the Bradford Beck within the Heaton township boundaries, the Batts leased similar rights in Idle, as specified in a survey of the Manor of Idle in 1584:-

> "Know that I (Robert of Whirington) have leased and granted to John (Batt) the son of Henry (Batt) of Heaton his free fishing throughout all my water of Idle as my land extendeth itself, to witt, from the mills of Eaton unto the meres and bounders of (illegible),
> And likewise having granted unto the said John my free fishing in the pools near to the house of Reynold (illegible), ... with a shove and netts fitt for him, ... reserving notwithstanding to me and mine heirs fishing in the dams of my Milnes   , and in the poole made adjoining my Dams, in which pooles the said John and his heires no fishing can have ..."

The lease, which was witnessed by "Adam of Heyton" (Heaton) and others, was a valuable privilege, as the Beck teemed with trout, eels and other comestibles.

A threatened attempt by John Batt to inclose part of Heaton Common for his own use aroused the freeholders to new action; not only did they resurrect the evidence presented against Thomas Folkingham in 1558 but also commissioned Christopher Saxton of Dunningley, "the first English cartographer", to survey and draw a map of Heaton Moor in

1591. Presumably the Bollings of Chellow led the action, as the map remained in their keeping for generations.

The danger of conflicts of a more serious nature, less likely now that the Scots had ceased to maraud the Dales and the Yorkists and Lancastrians had fought their last battles, remained a constant source of concern to the government, and townships always had to be ready to supply armed troops if the need arose. The troops and their armour were inspected from time to time by royal commissioners. Thus on the 13th and 18th of April (year unknown, but in the reign of Henry VIII) Sir Robert Neville and Sir Thomas Tempest attended

"... the muster or showing and view of men of arms, men armed (and) able to bear them, as well (as) archers and other men on horse and on foot ... viewed and seen in ...Bradfordale in the Westriding of the County of York."

There they "viewed" the Heaton muster: -

"HEYTON

Archer	Richard Baildon, horse and harness;
	Thomas Rhodes, a horse, a jake, a bow and arrows;
	Thomas Jowett, a bow and a horse
Bills	Thomas Dawson, a jake, a salet and a bill
	Robert Craven, a jake and a salet, a bill
	Denis Leadbeater, a jake and a bill
Archer	Richard Smyth, bow and arrows
Billmen	Richard Capps
	James Capps
	George Capps
	John Learoyd, a jake.

Number of men able to wear harness - 9; men furnished with horse and harness - 2; horses not furnished - 1; number of jakes - 4; salets - 1; bills - 3; archers - 4; billmen- 4;"

Happily, their services were not needed, although from time to time they were warned to be ready in case of a sudden emergency or assault.

The use of local stone for building purposes was recorded as early as 1613, and it is likely that by the end of the century the old, timber -framed dwellings and barns had been replaced by or encased in more substantial structures. Heaton sandstone was of the "cleavage" variety with a well-defined grain which allowed it to be split into regular-shaped wallstones, flagstones and roofing-slabs. The new roofing materials, sometimes illogically termed "stone slates" replaced thatch in the eighteenth century. The quarries, known as "delphs" were worked by "delvers" who hewed the stone and sent it to the surface for dressing by masons, but it was not until about 1770 that any delph began to operate as a commercial venture.

Stone was used to encase the 16th century timber frame of Heaton Royds Farm in two stages - gables first and other walls afterwards, with wings which were complete by 1559. "J. H." built Cross Hill Head Farm in 1637 at the junction of Cross Hill (Heaton Road) and Emm Lane, while at the summit of Town Street in 1681 James Garth erected the long, stately farmhouse which bore his initials and which the Baptists subsequently used as their first meeting place. Part of Chellow Grange was reconstructed in stone in the same year. Other undated buildings were soon to be found elsewhere, and in 1632 John Dixon erected a solid farmstead opposite Heaton Royds Farm but in Shipley township, which still bears his initials and is still owned by his descendants.

Emm Lane (Cross Hill Head) Farm, built in 1637 and photographed about 1900 when the tenant was Bairstow Tetley, seen (right) by one of the blossoming apple and /or pear trees in his garden, which was separated by a stone 'bank' (bench), on the left, from the farmyard.

(Courtesy of the late Mr Arnold Pickles)

In 1581 John Batt conveyed his manors of "Heaton in Bradford dale" and Oakwell to his son Henry, but as the latter predeceased his father in 1603, shortly after "Good Queen Bess" herself had passed away, John Batt was still in possession of his Heaton lands at the time of his own death four years later.

The new lord, Robert Batt, Bachelor of Divinity, was the second son of John Batt. Sometime Fellow and Vice-Master of University College, Oxford, he seems to have been a cheerful, family-loving man unlike his acquisitive father and grandfather, as he married three times and had four sons and eight daughters. At the time of his father's death he was rector of Newton Tony in Wiltshire, where he remained for the rest of his life.

By this time the ancient system of open-field farming was rapidly falling into disrepute. In theory the system was fair and even-handed, as the process of allocating "stints" and "doles", i.e., shares of the pastures and ploughlands awarded by the Court Baron, gave each customary tenant a share of the good land as well as the bad.

Human nature, however, ensured that ultimately the system degenerated into a source of dispute and "fratching", as the daily toil of hard working yeomen was directly affected by the greed or slothfulness of their neighbours.

> Little boy blue, come blow up your horn,
> The sheep's in the meadow, the cows in the corn.
> Where is the boy who looks after the sheep?
> He's under the haystack, fast asleep!

Equally frustrating, weeds from neglected strips wafted gleefully across well-tended strips, and careless ploughmen encroached on other men's furrows.

Tenants therefore pressed the Court Baron to redistribute their scattered strips and to consolidate them into compact units or "closes", i.e. inclosures from the common field. In this way the slow process of inclosure began, as the "closes" were conveyed to the tenants as freehold, unlike the "doles" which were held as copyhold from the manor. The new freeholders of the manor paid a capital sum as well as an annual Lord's rent in acknowledgement of their privilege, and were bound to attend the sessions of the Court Baron at which they could be called upon to serve on the "homage", i.e. the jury.

This was the process used by the lord, Robert Batt, on June 25th, 1613, when he "grannted, barganed, soulde, aliened, enfeoffed and confirmed" to William Clarkson, tanner, of Heaton, for the sum of £155, a half part of the house in which William Clarkson dwelt (it was divided from the other half by a stone wall), the "east moytie of the lathe or barne" belonging to the house, half of the adjoining "foulde or backside", "the herbage and grasse of one lane called the Towne Lane", (i.e., Highgate), half a garden, "one garth called the Pittgarth", "the lower ende of a crofte", "one ynge or meadowe called Emmefielde", "one close or meadow called the Ashwell, lyinge and adjoyninge in the east parte one well or springe there called the Ashwell", "one close of lande and meadowe called the Overspringe" and the neighbouring "Pighell", the western half of "Springe Wood", also "foure other closes of land called the Westfielde or fieldes lyinge all together and adjoyninge to one Fielde there called Olde Manningham", together with "common of pasture for all manner of beasts, sheepe and cattell" normally kept on the common or moor, common of turbary, i.e., the right to dig turf for fuel "to be burnde and spent" in William Clarkson's home, "libertie to digg for and gett wallstones" for the repair of his buildings and walls, and

> "Free libertie to plowe and sowe from tyme to tyme for three years together two parts of such rateable and proportionate parts (the whole beinge into Three parts devided) of the Commons ... as shall from tyme to tyme hereafter be lymitted and allotted to the said William Clarkson ... in respect of the Premises hereby bargaaned and soulde ..., so often as the same moores ... shall by consent of the said Robert Batt ... and of all the Freehoulders ... be plowed and sowne with corne or grayne".

In acknowledgement of these privileges, William Clarkson bound himself to pay the lord 30s in two equal portions at Pentecost and the feast of St.Martin-in-winter, to

> "doe, observe and performe therefor Suit and Service to and at the Courte Baron and the Corne Mille of the said Robert Batte",

paying one bushel of grain for every 16 bushels ground there, for the first six years, and thereafter 1 bushel in every 20. Also, he must maintain the hedges and fences of the portion of common allotted to him.

Finally, if the commons and moors were at any time to be inclosed by mutual consent and divided between those who had common rights, the portion which William Clarkson had agreed to fence would be shared equally between him and the lord.

Two of the witnesses to the above deed, John Midgeley and Richard Batt, later in the same year served on a Royal Commission held at Wakefield for the purpose of examining all Military Tenures, i.e., tenure by "knight service" in the wapontake of Morley. They found that in Heaton the tenant of the manorial lands was James Garth, who leased "lands and tenements at Heaton in Bradforddaile, formerly belonging to Roger de Leedes, then to Lord Hussey and latterly to Henry Batt, gentleman, for which he pays yearly 1d." The land thus leased amounted to an eightieth part of a knight's fee, and seventeen other Heaton freeholders paid a similar sum, among them being Edward Field of Shipley. Eight other

Heatonians held a 1/160th part and therefore paid a halfpenny each.

When Robert Batt died in 1618 his son John, being only eleven and a half years of age, automatically became a ward of the Crown, but his wardship was quickly redeemed by his mother, Elizabeth, and his step-brother in law, George Parry, for the sum of £150 and an annual payment. At about the age of twenty John married Martha Mallory, daughter of the Dean of Chester, and purchased a captaincy in the local Regiment of Agbrigg and Morley.

The Craven family of Frizinghall, who had farmed land in the hamlet since the days of Queen Elizabeth, began their long association with the corn mill by a lease from the lord on April 30th, 1628. The lessee was George, a younger son of Robert Craven, yeoman, to whom Mr. Batt gave a thousand-year lease of the

> "… Water Corn Milne, Kilne and Close called the Milne Holme … situate,
> lyinge and beinge in Frisinghall aforesaid and within the Townshippe of
> Heaton, now or late in (the) tenure of one John Hurdson …"

The rent was "one redd rose in the tyme of roses, if the same be demanded" and an annuity or rent charge of 6s 8d payable from the income of the mill and from woods, meadows and pastures in Bolton.

By the time that Captain Batt officially came of age at 25 in 1631, his household included not only his wife and children but also his mother, stepfather, brothers, sisters, his half-sister, her husband and their children The alterations thus needed at Oakwell Hall may have been the reason for his sale of Heaton manor to John Smyth, Esq., of Miryshay, Bradford, in 1634.

For the first time in recorded history the lord of Heaton was a local man; how many of his predecessors had ever visited their remote Heaton estate is a matter for conjecture, as the manor consisted merely of undistinguished farmsteads, cottages, fields, woods and moors, and the steward who presided over the Court Baron was the only regular link between the lord and the tenants. Mr. Smyth's ownership was of brief duration,as on September 5th, 1634, he re-sold the manor "for a valuable consideration" to Joseph Field, Esq., of Shipley, son of Edward and William Midgley, Esq., of Baildon.

The complicated nature of manorial land transactions is exemplified in a grant made by the two joint lords on June 26th, 1635, to William Robinson, yeoman, of Bradford. In return for a payment of £4 4s 2d Mr. Robinson was granted:

> "Three whole parts and the eleventh part of another part of the commons,
> moors, the soil and ground of the common and moors, and of all mines and
> quarries and other profits, all of which were to be divided into 660 parts;
> > The Pease Close and the East of the Spring Close; A yearly rent of 2/- due
> from the under-tenant of Pease Close and 1s 11d from the other close."

The lessee would have to render suit and service at the Court Baron, which was held twice a year.

Many other references occur in the manorial records to the division of the commons, moors, waste grounds, mines etc. into 660 parts. These clearly related not to any form of physical division but to a proportional entitlement to the number of beasts allowed to graze, the quantities of turf which could be dug for personal use and the amount of stone which each tenant could excavate for building work. How the basic figure of 660 had been agreed upon in the first place is unclear.

On October 30th, 1635, William Midgley sold his share of the manor to Mr. Field, who thus became the sole lord.

Joseph Field was born in 1601 and baptised at the Parish Church in August of the same year. His father, Edward Field, was tenant in chief of land at Shipley, which he had inherited from his brother Robert in 1599, the year in which he married Janet Thornton of Bradford. Mr. Field senior died on April 6th, 1641, leaving to his son Joseph land at Heaton, which he had bought many years previously. Joseph Field was therefore a substantial landowner in the township, and his wife Mary, whom he had married in 1625, was the daughter of William Rawson, Esq., of Bracken Bank, Keighley.

The principal freeholders of the period were James Booth, William Capps, Richard and William Clarkson, Edward Cousen, Edward and William Crabtree, Thomas Exley, James Garth, Peter Gledhill, Richard Green, John and Samuel Holmes, John and William Jowett, Edward Midgley, Widow Northrop, Thomas Pighells, Richard Pollard, Robert Ramsden, William Scott and Richard Wilkinson. These were the leading men in the township, whose surnames recur in deeds and testaments, and one - Crabtree - survived until 1997 with at least four centuries of continuous residence in Heaton.

Edward Crabtree sometimes visited Adwalton Fair in search of a mount: -

"June 2nd, 1631: John Lewis of Barnborough, York, husbandman, soulde one mouse-colour fillie, trots unto Edw. Crabtree of Heaton in Bradford Dale."

On the same day, "John Dickson", probably of Heaton Royds, "exchanged one white-gray mare with Abraham Thomas of Manningham, clothier, giving 6d in exchange." Two and a half centuries later. After Adwalton Fair had faded into history, Wibsey Horse Fair was a favourite venue for the sale and purchase of horses, but Ted Greenwood of Parkside farm, Heaton (d.1968), a regular attender, soon learned to avoid dealers from Leeds who, he averred were "worse than the forty thieves" of Arabian legend.

A survey of the value of tithes due to the Parish Church by the townships within the parish was made in 1638 by Sir John Maynard, who reported that:

"The Tenants of Heaton plead prescription: they neither pay corn nor hay in kind but certain composition money which is part of the Easter Book. There is good common in Heaton, containing about 300 or 400 acres, part whereof may in time be enclosed, and so some benefit and profit may thereby arise."

In other words, the tenants had compounded (reached an agreement) with the Vicar whereby they made a monetary payment which was considered as part of his Easter dues.

Heaton had grown into a quiet rural area where breaches of the peace were rare. Thus, although Richard Cappes was convicted on October 11th, 1576, of having assaulted the constable, Willian Bayldon (alias Hobsonne), no other affray was recorded until 1628, when Christopher Pickard of Heaton Roydes was fined 10s for assaulting John Barraclough and drawing blood.

With the passage of years, much public business was transferred from the Leet to the Quarter Sessions, which, as their name implied, were held quarterly in rotation at the principal towns in the Riding. At the Sessions held in Halifax on October 2nd, 1637, Miles Wallis, blacksmith, of Horton, was tried for the theft of "one sacke, value 2d., the property of Mary Pearson" of Heaton. Subsequently in the same town Robert Wood, labourer, of

Wakefield, was summonsed "for stealing at Heaton on 20th September, 1638, a ewe sheep, value 3s, the property of Richard Mills." Had Wood intended to walk the ewe back to Wakefield or sell her to the nearest butcher? William Cappes, clothier, of Heaton, together with an Allerton farmer and a Manningham labourer was fined 2s 6d at Wakefield "for assaulting and maltreating on 10th November, 1640, at Bradford, Samuel Guy."

The late William Garth of Heaton had had a poor apprentice put to him by the Overseers of the Poor of Heaton, and when a dispute arose between his widow Mary and his heir James Garth as to the future custody of the youngster, the Sessions on October 3rd, 1638, ordered that Mary Garth "shall take and keepe the saide apprentice as by lawe she ought", because she had received a jointure of £14 from her husband's will in addition to £90 towards the administration of her late husband's personal estate.

Chapter 4 – Civil War, Restoration and Toleration

Troubled times lay ahead. Good Queen Bess had died thirty years earlier, and the policies of her unwise successors had divided the country between the adherents of the Crown and the upholders of Parliament. Civil war between "Cavaliers and Roundheads" erupted in 1642, bringing to the surface distrust and hostility between the Established Church and the Puritan dissenters, and, sadly, between members of the same family.

For the first time since the Wars of the Roses armed conflict threatened Bradford Dale. In October, 1642, and June, 1643, the town of Bradford was besieged by the Royalist army who bombarded the Parish Church tower and engaged in fierce battles, all of which would be clearly audible on Heaton's hilltop. Although the Bradford Beck did not run red with the blood of the slain, fugitives fled westward to Colne, and reinforcements from Bingley hastened to the battle.

Again on March 3rd, 1644, Bradford was the scene of battle, when a column of Parliamentary troops commanded by Major-General Lambert marched "out of Cheshire to Sowerby and from thence to Halifax and back to Keighley and so to Bradford." During one of these skirmishes a Royalist troop rode "through some of the parish villages" to deter Parliamentary sympathisers from joining the Bradford garrison, but withdrew when "some club-men from Bingley" arrived on the scene. It is likely that all these journeys to and from Colne, Bingley and Keighley were made by way of Toller Lane, so that Heaton, although not the scene of battle, experienced considerable activity. Interestingly, James Lister, historian of the Siege of Bradford, in his will dated March 4th, 1709, bequeathed £5 to Peter Crabtree of Heaton.

When both houses of Parliament resolved in May 1641 that loyal subjects should be required to support a Protestation in defence of the reformed religion, the commissioners despatched to Bradford dale in the following March reported that, "There are none within the severalle parishes, townships and hamlets contained in these schedules that have refused to take the protestation . . ." For Heaton forty-five heads of families attested to the commissioners, with Edward Bolling heading the list and Ferdinando Brown bringing up the rear. Crabtrees, Jowetts, Garths, Marshalls, Midgleys, Cravens, Greengates and Scotts were all emphatic in their loyalty. But which side did they take during the civil war? Official records provide a few clues.

At the Quarter Sessions held at Pontefract before Sir Thomas Fairfax, Thomas Midgley of Heaton, yeoman, together with three other men and no fewer than nine women from other parts of Bradford parish, was indicted for his part in "riotously assaulting and maltreating in the parish church - - -Nathan Bentley, clerk and preacher of God's Word, in the time of Divine service," on March 2nd, 1642. Mr. Midgley and his associates were evidently Anglicans scandalised by the dissenting doctrines being preached from the ancient pulpit.

Religious differences remained after the restoration of King Charles II in 1660, although surprisingly the York Depositions for 1665-1671 recorded only four persons in Heaton-cum-Clayton as nonconformists – James Bradley, John Bradley, Widow Jowett and John Kellet, of whom the last-named was probably a Claytonian. Doubtless many Puritan sympathisers were "occasional conformists" who attended the Parish Church from time to time, whereas the Bradleys, Jowetts and Kellets were among those who resisted the Established Church at all costs-Quakers, Independents and the like.

Nevertheless, the Parish Church remained indispensable to all believers, as for generations to come it was the only place at which baptisms, weddings and funerals could lawfully be performed, as all the above functions were arranged by the township churchwardens, it was not uncommon for whole batches of infants from the same township to be baptised on the same day. A rate or "lay" for the upkeep of the church was levied or "laid" on each township (and collected by the church warden) until Victorian times – "1667/8 Received of Heaton-cum-Clayton £1-16-0" – which implied that the two villages were assessed as separate townships for church purposes, as the "lay" that year was 18s per township. Similarly, "Allowed to the Churchwardens of Heaton and Clayton for their charges to visitations £0-6-0d", where the allowance was 3s per township.

The accounts for 1676 included the first reference to the fore-runner of the most prolific of all Heaton families, as well as a glimpse of a churchwarden's additional responsibilities: -

"Allowed to Daniell Greenwood, Churchwarden of Heaton, for two foxheads, 2s."

Victorian historians credited John Field, who succeeded to his father's manorial estate in 1660 - the year of the Restoration -, with the erection of Heaton Hall, the stately mansion which for generations was the family seat. However, records show that the family continued to reside at Shipley until the end of the century, and although the Hearth Tax records for Lady Day, 1666, list 178 hearths in Heaton-cum-Clayton, none belonged to the Fields. The only householders owning three hearths or more were:-

> Mr. Edward Bolling (Chellow) 6, Timothy Royds (Heaton Royds) 4,
> Jeremiah Holmes 4, Edward Marshall 3, Matthew Craven (Frizinghall) 3,
> James Lister (Frizinghall?) 3, William Bradshaw 3, John Midgley 3,
> Isaac Hollings 5, John Hirst 4, William Blamires 3, Richard Webster 3
> and Richard Holdsworth 5 -

of whom the five last-named were probably Claytonians. The houses of Edward Bolling (Chellow Grange) Timothy Royds (Royds Hall Farm) and Jereiah Holmes (possibly at Cross Hill Head) were obviously the largest houses in the township at that period.

Straying cattle and misuse of the commons continued to provoke discord between the freeholders of Heaton and their neighbours in Manningham and Shipley. In October, 1662, the Leet was obliged to order,

> ".... that the inhabitants within the Townshipp of Heaton doe Keepe and
> mainteyne one sufficient yate hung at a certaine place dividing betwixt
> Manningham and Heaton from tyme to tyme and at all tymes hereafter. Or
> in paine of not soe doeinge to forfeit the sum of 6s 8d."

The "certaine place" was probably the summit of Heights Lane, where the "yate" or gate served to prevent beasts from straying across the boundary, which was probably defined elsewhere by hedges.

Edward Bolling of Chellow was particularly vigilant against infringements of common rights. In April, 1665, he persuaded the Leet to order,

> ".... That no person dogg any Sheepe with any dogge upon Heaton Moore
> belonging to the freeholders or tenants in Heaton upon payne of 39s 6d."

A few months later, in company with his fellow freeholders Edward Marshall and James Lister he laid a complaint against Jonathan Jowett of Heaton Royds in Shipley, who, he alleged, "hath digged turves" on Heaton Moor and carried them away despite previous warnings. Not content with that, he had also "ffoddered his cattle" upon the moor, which as a Shipley dweller he was not entitled to do. These charges were stoutly refuted by Jonathan Jowett.

Nevertheless Mr.Bolling was himself not entirely beyond reproach. In October, 1677, he was fined 40s (£2) upon the complaint of Robert Holdsworth, constable of Heaton-cum-Clayton, because (in Latin which would have baffled Augustus Caesar),

"…. non dejecit (Anglice, hath not taken downe) stagnum molare ad usual altitudinem in ffrizinghall …"

The inference is that the weather in the summer and autumn of 1677 had been dry, causing the level of the Bradford Beck to fall. The mills higher up the dale - Leaventhorpe, Sam's Mill, the Bradford Soke Mill and Frizinghall (Upper) Mill in Bolton township - had accordingly raised their dams in order to impound a sufficient head of water for their waterwheels. However, when Mr.Bolling, then tenant downstream at "ffrizinghall lower Mill in Heaton" (i.e., Dumb Mill) followed their example, he raised his "Mill damm" so high that not only did he succeed in grinding all his grain but also caused "the water called Bradford Beck or ffrizinghall Beck which runneth to the said Mill to flow across the King's Highway leading from Bradford to Otley, to the peril of travellers being subjects of the King who were travelling upon the same".

The judgement was, "That Mr.Edw.Bollinge do before the four and 20th day of June next (i.e., nine months hence!) take downe one Mill Damme called ffryzinghall lower Mill to its usuall height, upon paine for every moneth's neglect 40s."

No doubt the nuisance - and the flood - eventually subsided, but disagreements about common rights arose intermittently between the lord (Mr.Field) and the freeholders, and between the freeholders themselves.

An attempt was therefore made in 1674 to solve the disputes by persuading the interested parties to enclose the whole of the commons and divide them between themselves:

"20 Charles II, 1674 [1]. Article of Agreement entitled An Article between the Lord of Heaton and the freeholders for dividing the Royalty.

Article of Agreement between John Field of Shipley, yeoman, and - - - Weddell of Bradford, gentleman, Lancelot Emott of - - -, John Craven of Bradley in the parish of Kildwick, yeoman, James Garth of Idle, yeoman, John Hall of Thornton, yeoman, James Lister of Phrisonell [2], yeoman, Christopher Freckleton, Jeremy Holmes, Samuel Holmes senior, Samuel Holmes junior, William Crabtree, John Jowett and John Crabtree, all of Heaton.

Whereas the said Partners to these Presents are and stand joyntly seized of an Estate of Inheritance in fee of All the Commons, Moors and Waste of and in the Town, Township or Lordship of Heaton and of the soyle of the same and of all the Mines,Quarries and profits thereof, and forasmuch as some question or dispute has lately arisen between the said parties by reason of the same not being divided but held in common between the said parties, it is hereby agreed that to resolve all doubts and disputes the said Commons, Moors and Waste Grounds shall be divided into two equal parts or moieties which shall be inclosed, and it is agreed that the said John Field shall have first ballot by drawing from a fair hat or bonnet one of two balls of wax, and shall hold to himself and his heirs only that part or portion as shall be mentioned in the scroll inclosed in the wax ball, and the other party shall do likewise."

The fair hat (or bonnet) was not needed, as the freeholders declined to sign. All were yeomen farmers (with the exception of Mr. Weddell who leased his lands - three Emm Fields and two Springs - to tenants.)

The old ways therefore continued, with the livestock on the High and Low Moors, Lord's Rents when demanded, and suit and service at the Court Baron each September.

One of the earliest references to the mining of coal in Heaton township occurred in 1665 when a "payne" was laid by the Leet,

> "that William Dixon of Bollinge and John Crabtree of Manningham shall Remove all the gravell of earth, stones and scale digged forth of the Harrie Rhods Coalpitts --- which by their procurement was throwne into the highwayes and ditches belonginge to Heaton, upon payne of 39s 6d."

William Dixon was born in 1619 at the family home at Heaton Royds. A strong Puritan like his father he had joined Cromwell's army at the outbreak of the civil war, eventually rising to the rank of captain as had his fellow townsman Captain Lister of Frizinghall. When peace returned he resumed his rural life, supplemented (as indicated above) by the digging out of shallow bell-pits at the top of Heaton Lane (Frizinghall Road). The coal, of indifferent quality, supplemented the wood fuel which was becoming scarcer as the population increased.

Country highways in the seventeenth century were winding, irregular and narrow, and great complaint arose when travellers found their way impeded by neglected and overgrown hedges. One such complainant was Edward Bollinge of Chellow who at the Court Leet held on April 20th, 1665 "layd a payne" to the effect that:

> "All the owners and occupiers of all such lands and tenements as do adjoyne from a certain place called Hill Clough alias Dean Hill Clough to a place called Chellow lane leading from Chellow houses to Heaton Moore and from Chellow lane end to the lane end leading from Heaton Moore to Theevesfore and from the said lane end leading from Haworth to Bradford and from thence to a place called Towlerlane end and from the said Towler Lane to a lane called Lillands and from thence to Heaton pinnfold, from thence to a place called Royds Clough beck, from thence to a place called Weather Royd nooke, from thence to the division betwixt Heaton and Shipley called North Clough, That they repair their fenses att all tymes and Keepe them so repaired upon paine of 39s 6d for everye default.
>
> Also that William Greengate remove all Rubbish out of Chellow lane and repaire the fenses of the lands in his possession before this day month upon payne of 39s 6d."

These were by no means the only attempts to prevent obstruction of the highways. At the Court Leet and View of Frankpledge held on March 29th, 1627/8 in the third year of the reign of King Charles I the townsfolk of Heaton had made complaint as follows: -

> "Heaton cu Clayton u villat' ibm. Jur. Psent. qd. Jacobus Garthe edificavit un domu furnae et un suit' in alta strata in Heaton ad nocum entu vicinij suos, Ideo &c."

In other words the township of Heaton-cum-Clayton (through its constable) made a sworn presentment that James Garth had built an oven-house in the highway in Heaton, probably on the brow of Town Street, to the annoyance of his neighbours, although the oven may have been for public use.

In October, 1662, the "Inhabitants of Heaton" were fined 2s at the Leet for having failed to maintain "the Church Way at the east end or side of Chellowfields." The neglected thoroughfare was presumably "the lane leading from Haworth to Bradford" complained of by Edward Bolling in 1665: indeed, he may have been the complainant on both occasions, as the ruinous condition of the lane impeded his weekly journeyings between "Chellow houses" and the Parish Church at Bradford.

Law and order were evidently in a sounder condition than the highways, as on the same day it was reported from Heaton-cum-Clayton that,

> "Josias Craven Const' et socij sui ibidem Jur' p'sent qd. Josephus Shoesmith de Clayton elect' est Const. ibidem hoc Anno et Jur', et quod Samuel Holmes Sen. Electus est deput' eius et Jur', et qd. Omnia sunt bene."

In other words, Josias Craven of Heaton, having completed his year's duty as constable of the joint township together with his deputies from Clayton, was reporting the election of Joseph Shoesmith of Clayton as the incoming constable and Samuel Holmes of Heaton as his deputy, after which both were sworn in and the retiring constables affirmed that all was well in both "hamlets".

Harryroyds were a source of contention again in October, 1686, when the Leet jurors were obliged to order,

> "... that no person or persons do pull downe any fences or drive any horses or any other goods whatsoever over the Harryroids, now in Daniell Greenwood's occupation, lyeing between Heaton and ffrizinghall, upon paine of 3s 4d for every offence."

No doubt impatient persons travelling between the two settlements were accustomed to "cut a corner" across the land in preference to fording the sticky quagmire which constituted the highway at that point.

A similar quagmire was created by Joshua Marshall of Heaton who, on October 4th, 1695, diverted Shaw Sike from its time-honoured course where it flowed from Bents Close towards the low common, with the result that it "invaded" and overflowed "the King's Highway leading between the Town of Heaton and the Town of Manningham", to the discomfort of horses and carriages. As the floods had not abated by the following May he was fined 4s 4d at the Leet.

Inundations of a more serious nature overwhelmed the valley bottom from time to time; a century later Dumb Mills were marooned in a vast sheet of water following continuous rainfall.

Among the most remarkable and distinctive disciples of the Reformation were the Society of Friends or Quakers, whose founder George Fox travelled far and wide to denounce "steeple houses" (Anglican churches) as well as other dissenters. His Journal for 1652 recorded that,

> "... wee passed away to Bradforde, and there wee came to an house ... ye woman was a Baptist, and after I had admonished her and ye people to turne to ye Lorde Jesus Christ and hearken unto him, their teacher, I passed away. And soe wee passed through ye Country preaching repentans to ye people ..."

His journey seems to have taken him along Toller Lane: did he turn aside to "preach repentans" at Heaton? If he did, his seed certainly bore fruit in due season, as the Quarter Sessions agreed in January, 1694,

> "... that the Dwelling house of James Askwith in Heaton be recorded as a place of

The township boundary, photographed on 11 May 1958, at the junction of Heaton Road and Parkside Drive, where Joshua Marshall created a quagmire in 1695. In the foreground (left), the wooden posts mark the pre 1939 site of the entrance gates to the park attached to Heaton Hall. Milford Place (right) was built in 1883 by Thomas Smith and Henry Dyson, of Heaton.

(Copyright: author)

Religious Worshipp for the people comonly called Quakers, pursuant to the late Act of Parliament intituled an Act to exempt their Majesties' protestant subjects dissenting from the Church of England from sundry penall laws".

Much more successful, however, was the preaching of William Mitchell, a Calvinist evangelist who undertook an extensive tour of Lancashire and the West Riding in the later years of Charles II and throughout the reign of James II, being arrested twice under the Conventicles Act for preaching the doctrine of Believers' Baptism. The second of these arrests was made near Bradford, probably either at Heaton or Rawdon; fortunately the good influence of Walter Calverley, Esq., procured his release from York Castle a few days before King James - for reasons of his own – proclaimed his Declaration of Indulgence on April 14th, 1687.

Thereafter on several occasions Mr. Mitchell broke bread for the small Nonconformist community at Heaton which met at James Garth's new house in Town Street, i.e., Garth House. Having failed to obtain ordination as a Presbyterian minister, he was induced by his cousin David Crosley to embrace Baptist teachings. The Baptist cause developed quickly, and its branches at Heaton, Rawdon, Gildersome and Hartwith were the earliest in the West Riding, snuffing out Quaker beliefs in Heaton. Their central tenet was the doctrine of adult baptism by total immersion, like John in the Jordan, except that for Heaton folk the humbler waters of Cliffe Dike in the upper reaches of Heaton Woods had to suffice.

The use of local stone for building purposes was recorded as early as 1613 (see above), and it is likely that by the end of the century the old, timber-framed dwellings and barns had been replaced by more substantial structures. Heaton sandstone was of the "cleavage" variety with a well-defined grain which allowed ti to be split into regular-shaped wallstones, flagstones and roofing-slabs. The new roofing materials, sometimes illogically termed "stone slates" replaced thatch in the eighteenth centuury. The quarries, known as "delphs" were worked by "delvers" who hewed the stone and sent it to the surface for dressing by masons, but it was not until about 1770 that any delph began to operate as a commercial venture.

(1) Faulty arithmetic: 1674 was the 25th or the 14th year of the reign of "the Merry Monarch", according to whether one's loyalties were Royalist or Parliamentarian.
(2) An exotic rendering of "Frizinghall".

Garth House, built by James Garth in 1681 and photographed by James Greenwood in August, 1932. The building behind it is the front of the 'Delvers' Arms'.

The Land Tax was first instituted by Parliament in 1692 at a rate of 4/- in the pound for the laudable purpose of "carrying on a vigorous War against France." (or, more precisely, its rapacious King Louis XIV).

Levied on the basis of a locally assessed valuation of land and property, the West Riding contribution was about £39,362, to which Morley wapentake contributed £5,327[1]. The earliest surviving Heaton assessment dated 1703, [2] aimed to raise £46-6-8d at the 4/- rate: -

Edward Bolling
William Bolling
John Field, junior
Robert Binns
James Booth, for Greengate Farm
Jeremy Dixon or occupiers
Benjamin Waugh
John Booth
Thomas Walker
James Hall or occupiers
John Gaukrodger
James Lister, senior
John Clapham, or occupiers
Joseph Gaukrodger
George Beanland
John Field, for Craven's Close
Joseph Field or occupiers
James Garth
William Bolling for Jowett's land
James Garth for Marshall's land
Joshua Marshall
Mr. Maison or occupiers
John Holmes
Jonas Crabtree
Jonas Craven

	£	s	d
James Lister, junior			
Occupiers of South Fields			
Occupiers of Exley Farme			
John Crabtree for Lower Moor			
Occupiers of Harry Royds			
John Field, senior			
William Crabtree			
James Garth for Jowett's land		4	9
James Lister and James Garth for parts of Weddell's land	1	6	7
Occupiers of Firth Carr		14	8
Josias Craven for Shaw Farme		15	6
William Crabtree for Lane End Close		2	3
James Lister for Capps land		10	6
for Freckleton's land		2	2
for Milne Holme		2	2
Jeremy Dixon for West Field		4	10
Josias Craven for Ryalls		2	4
James Lister for Mr. Garnett		17	0
John Field for his free rente		14	0
	£46	6	8

William Bolling)
John Crabtree) Assessors

May 15th, 1703
John Holmes, Collector

Two years later the assessment made by Joseph Gawkrodger and Joseph Field was confirmed by James Farrer, Michael Firth and Richard Richardson, justices, on "May ye 18th, 1705."

(1) "Search Guide to the English Land Tax" - West Yorkshire Record Office, 1982.
(2) Archives of the Earl of Rosse.

Village life in Heaton assumed a new significance with the construction of Heaton Hall in the reign of Queen Anne. A stately, imposing residence situated on the brow of Town Street with a gently-sloping southerly aspect, it bore a close resemblance to other mansions in the locality such as Bradford Manor House (1705), Tong Hall (1702) and Shipley House (1710). More importantly, its owners were Mr. John Field, the lord of the manor, and his family, who were to play a significant role in the life and development of the Township. Mr. Field died in October, 1712, being succeeded by his unmarried nephew Joseph (born 1660) who died in 1733, leaving as his heir Mr. John Field, junior (born 1701), who was the son of another John Field (1661-1731), yeoman, of Chellow, and his wife Grace, daughter of Timothy Rhodes of Heaton Royds.

Throughout the length and breadth of the country the ever-growing burden of the Poor Rate was causing dispute and dissension among township ratepayers, particularly those who resented paying for "other folk's poor". The post-1660 Restoration Parliament had accordingly enacted a law of settlement and removal whereby those who chose to take up residence in a township had to find sufficient surety to guarantee the ratepayers against any demand on their purses. Anyone who visited a district even for a short period, e.g., for the harvest, had to produce a certificate testifying that the township wherein he had a lawful "settlement" would receive him back afterwards.

Vigilance was therefore exercised by the overseers against subterfuges such as over-long visits, payment of rates or the acceptance of office, all of which could confer a right of settlement. If it were thought necessary to remove an individual, a magistrate's warrant could be obtained (as a last resort) in the event

John Field of Heaton Hall, lord of the manor; born in 1701 and died in 1772. His monument can be seen in Bradford Cathedral.
(Photo: author, courtesy of the Earl of Rosse)

of a refusal to depart, when the "stranger" would be escorted on his way by the constable of each township through which he (or she) was due to pass. In this way the Heaton constable would meet his Manningham, Allerton, Bingley, Shipley, Idle or Bolton counterpart to hand over or take charge of paupers or beggars on the next stage of their reluctant journey.

Strict though the system undoubtedly was, it was not entirely devoid of mercy; illness could bring a stay of execution, and carts were provided for those who were unable to walk, while appeals could be made against a removal order. In later years William Stead was one of the successful appellants. Born at Shipley in 1773 and trained as a weaver, he went to Scriven-with-Tentergate in 1791 as a servant in the house of a Mr. Atkinson. A year later he removed to Bradford to serve Samuel Crossley, spirit merchant, but left his post within seven months to marry at Leeds, subsequently working as a weaver at weekly wages for anyone who would employ him. In 1798, having removed to Heaton and unable to find work he returned to Scriven and applied for relief, whereupon the overseer gave him a night's lodging at the workhouse and a parting gift of £1-9s-0d. Returning to Heaton, he plied his trade until 1842 when at the age of 69 he applied to the Heaton overseers for assistance. The magistrates upheld the overseer's view that his legal place of settlement was Scriven and ordered his removal, upholding their decision on appeal.

The tale had a happy ending, as his family took him in. Nine years later he was recorded as a lodger with his son Samuel and his wife, their son, three daughters and another lodger in a cottage at Garter Row whose accommodation was so limited that several people must have slept in the same bed and others in a "shut-up" (i.e., fold-away) bed in the living-room! Subsequently on June 5th, 1865, "Mr. Samuel Stead entertained his family at Mr. Nathan Firth's, the 'Hare and Hounds', Heaton. The occurrence is worthy of note, as the party included five generations, viz., Mr. Stead's father (92) with all his faculties perfect, Mr. Stead himself, eight of his children, their children and grandchildren, total sixty. This was to celebrate Mr. Stead's fiftieth birthday, and the novelty and rarity excited great interest in Heaton. Mine host of the 'Hare and Hounds' fully maintained his credit as a caterer - the 'spread' was in every respect worthy of the occasion."

Evidently "the changes and chances of this fleeting world" had a beneficial effect on old William Stead, who at the age of 94 later achieved fame as the oldest participant in the "Old Folk's Gathering" of 1868 (see below)!

Two centuries previously, however, the workhouses of which Mr. Stead had so brief a taste were in their infancy. Finding the expense of a separate establishment unjustifiable, Heaton's overseers had approached their counterparts in Manningham whose accounts noted the agreement which they had reached:-

> "1699 - Paid for half of goods when Heaton joined in the Workhouse
>
> £6 11s-8d"

This new partnership with their near neighbour enabled Heaton's officers to realise how irksome the joint arrangements with Clayton were; one can imagine that the endless weekly journeying to and fro must have proved a weary burden for the overseers in the wet and wintry weather. A petition from "the Freeholders and Inhabitants of the Township of Heaton cum Clayton" was presented to the Quarter Sessions held in Leeds in July, 1701, when the jury heard that the Township

> "...consists of two Distinct Hamletts lyinge a considerable Distance from each
> other, so that the Churchwardens and Overseers of the Poor and other
> principal Inhabitants and Freeholders residing in each Hamlett, being
> necessitated to have frequent meetings abt. making Assessments, passing
> Accounts and other necessary occupations relating to the maintenance of the
> Poor within the Townshipp, do not only spend yearly considerable sums of
> money but are often also involved in differences and dissensions, by reason
> whereof the joint charge of maintaining the Poor of this said Townshipp is

much unsettled, and they not so well provided for as they might with lesser charge to both Hamletts in case the said Hamlett of Heaton and the said Hamlett of Clayton were for some tyme allowed, each of them to maintain and provide for their own poor severally, without being accountable the one to the other." . . .

The magistrates agreed to allow both "hamletts" to revert to their former status as "two Distinct Towns" for "one and twenty years", and awarded to Clayton the interest on a sum of £30 belonging to the township which had presumably been the bequest of a Clayton resident.

Second thoughts must have prevailed, as an agreement probably made a few years later [1] set out new arrangements, i.e.,

"Terms of Agreement Establisht and settled betwixt and amongst the town officers and inhabitants of Heaton-cum-Clayton touching the joint Management of their Affaires relateing to the Poor:-

That the Overseers of the Poor and two or three at most of the Principall Inhabitants out of each Hamlet meet every two monthes to view the State of the Poor, increase or Mitigate theire allowances, give or receive Certificates, put out poor Apprentices, and amicably join in makeing Rates, passing accounts and other necessary acts relateing to the poor.

That all these meetings shall be at Nine of the Clock in the morning in one of the Hamletts, and after the viewing the poor in that Hamlett the Company to part for two houres, dine at their respective habitations, meeting againe about two in ye afternoon in the other Hamlett to carry on the same business, which being ended, each overseer shall expend and pay for himselfe and those he takes with him four pence apiece, and noe more to be allowed by the Towne.

That noe Overseer in either Hamlet presume to disburse anything to the poor but according to his View Bill [1], except in case of sicknesse and with the consent of such townesmen in his Hamlet as assisted at the foregoing View, or by order of some Justice of Peace, and that the Overseers mutually communicate to each other and to the townsmen at theire next meeting an honest account of theire disbursements and proceedeings in their office[2], that the good and welfare of the whole Township may be better consulted and promoted."

Rumblings and "fratchings" must have persisted, however, as the Sessions held at Wakefield on October 5th, 1704, requested Walter Calverly, Robert Ferrand and Francis Lindley[3], justices,

"... to examine the Assessment for the whole Townshipp ... to the poor, and all other matters, and to settle the same equally, and that all Assessments to be made for the future be made according to such regulation."

The parting of the ways, for poor-law purposes at least, came on October 6th, 1726, when the Sessions at Leeds received

"... a Certificate of an Agreement under the hands of the principall and major

(1) the list of observations made when the officers viewed the poor.
(2) i.e., their official capacity.
(3) Of Calverley, Bingley and Bowling respectively

part of the Freeholders and Inhabitants of Heaton cum Clayton in the said Riding, purporting That the Hamlet of Heaton and the Hamlet of Clayton, Each of them, shall maintain their own poore separately without being accountable one to the other, in such manner as if the said Hamletts were two Distinct Townshipps from henceforth until both the said Hamletts do agree to join in the maintenance of their said poor."

A later reference to the joint township was made on July 12th, 1733, when the Sessions held at Bradford decreed that

"... the Surveyors of the Highways of Heaton cum Clayton and Manningham Be summoned to ... give account of the Highways within their respective Townships."

But the Highways Surveyors like the Churchwardens and Constables must already have agreed to part company, as when the "presentment or indictment" was reviewed and deferred in January, 1734, the reference was confined to the townsfolk of Heaton and Manningham. The "marriage" was at an end.

Since the Middle Ages Bradford Dale had been engaged in the wool and clothing trade, and when the parish registers began to include references to occupations in 1713, Heaton's Joseph Shaw, Samuel Kitching, John Jowett and John Broadley were recorded as tailor, clothier, woolcomber and weaver respectively. The task of producing the necessary yarn was usually left to the ladies; Mary Morvel was listed in 1717 as "spinster", a term which probably indicated her status as well as her trade,

The increasing importance of commerce began to promise greater benefits to ordinary folk than the immemorial habit of self-sufficiency, but the difficulty of transporting goods to other parts of the country was not solved until the evolution of the pack-horse system of travel. Eventually long files of laden animals could be seen wending their way over the moorland tracks, headed by an experienced horse whose tinkling bell marked him (or her) out as the leader. Hence the old rhyme familiar to children until the mid 20th century:-

"Bell-horses, bell-horses, what time of day?
One o'clock, two o'clock, three - and away!"

Hence, too, the expression, "laden like a packhorse." The highways, however, were seldom satisfactory. At Leeds Quarter Sessions in October, 1736, Josias Craven of Frizinghall, yeoman, was

"... indicted for a Nuisance in erecting several Wood Stoops in a certain place called the Low Lane in Heaton, to the Stopping of the Passage of Loaded Horses. It is ordered that it be recommended to Sir Walter Calverley, Baronet, to View the said Way and certify the State and condition thereof at next Wakefield Sessions."

Even without the wooden posts Low Lane (later Frizinghall Road) was narrower than "the Breadth allowed and required by Law", and eventually in July, 1763, the Bradford Sessions impanelled Mr. John Field, James Hodgson, Benjamin Hird, John Bailey, Samuel Lister, David Binns and John Cordingley, all local townsmen, as a jury charged with assessing compensation payable to landowners for land needed to widen the lane "to the Breadth of Eight Yards, pursuant to an Act for enlarging Common Highways made in the 8th and 9th years of the reign of his late Majesty King William III (1696). No house to be pulled down nor the Grounds of any Orchard, Court or Yard to be taken away."

Having viewed the site, the jury resolved as follows:-

"Township of Heaton and Frizinghall

Owner	Tenant	Value of lands by the acre	East & West sides of roads	Expense of fence removal, by the rood
Mr.Benj. Hird	–	£ 1- 5-0	East	£ 0- 6-0
James Lister	Joshua Hainsworth	£ 1- 5-0		£ 0- 6-0
John Redshaw	Joshua Tetley	£ 1- 2-6	Both	£ 0- 6-0
James Lister	–	£ 1- 5-0	West	£ 0- 6-0
Benj. Hird	John Spence	£ 1-10-0	East	£ 0- 3-0
John Dawson	Abraham Hustler	£ 1- 5-0		£ 0- 7-6
		£ 7-12-6		£ 1-14-6

The lane was duly widened, but persistent complaints from wayfarers led to a fine of £300 in April, 1787, "... to be forthwith estreated and levied" upon the ratepayers for the repair of Low Lane,

"... leading from Halifax in, through and over the said Township of Heaton to Otley, (to wit), for the Space of 880 yards in length and 8 yards in breadth ... from a certain Ditch and Watercourse named Carr Sike, dividing the Township of Heaton and Manningham in the said Riding ..."

In the reign of George I other highways were traversed by John Warburton in preparation for his " Map of Yorkshire from actual Survey, with a list of the nobility and gentry and their Coats of Arms", which he published in 1720. On the morning of May 8th, 1719, he walked "from ye Cross" in Bradford over the hills to Halifax, observing "Heeton o' th' Hill" to the north as well as "Clayton town" and "Thornton town". Five months later he took bearings from suitable viewpoints such as Bradford and Keighley church towers, whence "Heeton oth Hill" or "Heeton Town" were said to be visible, and afterwards he surveyed the wider panorama obtainable from the "Hill on Heaton Moor called Stony Rigg", including Denholme Park, Harden, Hope Hill, Hawksworth, Yeadon, Guiseley and Idle.

Meanwhile the religious life of the township was being reinvigorated by visiting Baptist preachers. A favourite visitor to Heaton was the Rev. John Moore, who is known to have preached in April, 1697, on Romans 5, v.1 ("Therefore being justified by faith, we have peace with God through our Lord Jesus Christ"). Again, on June 29th, 1711, he delivered a sermon which was a testimony to the enthusiasm and endurance of his Heaton friends, as in the estimation of the Rev. Richard Howarth who saw it 170 years later, its duration was one and a half hours! The title, "Christ the Mediator", was based on Colossians 1, v.19 ("For it pleased the Father that in Him should all fulness dwell").

Increasing numbers emboldened the members to erect a small chapel and graveyard, believed by a later minister (the Rev. H. Dawson) to have been about a hundred yards north of its 1824 successor. Demolished about 1795, its site was long known as Chapel Fold, where John Gott, who tilled the soil at the time of the Napoleonic Wars, occasionally turned up evidence of man's mortality. A quarry engulfed the site about 1870.

In 1712 William Rawson of Heaton, physician, was appointed one of the first trustees of the Rawdon chapel, and two years later the four West Riding fellowships seceded from their Rossendale mother church to form a separate body under the pastorate of the Rev. John Wilson. Among the original Heaton members was the Rev. Alvary Jackson, who was received into fellowship in 1715 and entered the ministry a year later. Fortunes fluctuated, and after 1751 the Heaton members joined the congregation which met at the house of Elizabeth Frankland in Manningham, later becoming founder members of the "Top o't Tahn Chapel" in Westgate, Bradford.

Widespread alarm pervaded the district in 1745 with news of an invasion of the Scottish army of Bonnie Prince Charlie; those who possessed valuables hurriedly buried them, and subscriptions were raised for a volunteer corps to uphold the House of Hanover. Fortunately the rebels approached no nearer than Manchester.

From time to time isolated farmholdings were created, with buildings erected either on the farmer's freehold land or on fields enclosed from the moor by permission of the lord in return for a "fine" and an annual rent. In this way several smallholdings collectively known as Heaton Shay had been built in the reign of William III on the edge of the common, close by the mediaeval hamlet of Heaton Royds.

At the top of Emm Lane the little settlement at Cross Hill Head where Dr. Rawson "practitioner in physick", was living in 1709, was added to from time to time – minute cottages known in later years as Stocks Yard, Emm Lane Top, and Hammond Square – and occasionally new cottages were built (or older ones rebuilt) in Back Lane, Back Fold, Town Street or Town End: grey, homely huddles which constituted the Town of Heaton.

On the southern verge of the township, between "Towler Lane" and the old "King's Highway" from Heaton to Manningham (nowadays called Heaton Road), John Crabtree was tenant of fields based on Low Moor Farm, built about 1700 and rebuilt in 1796. Not far away, at the foot of the Holt, old Richard Thompson, carpenter, had built his own farmstead on land which he had bought in 1729. The house still bears his initials and those of his wife Mary (RMT, 1734), but as his personal holdings were too small to support his family, he rented fields from the more affluent Marshall family. Mr. Thompson's new house was pleasantly situated on the north bank of the Syke, adjacent to older cottages described in 1760 as "three several cottages at Heaton lately enjoyed as a cottage and shop with stable and garden", which had been listed a generation earlier (1716) as "two cottages under one roof where Michael Escolme and Mary Isitt dwell, with the foldstead and shopp or smithy shopp, formerly cottages, in the occupation of Joseph Woodhead". The two cottages, and a stable on the south bank, were subject to a Lord's Rent, having been built on land enclosed from the common.

Joseph Woodhead was the first Heaton blacksmith of whom any record survives, although George Booth, mentioned in parish records between 1719 and 1729, had occupied a smithy elsewhere in Heaton. Mr. Woodhead's successors appear to have been James Mortimer and his son, who were plying their trade in the "shopp" at the Syke between about 1779 and 1812, the father of James the elder having bought it from Abraham and Joseph Kershaw of Skircoat, Halifax, in 1765.

Frizinghall too was little more than a scattering of farmsteads between Frizingley Hall, rebuilt in 1728 by James Lister, tanner, and Old Castle, a large quaint farmstead in Buckstalls Lane. Higher up at Firth Carr, Joseph Child farmed the steep fields which ascended towards Heaton, whilst another group of cottages occupied a pleasant site on the northern bank of Carr Syke, the eastern branch of the Syke which flowed down from Heaton.

A glimpse of the prolonged excitement aroused by a parliamentary election campaign is

Firth Carr Farm, photographed from Heaton Grove on 5 May 1958. The site is now covered by the Aireville Rise (etc.) estate.   *(Copyright: author)*

Frizingley Hall, erected by James Lister in 1728, and photographed by the author on 21 April 1973.

provided by an anonymous "List of the Freeholders in and near Bradford with Coll'suns shewing how it is expected they will vote and act at the next Election for the County of York which is to begin May 15, 1734. Sir Rowland Winn, Chomley Turner Esq. and Sir Miles Stapleton, Candidates."

<u>Heaton on the Hill and Frizinghall Freeholders.</u>

U	P				W	T	S
1		Peter Crabtree		Old			
		Richard Thompson		Old	1	1	
1		Mr. Field				1	
1		Mr. Bradford		Mort.			
1		Joseph Gaugroger		Mort.			
		Joseph Drake			1	1	
1		Jno. Crabtree					
			Abm. Rhodes	Mort.		1	
		James Lambert	Jere. Rhodes			1	
		Peter Watkinson					1
1		Geo. Beanland		Mort.			
1		James Booth		Mort.			
1		George Booth					1
		Josiah Craven			1		1
		James Lister					1
		Saml. Lister					1
		Abraham Rhodes			1	1	
1		Joseph Beanland			0	0	
	1	Matthew Cordingley				1	
	1	Peter Atkinson				1	
1		Jno. Rawson				1	
		Jno. Beanland				1	
		Joseph Beanland			1		

The names of those that want Horses –

Jos Drake and Matthew Cordingley of Heaton.

(Key – P = polled, i.e., canvassed; U = unpolled; Mort = deceased, and W, T and S = the candidates' initials).

The problem of transport for voters was particularly important before the Reform Act of 1832, as the election was held at York Castle!

The delightful title of "Heaton on the Hill" was often used in the 18th century to distinguish the township from its lesser rivals, the Cleck-, Kirk- and Hanging Heatons elsewhere in the Riding. It was also used by the Moravians who about 1742 established a small but short-lived "society" in the township; their teachings were superseded by those of the Methodists, who, under the influence of John Bennet, established a foothold in Heaton in 1744.

Chapter 7 — Turnpikes

The outside world was brought appreciably nearer by the creation of Turnpike Trusts. Hitherto, narrow causeways and country lanes scarcely meriting the title of "The King's Highway" had wandered casually from village to village, and paving materials were deemed unnecessary on the grounds that roads would improve spontaneously if left to their own devices! Small wonder, then, that when Squire Field journeyed to Bradford, he needed a team of six horses to drag his carriage through the sloughs which constituted the highways of Manningham.

"Every season of the year brought to the roads a different and unenviable character," wrote Joan Parkes in 1925. "In summer there was a smothering dust; in spring and autumn ruts filled with water; in winter the mud levelled road and ditch to a quagmire, except during periods of hard frost when it turned to ice - until a thaw brought its own peculiar dangers. Sometimes a rider would be up to the saddle-girths in mud, and the humble wayfarer would think it no uncommon hardship to walk in mud to the ankles."

The ancient packhorse track past Chellow to Haworth, Two Laws and Wycoller Causeway to Colne and Clitheroe, probably little altered since the days of John of Gaunt, gave way after 1755 to the Toller Lane, Haworth and Blue Bell Turnpike Trust whose starting-point, an engraved stone at the bottom of the new Haworth Lane, proclaimed the distance to Colne as $17^1/_2$ miles. The former condition of the road was ruefully described in the preamble to the Bill laid before Parliament:

> "Whereas the Road leading from the West End of Toller-Lane near Bradford, over Chelleyheight and Cullingworth Moor, through Haworth and Stanbury to a place called The Two Laws, in the County of York, and so, by Lanshaw Bridge to a Place called Blue Bell near to the Town of Colne in the County Palatine of Lancaster, and the Road branching from the said Place called the Two Laws to Keighley ... where the Roads from Bradford and Keighley to the said Town of Colne unite, are in a very Ruinous Condition, and in some places not only very narrow and incommodious but almost impassable for Wheel-carriages, and sometimes very dangerous for Travellers, and are incapable of being effectually repaired and widened by the ordinary Course of Law,
>
> May it therefore please your Majesty etc."

His Majesty (King George II) duly saw fit to sanction the measure under the auspices of Trustees who owned property in the areas which might be expected to benefit from the turnpike. Locally, the Fields of Heaton Hall and Shipley Fields together with their neighbours Samuel Lister (Manningham), Edward Leedes (Royds Hall, Low Moor), Thomas Busfield (Harden), Abraham Balme (Bradford), Gilbert Brooksbank (Horton), John Hird (Cottingley) and Richard and William Hodgson (Whetley, Manningham) were amongst the earliest trustees and subscribers.

Work began in earnest on July 30th, 1755, when an estimate was sought "for repairing the road from the Toller Lane Gate to the Two Laws, to cast the bed 21 feet between ditches, to be stoned 12 inches thick in the middle (for a breadth of 15 feet) and 6 inches at the edge, the stone to be small broken, with 3 inches of (stone) gravel."

The length within Heaton, from Haworth Lane Bottom (i.e., Toller Lane End), "over Cottingley Moor" (actually Chellow Height) was estimated as 1½ miles at 10s 6d per rood, totalling £197-13-4d. Much levelling was needed to smooth out the worst of the undulations ("hills and slacks"); progress was slow, and in April, 1757, the trustees had to order, "that the road from Chellaheight to Cullingworth Field Low Corner on Cullingworth Moor be finished".

Tolls were levied upon "any horse or other beast" (i.e., ox) drawing carts or conveyances over the road, and when confronted by damage to the soft surfaces, the trustees decreed in 1769 that no more than ten horses be allowed for any waggon with wheels of 9 inch breadth, or six horses where wheels of lesser breadth were used. Property owners who had borne a "ratio tenure" liability for repairs to the old road did not escape liability for the new, the Trust being responsible for the rest.

Other horizons opened in 1760 when the Keighley and Bradford Turnpike Trust transformed Toller Lane into a passable thoroughfare and carved out a new highway (later known as Bingley Road) past Low Thorn Slack and across the High Moor, whence it descended steeply to Stairfoot and Cottingley. The jingle of packhorse bells faded before the stirring notes of the post-horn as the fast mail-coaches rushed by on their triumphal progress to Skipton and Kendal, bringing in their wake the new excitement of long distance travel as well as the novelty of up-to-date news from the outside world. By 1779 the mails

Memories of coaching days – the old 'Hare and Hounds' in Toller Lane shortly before its replacement in 1940 by the new building (left). The drivers of the two horse-drawn carts (left) are drinking 'Hammonds' Bradford Ales' inside the hostelry, and in the far distance Sharpes' new factory is girding itself for war. *(Bradford Libraries)*

were being conveyed thrice weekly over the Keighley road to Settle for onward transmission to Kirkby Lonsdale, and to Crosshills for the towns in East Lancashire, thus depriving the Haworth and Blue Bell Trust of much of its hoped for through traffic, and relegating it to purely local use. One of the more notable travellers over the new roads was John Wesley, the founder of Methodism, on his journeyings between the parish churches of Bradford, Bingley and Keighley.

Now silent and forgotten, the old Roman (?) track and packhorse road over Noon Nick and Guide Post faded into the grass before being obliterated by the pick and shovel of the Heaton delvers.

The Quarter Sessions held at Bradford in July, 1763, heard " . . .a Petition of George Craven of Bradford, salter, setting forth that on Tuesday the 5th day of July instant, in the night, a sudden and terrible fire accidentally broke out in the Rasping, Grinding and Flour Mills of the said George Craven at Frizinghall in the township of Heaton . . .which in a short time (notwithstanding the utmost endeavours of the said George Craven and his neighbours to extinguish the same) burnt down to the Ground and consumed the said Mills together with the Rasping Engine (which had been made and brought to great perfection at the extraordinary expenses and pains of the petitioners, and was the most complete for rasping wood and dyeing of any in the kingdom), Corn Mill, Chipping Engine, Sack, Tackle, Wheels and all the other going gear ' . . .with all the Millstones . . .for grinding of Wheat and other Grain - - - and grinding and finishing of Wood for dyeing, to the amount of £1,128-7-0d and upwards.

The truth of which allegation being proved on the Oaths of Thomas Shaw and Samuel Strickland, millwrights, Benjamin Ledgard, carpenter, John Fearnley, mason, and Michael Nicholson, glazier . . ., James Lister and James Driver, substantial Inhabitants of the Township of Heaton . . .

This Court orders a certificate to be made to the Lord High Chancellor of Great Britain on behalf of the said sufferer . . . to procure for him His Majesty's most gracious Letters Patent . . . to impower him to ask, collect and receive the Alms of charitable Christians throughout England and Wales and Berwick upon Tweed, and from house to house throughout the Counties of York, Lancaster and Lincoln."

An Estimate made of the loss by fire at a Mill called Dumb Mill belonging to George Craven situated at Frizzinghall nigh Heaton . . . .

	£	s	d
To Rasping Ingine finishing stones as by plan at	600	–	–
Corn Mill as by plan	110	–	–
Chipping Engine as by plan	95	–	–
Grind Stones and Gears as by plan	12	–	–
One new Wheel	10	11	0
Utensils and drivers	15	–	–
Dyeing Wood of different kinds	203	10	0
Corn distroy'd in the Mill	1	5	0
In the Roof 10 Square at £2-2s per foot	21	–	–
In the Floor 80 yards at 6s per Yard	24	–	–
Slating 150 yards at 8s-2d per Yard	8	15	0
12 Yards of Digging Stones at 1/- per Yard		12	0
Stone Walling 25 rood at 12/- per Rood	15	–	–

80 yards of Flagging at 1s per Yard		4	–	–
Two stone door stands at 8s each			16	0
100 feet of Glass at 7d per foot		2	18	4
Two double doors at 15/- each		1	10	0
Wood Windows and Shutters to same		2	10	0
	£ 1,128		7	4

Whether the alms and oblations of sympathetic individuals sufficed to restore the unfortunate George Craven's fortunes is not recorded, but in September, 1780, his son and heir George junior was able to sell to the Bradford Canal Co. the "Water Corn Mill called the Dumb Mill . . . formerly occupied by the late George Craven, later by the late Thomas Ledgard and now by the Canal Company," together with a new cottage and two new warehouses. Business continued as before, with John Kitching, John Mallinson, Stephen Holroyd and Matthew Phillip successively the millers.

A mid-eighteenth century list of tithes payable to the Vicar of Bradford reveals that "The Tyth of Wool and Lamb in Shipley and Heaton" comprised "3d per lamb lambed; $1^1/_2$d per fleece of sheep wintered there; $^3/_4$d per fleece of sheep wintered elsewhere. Except for Hog Lambs." For the ex-abbey lands at Chellow different customs ruled: "The four farms there pay 5 shillings a year and a dinner for the tytheman, whereof Mr. Edward Bolling's farm pays one half." The agreeable custom of providing a dinner was superseded by more mundane arrangements when in 1761 the Bolling farm was sold by Mrs. Prescott (cousin of William Bolling) to the Hodgsons of Whetley, Manningham: –

(1) Richard and William Hodgson	2s 6d
(2) Mr. John Field of Heaton Hall, for the 100 acre farm bought by Edward Field in 1620	10d
(3) Thomas Fenton (formerly owned by James Garth)	10d
(4) William and Mary Thomas of Marylebone for premises bequeathed by Mary's grandfather William Bolling	10d
	5s 0d

The Hodgsons were not slow to assert their claim to the mineral rights in Chellow, and in 1765 they entered a suit with the Master of the Rolls to prevent Mr. Field from mining and quarrying there. Their witnesses were Nicholas Pollard, a Manningham yeoman (1682-1766), Gilbert Brooksbank (1693-1765), David Binns, a Manningham labourer, Peter Watkinson (born about 1688, tenant of Mr. Bolling's farm 1724-1754) and William Bolling of Ilkley, born 1711, eldest son of John Bolling.

The basis of their testimony was that about 1694 Edward Bolling had dug for coal on "Chellow Common", from "a little under Chellow Field Nook all under the hillside to . . . Noon Nick", and had also quarried millstones for his malt mill.

They agreed that,

" . . . that part of Heaton Common which adjoins on Chellow inclosures and goes by the ridge of the hill there to a place on the said moor called Stainwell Clough, from there to another place called Ducksikehead from thence to a place called the Hermit Holes, thence to an old guide post which formerly stood at a place called Noon Nick, thence in a direct line to the point of a small snip of common belonging to Allerton called the Long Tail end, and thence to the lane leading to Allerton, belongs to Chellow."

William Bolling alleged that about 1748 when he had been acting as his cousin's steward, Abraham Rhodes of Heaton Royds, "who farmed (i.e. leased) of Mr. Field the coals lying within the wastes of the manor of Heaton" and who had already drained Mr. Bolling's flooded pit (intentionally or otherwise) by sinking a shaft just over the Shipley boundary, also sank a new pit near Noon Nick. As Mr. Bolling considered John Field to be "a rich man and very litigious," and the coals having little value, he had advised Mr. Prescott to take no action. Nevertheless on June 21st, 1757, Mr. Prescott had accused Mr. Field of taking his wife's property "by violence," to which Mr. Field had replied that "he verily believed that Mr. Prescott knew he had no right to the coals."

The Master of the Rolls declined to grant an injunction, as Mr. Field had obviously enjoyed long possession, whereas the Bollings' title appeared disputable. Tantalisingly, Christopher Saxton's map of 1591 was claimed to be in Mr. and Mrs. Thomas' possession, but sadly it has never been traced subsequently.

A further lawsuit by the Hodgsons was dismissed with costs in 1767, when John Field counter-attacked with a suit against William Hodgson, merchant, and Henry Mitchell of Chellow, farm labourer, as well as two of the freeholders, Richard and Joseph Tetley of Manningham, yeomen, who had infringed the lord's right to cut brackens on Heaton Common.

Simultaneously Mr. Field sued William Kitching, yeoman, of Heaton, in company with other men from Shipley and elsewhere, as a means of determining the Heaton/Shipley boundary which, when it was perambulated in 1765, had been defined by the Heaton jury as lying along the bottom of the deep cloughs or ravines on the southern side of the present-day High Bank and North Bank Roads. Mr Field had sunk some pits near Dungeon Woods, but one night in March, 1767, the doughty Dr. Cyril Jackson, lord of the manor of Shipley, sent his agents to wreck the blacksmith's shop and cast its contents down four of the shafts. This time Mr. Field was unsuccessful, as the judge considered the true boundary to lie slightly further to the south of the shafts and ravines.

Chapter 8 – The Squire

When John Field died in January, 1772, he was succeeded by his youngest and only surviving son Joshua, who was destined to be remembered far into the 19th century as Squire Field, a good friend to the lowliest cottager, a man who knew everyone in the township and a genial host who played an active part in the Town's affairs as well as in the wider social and commercial life of Bradford and the county.

At the Town's Meeting in 1772 he accepted appointment as Highway Surveyor for a year, and thirty years later served as Overseer of the Poor. From 1776 he was partner with his Cottingley neighbour Henry Wickham in the Leeds New Bank, participating at a later date in the London banking firm of Wickham, Field and Cleaver. His abilities were recognised in 1778 by his appointment as Deputy Lieutenant for the West Riding; the trustees of the Manningham Poor Lands invited him to join their number, and as late as 1818 he was made President of the new East Morley and Bradford Savings Bank.

In 1774 Mr. Field married Mary, youngest daughter and eventually sole heiress of Randal Wilmer of Helmsley, a descendant of the mediaeval baronial house of Thwenge. Like their fellow townsmen, their married life brought them both joy and sorrow, as Joshua Field's diary reveals: -

Joshua Field – Squire Field of Heaton Hall. (*Photo: author, courtesy of the Earl of Rosse*)

> "August 20th, 1775. My son John Wilmer was born at York half after 5 in the morning (he had the Smallpox very young by inoculation and the Measles soon after.)
> January 6th, 1777. My son Zachary was born at York at 11 in the morning and died about half a year old. (n.b., as Zechariah Suger Field he was buried at Bradford on April 30th, 1777).
> May 10th, 1778 my son Joshua was born at York at 9 in the morning.
> May 8th, 1772. My daughter Mary was born at 1 o'clock in the morning.
> July 14th, 1780. My daughter Delia was born at 6 o'clock in the evening.
> April 9th, 1791. Mrs. Field was brought to bed of a boy that was stillborn, and Mr. Outhwaite was of opinion that he had been dead a week at least and was nearly at the full term."

Mr. Field inherited not only his father's considerable estates but also his long-running feuds. In 1770 the Hodgsons of Chellow leased their farm to Jonas Greenwood who carried out his landlords' customary practice of keeping 12 to 14 head of cattle which he turned on to the Common for grazing. In addition however, he began to graze other farmers' cattle on the common for a fee of 3d or 4d a week per beast, a questionable activity which did not escape notice.

In late October, 1773, Mr. Field observed 16 oxen or Scotch bullocks "depasturing near his Mansion House," whither they had strayed over the unfenced common from Chellow "at a distance of a mile and upwards." He summoned the township pinder and had the cattle "distrained" or placed in the pinfold, whence they were claimed almost a fortnight later by Jonas Greenwood, who admitted that they belonged to John Cunliffe of Addingham and John Margerison of Ilkley who had no common rights in Heaton.

Urged on no doubt by the Hodgsons, Jonas Greenwood entered a writ in the King's Bench alleging "trespass and replevin" and claiming £60 for the temporary loss of the beasts whose disappearance he had been so slow to notice. In evidence the Hodgsons asserted that they were "seised in their Demesne as of fee of 100 acres of land well appointed, lying and being in Chellow otherwise Chellow Grange in the Township of Heaton," in addition to which as freeholders they were "seised in fee of 10 undivided parts (the whole into 660 parts to be divided)" of Heaton Common and to possess pasture rights for "all their commonable cattle levant and couchant upon the common at all times of the year at their pleasure."

Contesting these probably exaggerated claims, Mr. Field argued that the practice of pasturing other people's beasts had increased to such a degree that "the Common would soon have been covered with Scotch and other Cattle belonging to Strangers, which would have eaten up all the grass." Supporting witnesses confirmed having assisted the Fields since 1738 to exercise their right to "drive the Commons" and "take up waifs and estrays" as lords of the manor; John Field's own accounts provided evidence that these rights were accepted by old-established farmers, viz.,

> "January 5th, 1767 – Received of John Crabtree for 11 years Rent for the liberty of driving over my Common to Shipley Common, 12s 10d.
>
> February 10th, 1771, – Received of Joshua Crabtree two years liberty of driving his cattle over Heaton Common to Shipley Common 2s 4d."

To Joshua Field's attorney, Henry Hemingway, witnesses testified to having bought bracken for burning from John Field in 1740/1746 for 3 guineas, while others described getting "great quantities of slate" from Height Delf for 6s to 7s a ton for him. Abraham Rhodes of Heaton Royds had obtained a 13-year lease for £26 in 1746 for the mining of coal, and not until he renewed the lease for a further 11 years for £22-10-0d had Mr. Hodgson objected.

These disputes were mentioned in passing in a letter to Henry Hemingway despatched from:-

> "Tadcaster, 11 o'clock Saturday evening, 29th July, 1775
>
> Dear Sir,
> I am this moment arrived here, and have the pleasure to acquaint you I've bought the Heaton Estate of Mr. Scott for £4,800, but would not have you mention it to any one. I have forgot to bring a waistcoat with me from Thos. Milner the taylor at Bradford, and shall esteem it a favour if you will bring it along with you.
>
> I remain, with respects to Miss Hemingway,
> Your Friend and Humble Servant,
> Josa Field.
> P. S. - I forgot to acquaint you, I heard this morning that Mr. Hodgson cut some brackens on the commons about 9 years ago, which was about the time

he had the Chancery Suit with my Father. I wish you would call on Tom Bastow of Leeds, who was my Father's attorney, and ask him what he knows about it, and perhaps it may be necessary to prove that suit in order to set aside their evidence. Please to ask him if he purposes being at York next week."

Happy indeed is the man who can employ his solicitor to fetch and carry waistcoats!

The Scott estate, once the inheritance of James Garth of Garth House, comprised about 100 acres of land at Leylands, West Fields and elsewhere, forming a substantial addition to Mr. Field's possessions and bringing with it Garth House which adjoined Heaton Hall and pre-dated it by fully twenty years.

Sporadic sinking of mineshafts having revealed an abundance of sandstone between Heaton and Chellow, Mr. Field began to extract the stone on a commercial basis. Most of the workings were small, as his records reveal: –

"September 9th, 1772. Paid Dan Greenwood and Hesletine for paving at Towler Lane Quarry in part – 6s.

(about 1780) James Harper has agreed to cart the stone from Weather Royd to fence the Bingley Turnpike from Towler Lane to Low Thorn Slack on one side @ 20s per yard 4 feet high."

Later in an attempt to improve output: –

"December 24th, 1801. I declined to give any more Drinkings to my Masons."

In 1805: –

"Solomon Clark is trying a Quarry in Emm Field."

The abundance of springs caused frequent problems: –

"July 8th, 1813. State of the Water in my new Quarry in Lillams (i.e.; Leylands) Lane:

5 yards 1 inch from surface of earth to surface of water;

5 yards 1 foot 1 inch from surface of earth to bottom of water",

from which one may deduce that the quarry, being a mere 16' 1" deep, had been

Thorn Lane, Bingley Road – originally a farm track serving the inclosures on Heaton High Moor – photographed shortly before being widened in 1969.

(Copyright: author)

temporarily abandoned until a means of diverting the numerous rivulets from Well Springs could be found.

Coalmining remained a small scale operation at the Shay Pit and the neighbouring Millstone Hill colliery: –

> "September 5th, 1772. There has been got 22 tons of coal at the Shay Pit this week, which comes to £4-8-0d.
>
> March 23rd, 1776. Weekly wages at Millstone Hill: colliers James Greenwood 10s, John Greenwood 10s, Luke Normington 7s 6d, William Clayton 10s, Richard Longbottom 10s, and the banksman, William Atkinson, 7s."

On April 14th, 1786, Mr. Field noted that he had

> " . . .agreed with Abraham Normington to sink me a coal pit in Ambrose Padget's Allotment at 8s a yard for every yard if the Pit requires Boaring in order to get rid of the water, but if there is no occasion to boar it, 7s 6d a yard only, to be about $7^1/_2$ feet long and 5 foot wide"

In 1792:

> "William Clark says they give their colliers $22^1/_2$d (i.e. 1s $10^1/_2$d) per dozen and 1 week load only, if they find (i.e. provide) their own candles and have no coals for this; they also find their own picks. For driving strate work 3d per yard for ending and 2d per yard for boarding."
>
> October 13th, 1796: "I hired James Greenwood and gave him £1-2-0d and agreed with him for 2 guineas to superintend my colliery in the bottom for a year, and to do any trifling work.
>
> And on April 12th, 1812: "Let a Coal Pit to sink to Elijah and Abraham Normington –
>
> To pay them 18s a yard for sinking and boaring;
>
> To find them tools (they to sharpen);
>
> To allow them 12s subsistence a week;
>
> To allow them 6s subsistence for Abraham's son.

Work began April 27th."

The opening of the Bradford Canal in 1774 provided a considerable stimulus for local trade, as the exporting of local stone and textile goods and the importing of cheap raw materials were now possible. At Heaton the freeholders soon recognised the benefit which they would derive from inclosure of the moors and commons with their mineral and agricultural possibilities.

An additional impetus was provided by the last of the wearisome land disputes in January, 1780, when the 430 year old grant of John of Gaunt and the 1621 Duchy of Lancaster evidences saw the light of day once more, and reminiscences of old inhabitants were heard.

They recalled that the Fields often impounded Manningham cattle which strayed over the ridge from Hazelhurst, and that Manningham folk were equally vigilant for errant beasts from Heaton. The gate which the Leet Court had a century earlier ordered Heaton folk to maintain at Old Manningham Nook had been forcibly removed by Manningham, so that "at the top of Toller Lane ... the Road to Allerton was always open to the Common, and the Cattle were generally turn'd on here." Evidently the term "Toller Lane" applied to the alternative route via Daisy Hill and The Heights as well as to the easier route across the West Fields.

There had, however, been dark deeds along the boundary line. John Brown, born in 1717, remembered three boundary stones.

> " ... 1st the Earthfast Stone in the West fields Fence, 2nd about the Mid-Way between that and Chellow Fields near the Road leading from Daisy Hill to Chellow, and the 3rd near the the place where Mr. Field's new House now stands, all nearly in a line ... He remembers a Mark cut out on the Top of the Middle Stone, believes it was the Letter M, for tho' he can't read, he observ'd that and the Earthfast stone were marked alike."

John Parkinson of Manningham recalled a visit to the house of David Binns in 1773 when Binns had told him that

> " ... very early the same morning he heard it as it were a rapping of Stones upon the common, and getting out of Bed he saw Henry Atkinson and John Broadley going away from near the place where the above mentioned (i.e. Middle) Boundary Stone stood, and one of them had a Mall upon his Shoulder ... that David ... desired the Witness to go with him and look at the place, which he did, and found the Stone broke to pieces."

However, unknown to John Field, David Binns had carefully concealed the third stone in the west corner of the barn being built alongside "Mr. Field's new House", i.e., Chellow Style Farm.

All these minor machinations were made irrelevant by the Heaton Commons Inclosure Award of October 26th, 1781, which not only incorporated a map confirming the ancient boundary line but also awarded "allotments" or allocations of land to the freeholders in proportion to their share of the common rights. The awards totalled 560 acres 2 rods 3 perches.

When the new owners took possession of their "inclosures" the face of the landscape altered dramatically. Gone were the timeless bracken moors, the rushes and rivulets where geese and cattle had wandered at will; in their place drystone walls and quickthorn hedges neatly demarcated the new farmlands. And when plough and spade, hoe and rake began to break up the bent-grass turf and the virgin soil, and sledgehammers shattered obstinate boulders left behind by primaeval glaciers, the old barguests, boggarts, guytrashes and suchlike "flaysome (frightening) things" retired unwillingly to remoter areas where their unwelcome activities had freer range.

Was the Inclosure fair and even-handed, or did it deprive cottagers of the right to turn a few ducks or geese on to the common?

> "The fault is great in man or woman
> Who steals the goose from off the common,
> But who can plead that man's excuse
> Who steals the common from the goose?"

The surviving Court Baron rolls contain no reference to cottage rights: perhaps they had been surrendered for a cash payment.

Social relationships had changed too. Gone were yeomen, husbandmen, customary tenancies and copyholds; Lord's Rents remained as an acknowledgement of earlier inclosures, but the time-honoured deliberations of the Court Baron no longer shaped the daily lives of the townsfolk. In their place came farms, farm labourers, cash rents and weekly wages, and cottagers who kept pigs or poultry did so in backyards or rented allotment gardens.

At Heaton Syke the Low Common was divided between John Fairbank (purchaser of Thompson's farm) and David Mortimer's trustees, who were ordered to provide a 40-foot wide cart track to give access to the old "smithy shop" and the row of "through light" cottages which the Mortimers built between 1790 and 1808 on the south bank of the syke which provided their water supply. The enlarged hamlet, pleasantly situated amid gardens long celebrated for succulent Heaton "peys", gave shelter to about 100 persons.

The most far-reaching changes took place west of the "town", where the High Moor extending from Well Springs to the Cottingley (or Swain Royd) Beck was reclaimed. At the Shay, the Royds and Chellow Grange the "inclosures" were used to extend the existing farms, but elsewhere new farmholdings were created: -

> Spring Head Farm, Chellow Moor; West House Farm, Chellow Moor;
> West Farm, also called Bay of Biscay Farm; Westfield House (originally
> called Cuckoo Nest and later New House, Haworth Road);
> High Park Farm, Haworth Road; Pyche Nook Farm, Chellow Heights;
> North Hall Farm (originally called West Hall) Plantation Farm, Bingley Road;
> Shay Grange, Long Lane; Gethsemane (later called West Farm, Toller Lane).

The owners of the new "allotments" retained the right of access to the streams flowing from Chellow Wells, Hartley Well at Hard Venture, the Syke and Town Well, whilst Mr. Field was ordered to provide a wayside trough (later known as "t'Bottom o't'Hill Well" at the foot of Highgate), which gathered the waters of the Well Springs for use by "the proprietors of lands and tenements within and the inhabitants of the Township of Heaton, with their Horses, Cattle, Carts and Carriages," in default of which they could enter the adjoining land in search of water.

Like the "ancient inclosures" the new fields often bore contemporary descriptive names such as "Cocked Hat" or "Spa Well Field", while "Boston" and "Bunkers Hill" with their

Bay of Biscay, with the Sandy Lane to Greengates bus climbing up to the ridge of Chellow Heights. Above, and to the right of the bus, can be seen a small ravine in the hillside, referred to as Salterclough in medieval deeds. Photographed by the author on 28 April 1957. *(Copyright: author)*

allusions to British reverses on "the American continent" revealed sympathy with King George's rebellious colonial subjects.

The sour, acid soil of the reclaimed moorland had to be "sweetened" with lime brought from Skipton via the new canal and burnt at Limekiln Close adjoining Roydscliffe Wood. Joshua Field's limekiln account books indicate that the cost of materials, transport and burning usually exceeded the price that farmers paid; the real profit lay in the improved productivity of the land. Low Moor and High Park farms, well tilled and thoroughly manured, prospered and yielded good, consistent crops, thus confounding local pessimists who had forecast that the inclosures would not be fully fertile for fifty years. Conversely, much-quarried Plantation Farm was dubbed "Pine-ation" by its depairing tenants, and the name "Hard Venture" – later known as Bay of Biscay in recognition of the wildness of the weather at its exposed elevation – needed no translation.

Production of fine grains such as wheat or corn was inhibited by the relatively high altitude (approximately 650 feet above sea level in the "town" and 850 feet at Chellow Grange) and the northerly latitude; oats fared better and provided part of the staple diet – oatcakes rolled into sheets were still being hung to dry on rope creels suspended from living room beams until the early years of the 20th century. Barley, a necessary ingredient of ale, was an equally successful crop. Winter fodder for the beasts in the form of hay, turnips and mangolds was grown on every farm, but the chilly chore of digging up the root crops on a frosty morning never enjoyed the same appeal as the warm, dusty labours of haytime and the joy of "the last load" and "harvest home."

The miles of drystone wall which were now a feature of the landscape provided work for delvers, masons and wallers. Joshua Field's accounts showed that on July 8th, 1792,

"John Padget agreed to make part of my Plantation Wall in the Park walling at 2s per rood, wheeling at 2s per rood, getting at 2s per rood; part of the stones are carted; the wall is to be 6 feet to the top of the cooping, and a cobble above."

Also, on December 16th, 1801,

"T. Tillotson to make a 4 foot wall from the corner of Sarah Brook's First Well Springs to the North Corner of Greenwood's Close at the Town End, to pull down the present wall and stub any trees and thorns."

The wall in question lay on the western side of Leylands Lane.

Wool and the production of cloth continued to provide valuable employment for men, women and children. Half a century later an "old inhabitant" recalled nostalgically that,

"The woolsorters and spinners of Bradford and district were in olden times an exemplary class, and in industry, frugality and the decencies of life could not be surpassed. Their indoor labours were at their own fireside, and while the father and his sons were engaged in sorting, combing and weaving, the matronly dame and her daughters were busily engaged in spinning and reeling."

In reality the "comb-shops" with the stifling atmosphere produced by the charcoal-fired "pot of four" and the melted wool-grease were unhealthy workplaces. The weavers fared better. Reminiscing in 1928 on the days of his youth, Mr. John Lee (1846-1931) recalled that,

"At all times there was the possibility of someone having a strong disinclination to work, and in such case it was not difficult to induce his neighbours to 'down tools' and come out for 'a bit a'sport',(i.e., football. cricket, knur and spell, arrow-throwing and snowball fights). These irregular habits often ... entailed long hours of overtime when the looms could be heard clattering away until long after midnight."

The womenfolk did not indulge in such frivolities; instead, on fine days they took their spinning-wheels into their gardens where they could "kall" with their neighbours.

Chapter 10 – Rural Heyday

Heaton Hall, the substantial family mansion of the Fields, had been extended and altered between 1765 and 1774 to suit its owners' growing status. The south and east frontages were remodelled on classical lines with dressed stone columns and pediments, and a servants' wing was added at a later date. The new Yellow Room was adorned with wallpaper, cornices and a stucco dado; mouldings, modillions, lozenges and stucco flowers enhanced the Dining Room walls, while the Red Room and study were somewhat plainer. Handsome Queen Anne style fireplaces warmed the principal rooms, and family portraits lined the walls. From the main entrance on the east front a carriage drive descended through the well-wooded park to a gatekeeper's lodge at the southeastern edge of the estate. The vast kitchen, long line of stabling, brewhouse and out-offices ministered to the wants of the family, and in addition to a numerous stud of hunters, Mr. Field kept a pack of hounds in kennels outside the park wall.

A steward was employed to oversee the estate - Michael Lancaster served in that capacity unitl 1805, F. Spanton until 1807 and Francis Lancaster thereafter - but Joshua Field kept the account books and journals which revealed the scope of his interests, ranging from the Bradford Library, the Bradford Auxiliary Bible Society and the fashionable York Assembly Rooms:-

"Oct.21, 1777 The Bradford Hunt, debtor to Joshua Field for 1 sheep and 2 foxes at Baildon, 12s 6d.

1789 - Condition of taking Cattle to graze: -

A 3 year old heifer is equal to a Cow Gate

Three 2 year old heifers are equal to 2 Cow Gates

One 2 year old calf is equal to a Cow Gate

Horses as above, but a Horse equals a cow gate and a half at least.

1797 - I pastured in my Park in the summer 1797 about 20 horses and cows or cattle equal to 20 gates, part horse gate and part cow gate, but they were too many; I suppose 16 are enough, 1/2 horses and 1/2 cows and young things.

1791 - I pay ratcatcher 1 guinea per year.

Oct.4, 1792 - Paid my shearers 5s 3d per day

(presumably collectively, not individually).

Dec.17, 1783 - To Oats threshed at the New Barn £4 - 8 - 0d (oats and grain were sent to Frizinghall, Wilsden or 'Lenthorpe' mills for grinding).

1792 - Accounts for sheep killed and mutton sold to Mr. Wickham.

Dec.3, 1810 - Sold my old Sow for £12 to John Binns on account.

Nov.3, 1810 - Sold my Barley to Mr. Tetley of Bradford for £2-8-0d a quarter.

Aug.16, 1813 - Exchanged clover with William Clark, he to give me £3 for the difference, and Henry Beanland is to take my four young pigs at 14s each tomorrow sennight. Wm Clark to have my sheep skins at 2s 6d each and the tallow at the price it is going at."

Artificial insemination being undreamed-of, Mr. Field sent his heifers to his neighbour's bulls:-

"Aug. 1781 - A third time by Mr. Wickham bull

A fourth time

Dec. 21st - The little Red Cow bulled at Frank Stead, and she pick'd her Calf."

The burdens of the Deputy Lieutenancy and the world of banking never diverted Joshua Field from the care of his land:-

"1810 - Memo - I manured all the Meadow from my house after Haytime in the year 1804; we had very dry weather for some time afterwards." (a rueful comment, surely?)

"Also the Footway Close or Hill on the North side and the field below in August 1805 I manured the small meadow next Firth Carr in November 1805, and the First Ash Well and the East side of the Meadow before the house next Crosshill.

Other manurings: the meadow adjoining Oddy Wood, north side of the Leas, and the First Ash Well and that small piece bounded on the West by the pathway and what is called Crabtree Close on the East."

The heated greenhouses and kitchen garden adjoining the west fence of the park were watched over with a zeal that would have delighted "Farmer George" himself:-

"Nov.12th, 1787 - Robert Moses (my gardener) debtor to Joshua Field for sundry sales of Herbs and Roots sold out of the Garden,

such as Sallads, Onions, Cabbages etc.	£2- 4- 6d
Gooseberries sold	1- 10- 0
To one year's Coals	1- 6- 0
	£5- 0- 6
By sundries bought -	
2 Pecks Early Potatoes for Sets	2- 0
Turnips bought when without in the garden	10
1 Peck of Beans	8
4 oz - Onion Seed	1- 0
	4- 6
	Net £4-16- 0d

Robert Moses received £18 annual wages in 1787, and in 1804 "Robert Mosey" (probably his son) was engaged as Mr. Field's groom at a yearly wage of 16 guineas plus of course free board and lodgings.

Miscellaneous domestic expenses in April, 1805, reveal an unexpected picture of good cheer:-

April 3rd	To Blacking		1s- 0d
..	Sisers and knife grinding		3
5th	To Washing at Heaton		7$^{1}/_{2}$
15th	To $^{1}/_{2}$ pint of Brandy	1	8
19th	.. .. ..	1	8
21st	To two letters		6
22nd	To $^{1}/_{2}$ pint of Brandy	1	8
..	1lb Hair Powder	1	6

..	1 pot Pomatum	1	0
..	Nanny Atkinson cleaning plate	1	8
27th	To ½ pint of Brandy	1	8

Perhaps Joshua Field had discovered the secret of long life, as he lived to the age of 77!

The ready availability of water from the local springs gave rise to unfulfilled hopes of a domestic supply. On October 25th, 1790, a draft agreement was prepared for:-

> " ... the laying of a conduit from a spring arising in Benjamin Bullock Ing (i.e., in Leylands Lane) belonging to ... Joshua Field, under the Town Street of Heaton to a reservoir at the upper end of the Town of Heaton, side pipes to be laid to the houses of subscribers, and all surplus water would run back into the trough (n.b., presumably the Town Well)."

Regrettably the novel scheme was not pursued, as the gravity flow would have been insufficient and the expense high.

However, twenty years earlier Mr. Field had provided several wayside troughs fed by streams from his pastures. The Syke Well and Middle Well (halfway up Cross Hill) supplied Heaton Syke, while the Town Well at the foot of Leylands Lane (a substitute for the reservoir, as it was fed via a pipe from Benjamin Bullock's field) sufficed for the "town" itself, although when it ran dry in summer the villagers had to resort to Bottom o't Hill Well. At Heaton Royds Mr. Field had installed a "trouf" which still bears his initials and the partly-obliterated date 177-. In respect of the Royds Well he noted on February 16th, 1818, that he had

> "Received 2 years Water Rent for the Water that comes to my trouf at a penny each, due at Candlemas last - 1s 8d",

Heaton Syke Well opposite the 'Fountain Inn' was set into the park wall erected by Joshua Field about 1792. Photographed by the author on 10 September 1955.

from which one may assume that ten households at the Royds depended upon it. Similar troughs existed at the Shay and at Chellow Heights, while the farms at Chellow Grange obtained their water from Chellow Wells at the head of the syke, which ultimately flowed through Heaton Woods as the Red Beck.

The eternal search for cures for "aches and pains" led local people to ascribe therapeutic properties to the local waters. The ancient Ash Well which lay at the junction of present-day Ashwell Lane and Wilmer Drive was considered to be beneficial for "rheumatics" - indeed, it had been a "holy well" before the Reformation - while Spa Field at North Hall, Spa Well Wood at Chellow Dene and the moss which grew on the door lintel of Mr. Field's farmhouse at Chellow Grange were all held in similar esteem. Ironically, the old house itself, built in 1620 with bedrooms so large that one could not throw a pillow from one bed to another, was so damp that its last tenant, Dan Craven, was driven out by chronic rheumatism against which his mosses were unable to prevail.

Chapter 11 – *Census, Taxes and War*

With the new century came the first Census, in 1801, when Heaton township was found to contain 951 inhabitants - 474 men and boys, 477 women and girls, 195 families, 881 persons in employment, 173 inhabited houses and 8 vacant.

A glimpse of life at the Hall in Mr. Field's later years is provided by his 1807 tax return:-

"Paid to George Frankland one quarter Assessed taxes, the first this year –

54 Windows	£7 - 13 - 9
Inhabited House Duty	12 - 6
3 Servants	2 - 5 - 0
Under-Gardener	1 - 3
Chaise	2 - 10 - 0
Riding Horses	4 - 11 - 0
Draught Horses	9 – 4 $^{1}/_{2}$
Dogs	10 - 0
Armorial Bearings	10 – 6
Hair Powder	5 – 3
For Wilmer: 1 Servant	
2 horses, 2 dogs	3 – 8 – 9
	£22 - 17 - 4 $^{1}/_{2}$ d

Strange taxes which valued coats of arms at eight times the worth of an under-gardener!

The Chaise and the horses were in regular demand. On April 2nd, 1805, their owner paid 7 $^{1}/_{2}$d in turnpike tolls on a journey from York to Heaton but only 7d on the return journey a fortnight later, while the tolls between Heaton and Horton cost him a mere penny.

But times were perilous. Wars with revolutionary France had been raging intermittently since 1794, with calamitous effect on the trade and commerce which formed Britain's lifeblood. Threats of invasion by Napoleon's armies seemed very real, and in 1802 - the year of the short-lived peace of Amiens - Mr. Field noted that on behalf of his various Yorkshire estates he had "subscribed to the Volunteer Corps as follows: - Heaton £100, York and Helmsley £50, Keighley £40, Baildon £10." The West Riding Volunteer Yeomanry Cavalry was wholly dependent on the efforts of fundraising committees in each of the wapentakes.

In addition, the families of local militiamen often had to be supported out of the rates. At the Pontefract Sessions in April, 1800. the Heaton overseer was ordered to reimburse the Treasurer of the West Riding out of the Poor Rate the sum of £6 - 17s - 6d "for the relieving of the family of John Barker, a substitute serving in the Militia of the said West Riding for the Township of Heaton". These payments fluctuated as the war ebbed and flowed; a maximum contribution of £74 - 0 - 7d was required in 1808, dwindling to £15 - 12 - 0 after Napoleon's retreat from Moscow and a final sum of £2 - 9 - 10 when the Duke of Wellington triumphed on the plains of Belgium.

Nevertheless Napoleon was not without a few English admirers. Perhaps it was one of these who determined to strike fear into the hearts of the local gentry who had signed a printed petition congratulating Mr. Pitt on his resolute war against the enemy. In his diary Mr. Field noted,

> "On Saturday, November 9th, 1811, several balls of perfumed paste were found in the yard, supposed to contain Poison - On the Monday following, a Peahen and two fowls was found dead; also a Turkey hen died in the night; the Turkey cock died on Tuesday."

Poor fowls - hapless victims of an unseen hand. Nevertheless, whatever the identity and motives of their assassins, life at Heaton soon resumed its tranquil course, although the harsh cries of the peacocks were probably heard no more.

In the closing years of the old century Mr. John Wood of Gethsemane Farm in Toller Lane had begun to build an attractive row of "through light" dwellings which constituted the first expansion of the "town" beyond Town End. Pleased with their setting and appearance, he named them Paradise Cottages. A narrow strip of land separating them from Town Street was leased from Mr. Field and converted into individual cottage gardens in return for a yearly Lord's Rent of 1s - 2d per plot.

Paradise was presently joined by Eden, a mixed row of single- and two-storey cottages erected by Mr. Field. At the foot of the row he decided to build a schoolroom (nowadays nos.96/98 Highgate), and in his diary for June, 1815, he recorded that an unnamed Haworth pedagogue had "offered himself as Master for my School at £50 a year". Following the example of the Foundry school at Wibsey whose charges to pupils were 1d per week for books and 6s a quarter for reading and writing, he noted in September,

> "Joshua Field re Heaton School Account -
>
> By cash received from Mr. Wilcock the schoolmaster for 4 weeks, being 1d per week for those that read in the daytime, being contingent money to defray expenses, and the surplus to be paid to him and all other receipts   17s - 0d
>
> Ditto October 2nd   13s - 6d
>
> November 6th   13s - 0d
>
> December 5th   13s - 7d

As the income from the pupils, evidently about forty in number, was insufficient to cover costs, the shortfall was paid by Mr. Field from a rent-charge on his 1781 inclosures:-

> "March 12th, 1818 - Paid the School Master, Jeremiah Craven, on old Assessment at 3s - 9 1/4 d per month for my New Land, £4 - 14s - 3 1/2 d."

For a number of years a group of Wesleyan Methodists had met for worship at the cottage in Paradise occupied by Samuel Broadley, handloom weaver. A regular visitor was the Rev. John Harland (1792-1870) who on October 10th, 1811, noted that he had "preached at Heaton last Sunday in place of James Worsnop, and had liberty" (i.e., of spirit). Again on October 13th, 1812, he wrote that he had "had a good time preaching at Heaton."

Initially there were 23 members with William Britton as leader, but when they decided to commence a Sunday School for the village children, Mr. Broadley's "chamber" (bedroom) soon had to accommodate 136 boys and 105 girls, in relays, one hopes! Books were provided by the London Sunday School Society, and benches were bought by public subscription in time for the opening on November 20th, 1813. By the summer of 1815 the "chamber" had "become insupportable to the Teachers on account of the number of children and their confined situation."

Mr. Field had already allowed the use of the Schoolroom as an occasional preaching-room for the curate at Bradford parish church, and when approached by the Wesleyans, "with his characteristic benevolence, let them have the free use of the School-Room" on condition that the Established Church should have priority if required. Mr. Richard Walker, a saddler from Darley Street, Bradford, served as secretary and teacher, lecturing the children with kindness and enthusiasm at "exceedingly small cost but extraordinary success." Punctual and cheerful, he embodied the Scriptural injunction to "Do unto others as ye would that they should do unto you." The first subscription list, headed by Mr. Field with a guinea, realised £9 toward the yearly expenses of £14 - 4 - 10d.

Not many weeks later the hurrying mail-coaches brought the glorious tidings of Waterloo with their portents of peace and prosperity. Joyous were the festivities in Hall and cottage.

With the post-war revival of trade the proprietors of the Keighley and Bradford Turnpike Trust laid plans for a new low-level highway to supersede the original Toller Lane and Bingley Road route with its slow, arduous ascent from the "Sun Inn" and Stairfoot to the summit at Long Lane.

Accordingly in 1815 they obtained an Act enabling them to utilise Low Lane, Manningham, as far as Clock House, with a new section of turnpike joining the old road at Cottingley Bar. Tenders for the first instalments were advertised for letting:-

> " . . . at the House of Mr. Wood, the TALBOT, in Bradford at 11 o'clock in the forenoon of Wednesday, the 14th day of February, 1816, (for) . . . the forming, stoning and fencing of a Piece of New Road commencing at or near Clock House and extending to Heaton Lane . . . Also the building of a small Bridge over Red Beck near Shipley Fields."

A tollbar inside the Manningham boundary near Carr Syke, costing £122, opened for business in October 1816.

Shortly after its completion in the summer of 1825 the new turnpike received an appreciative comment from a local user. "We have seldom, if ever, seen," he reported, "a better road than that which now exists between this town (Bradford) and Keighley. But a few years ago the only communication between these two towns was the old road over Cottingley Moor - a road never good, but in winter always dangerous. There is nothing that can be fairly called a hill in the whole line of the road, and . . . the surface nearly equals the smoothness of a bowling green."

The New Road, or Keighley Road as the Frizinghall sector became known a lifetime later, deprived Toller Lane of most of its traffic and its taverns of all but local trade. The original hostelry in Toller Lane, the "Brown Cow", was kept by John Crabtree who died in July, 1827, at the early age of 31 as a result of over-exertion while serving in the Yorkshire Hussars during the anti-machine riots at Horsfall's Mill, Bradford, a year earlier. When his widow, Betty, removed to the newly-built Branch Hotel at Shipley in 1828, Benjamin Silson persevered for a season or two under the now-obsolescent title of the "Coach and Horses", but finding agriculture more rewarding than ale, he gave up the business and converted the old buildings into Toller Lane Farm. Wayfarers then resorted to the adjacent "Hare and Hounds" inn, which had been built before 1800, and was noted forty years later as "an old respected public house." Owned by Mr. E. C. Lister of Manningham Hall, its publican Nathan Firth, had probably been born there in 1786 when his father John and grandfather "Sammy" were the tenants. Mr. Firth soon established his reputation as a genial host whose "good dinners" were widely renowned.

At Frizinghall the ever-present threat of thirst, real or imaginary, prompted the erection of new hostelries. At Carr Syke, now bypassed by the new turnpike, Mr. Richard Fox Lister of Frizingley Hall had built the "Three Jolly Boys" in 1803 and leased it to John Beanland, blacksmith and innkeeper. Subsequently re-born under the splendid name of the "Flower of England", the little inn adjoined the "Bonnie Stone House" erected by "M. T." in 1769. When traffic forsook the old Otley road (Low Lane) for the new turnpike, Mr. Beanland transferred the licence to the new "Horse and Jockey" which he had built on his pasture at the foot of Emm Lane, but in 1822 the premises were bought by Mr. Benjamin Marriner, a descendant of Richard Fox Lister, who re-named them the "Turf Tavern" in honour of the "sport of kings". The first landlord, John Sunderland, was followed by John Hammond (born 1812) and subsequently by Robert Williamson.

Further along New Road, at Peacock Close, another Beanland, James, built a beerhouse called the "Craven Heifer" about 1841. Tenanted by relatives, the inn had a brief existence of about twenty-five years. A nearby roadside horsetrough was the scene of a fatality in July, 1855, when a passer-by observed what he took to be a cabbage floating in the water; sadly, it was the green-coloured frock of two-year old Benjamin Smith who had overbalanced and fallen in while "dabbling his hands in the water."

Modern disputes about rates, poll taxes and council taxes have their roots in distant history. The downfall of Richard II in 1399 was hastened by his financial demands, and in Heaton a fierce dispute over property assessments in 1704 led to arbitration and revaluation. In 1736 "four respectable gentlemen" from other districts heard an appeal by Edward Bolling against his poor- and church -rates. Eighty years later great complaint was made by James Beanland the publican and his Frizinghall neighbour William Hargreaves, a spinner and weaver at Old Castle, who claimed that properties erected since 1781 on the former Common were being unfairly rated in comparison with other developments on the "ancient inclosures", and a fresh assessment was made. Still dissatisfied, Mr. Beanland appealed again in 1822, and once again every property in the township was reassessed, to the joy of some and the grief of others. William Hargreaves and his brother James were involved in the wool industry disputes which had caused the death of John Crabtree (see above); they were among the few manufacturers who withdrew from the Masters' Association when it decided to close the mills and lock out the strikers rather than submit to their demands.

Up at the Hall, Joshua Field continued cheerfully busy even in old age. "Dear Madam", he wrote to an un-named friend on June 18th, 1819,

"Inclosed I send you a Bill for £45 a year Interest, and shall esteem it a favour if you will acknowledge the receipt of it as soon as convenient, and say when it was due.

I'm sorry to say I continue much indisposed, but shall be glad to hear yourself and Family are well, to whom with our united Regards I remain
Your sincere friend, J. F."

Equally his sharp eye remained undimmed. When Samuel Crabtree, farmer (1754-1831) "hung a Gate" giving access from his field "into the Nog Lane belonging to Joshua Field Esq.", he was reminded that wayleaves over other people's property were a privilege and not a right. An annual rent of 1s was agreed upon.

Shortly afterwards, on September 25th, 1819, Mr. Field passed away. His memorial tablet can be seen at the West door of Bradford Cathedral, the old parish church.

Squire Field was succeeded by his elder son, Mr. John Wilmer Field, born August 20th, 1775, and baptised at Holy Trinity Church, York, where his maternal grandparents Randal and Jane Wilmer resided. Probably he attended Bradford Grammar School, graduating to university where he gained a Bachelor of Arts degree. A period of military service followed during the Napoleonic Wars, when he purchased a commission as captain in the Royal Horse Guards (Blue).

On September 3rd, 1812, Captain Field married Anne, daughter of Robert Wharton Myddleton, Esq., of Grinkle Park Easington, North Riding, having no doubt first met her at a County ball or similar function at York, which was then the social and fashionable capital of Yorkshire. Two daughters were born of the marriage. The elder, Mary, first saw the light of day at Heaton on July 21st, 1813, an event which doubtless provided the occasion for a "treat" for the tenantry. The younger daughter, Delia, was born on October 22nd, 1814, at Whitwell on the Hill, near Malton, being baptised at Whitwell and subsequently christened on July 24th, 1815, at Bradford, where she suffered the temporary indignity of being recorded as "Delilah" in the parish register.

Unfortunately, Mrs. Field had passed away several months earlier, and feeling her loss keenly, her husband immersed himself in the affairs of Heaton and the surrounding districts, serving as a magistrate, a commissioner for the Bradford to

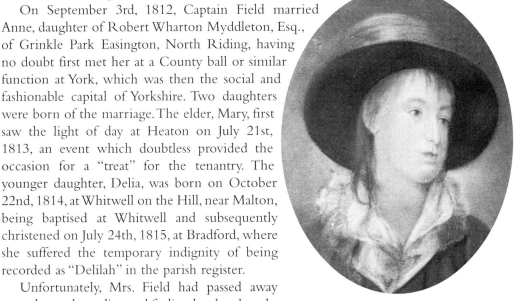

A portrait of nine-year old John Wilmer Field, painted in 1784.
(Photo: author, courtesy of the Earl of Rosse)

Eccleshill turnpike, a supporter of early railway projects in the area and a govenor of Bradford Grammar School, where his Commercial acumen enabled the school to reclaim property tax worth £271. A subscriber to the Bradford Philosophical Society established in 1822, he took an interest in the history of his family. An enquiry to the College of Arms resulted in 1819 in a beautifully illuminated pedigree, which proclaimed its owner's descent not only from the Fields but also from "the ancient families of Wilmer and Thwenge, Lords of Over Hemlesey, Barons Thwenge of Kilton, Bruce of Skelton, Lancaster, Barons of Kendal and Gundred de Warren, youngest daughter of William the Conqueror." A coat of arms of sixteen quarters hung at Heaton Hall for almost a century.

In the stirring and robustly-outspoken 1826 General Election campaign in Yorkshire, Mr. Field took a leading part in the success of Richard Fountayne Wilson of Ingmanthorpe and William Duncombe of Helmsley, staunch upholders of the established Protestant Constitution. As their opponents, Lord Milton and Mr. John Marshall, advocates of Catholic Emancipation, were also elected, it may be assumed that everyone was reasonably satisfied!

Festivities of a different kind surrounded the opening of the new church of St. Paul at

Shipley, whose site had been given by Mr. Field as lord of the manor of Shipley. The church bells were first pealed on August 11th, 1826, on the occasion of the birthday of King George IV, and thousands attended the consecration by the Archbishop of York on November 1st. Spectators admired "the unrivalled beauty of its situation ... at the junction of three of the most beautiful valleys in the West Riding", as yet unsullied by industry or scarred by railways. As the building had been set aside as the centre for a new parish of "Shipley-cum-Heaton", worshippers no longer had to jostle for space in the old, overcrowded church at Bradford.

The summer of 1826 had been long and hot, and drought had scorched the hay, peas, beans and early turnips, but the farmers' fortunes were saved by a bumper corn harvest; "Larger crops have seldom been gathered," they said. But trade was poor, with much unrest in the growing industries of Bradford and little work for the hand-combers, spinners and weavers in the villages; relief committees were formed for the distribution of goods sent by the London Committee for the Relief of the Poor, and Heaton's workless were allocated 16 waistcoats, 27 "trowsers", 50 pairs of gaiters, 13 pairs of stockings and shoes, 8 greatcoats, 18 blankets and 6 flannel waistcoats. By the end of the year, however, it was felt that trade was beginning to recover.

Heaton's population was slowly expanding, from 1088 in 1811 to 1217 in 1821 and 1452 in 1831, and groups of cottages were springing up here and there, at Heights (Moorside), Toller Lane End, Garter Row (Haworth Road) and Frizinghall. Beyond the ridge of Chellow Heights the rough moorland tumbling down towards Cottingley Beck had been awarded at the Inclosure to James Driver, tanner, of Frizinghall, and Benjamin Hird, gentleman, of Cottingley. Mr. Driver's "allotment" was ultimately bought in 1804 by Jonas Hardy who built and settled at West House Farm and about 1824 built seven cottages

The curiously named Garter Row in Haworth Road was built soon after the inclosure of the Commons, and survived until 1963, when it was demolished in favour of a bus layby. Photographed by the author on 28 October 1961.

Old Sandy Lane Bottom – cottages such as those seen here at the top of Cottingley Road (Small Tail Road) were among the first to be built in the original hamlet. They were demolished for road widening in 1972. *(Copyright: author)*

nearby, at Small Tail and Bay of Biscay. Mr. Hird's share was disposed of piecemeal. The long, narrow strip of wasteland between Small Tail Road and the beck ("not worth the expense of fencing", according to the inclosure commissioners) was sold about 1825 to Jonathan Anderton, Joseph Waddington, William Tetley and John Greenwood, who built a dozen cottages there.

Thus a new hamlet was evolving, with fourteen cottages, a farm and a small Baptist chapel. Seven further dwellings arose shortly afterwards, including one at Spring Head alongside the Sandy Lane and ten more by 1839, including a comb-shop at Small Tail Bridge where the beck flowed under the road. At first the new settlement lacked a name, being referred to variously as Swain Royd or Swain Royd Bottom, but perhaps as these were "borrowed" Allerton placenames, the more local title of Sandy Lane Bottom came into use. Even so, individual names persisted for many years – "Wonderful", alongside the beck, "Small Tail" (later renamed "Woodhouse Grove") and the Sandy Lane cottages opposite the head of Chellow Dene.

In Heaton village the original Particular Baptist cause had revived to such an extent that a new chapel and graveyard were constructed at a cost of £700. Eighteen members were transferred from the Bradford chapel and three from Shipley, the first recorded chapel meeting being held on January 27th, 1826, when "Martha Craven and William Pilkington came before the Church and related their experience in divine things to our satisfaction; agreed unanimously to receive them next Lord's Day by baptism" – not, as in former days, in a beck: the new building included a suitable baptistry.

The first minister, the Rev. John Spooner, was ordained at Heaton in September, 1828,

Heaton Baptist Chapel, erected in 1824 and demolished in 1893. On the left can be seen several graveyard monuments as well as the Baptist Sunday School (1872-1962) in Paradise Road, while the building on the right forms part of the present-day Clark's Restaurant.

(Courtesy of Mr F. D. Richardson)

when, according to the minute book, "The day was favourable; the attendance was numerous. The impressions produced were of the most desirable kind. May great good result from the whole. Amen."

Unfortunately the "disordered state of the church" and lack of adequate income obliged the pastor to resign in 1832, and in March, 1840, the church was formally dissolved, the 32 members being received at Westgate once again. Nevertheless, the building was retained and used as an occasional preaching station.

In 1822 Dr. John Simpson (1793-1867) took up residence in Bradford and established a medical practice in the town.

A native of Knaresborough and a country-lover at heart, he quickly conceived a detestation of Bradford, its people and its trade. (" . . . everyone being engaged in trade and thinking of nothing else . . . little removed from the brute creation, being the rudest and most vulgar people under the sun. I have been told that they are worse at Halifax and Huddersfield but think it scarce possible." Local aspirations were coolly dismissed "People imagine that Bradford is to be a second Manchester, but . . . that is all nonsense.") Adjacent towns fared little better. Skipton was "one of the shabbiest dullest towns I ever was in", and Idle "one of our worst manufacturing villages." Understandably, therefore, he visited "the country" when his professional engagements allowed, and among the rural retreats which afforded him the greatest pleasure was Heaton, as his diary records.

1825, January 2nd.

I was to have dined at Heaton, where for some time I have generally dined on a Sunday, but the rain prevented me. I rode up in the evening when it was fair, as I wanted to see Mr. Field on particular business.

January 5th.

Dined at Heaton to meet Mr. John Preston of Barton and the Rev. Mr. Eamonson. Mr. Eamonson and I generally have a game of chess when he comes over to Heaton, being pretty equal players, but today out of compliment to Mr. Preston we did not play - who by the bye returned our politeness by falling asleep.

January 9th.

At church in the morning. Dined at Heaton. We had Mr. Preston, old Mrs. Field (widow of Joshua Field) and Mr. Field's two daughters. The late Mrs. Field (wife of John Wilmer Field) died five years ago.

(N.B. dinners at private houses were generally in the middle of the day, whereas public dinners, e.g. at the Exchange Rooms, Bradford, were evening affairs)

The present Mr. Field is a widower, and his mother lives with him. I suppose the late Mrs. Wilmer Field was a most amiable and beautiful woman. She died very young, leaving two daughters Mary and Delia; they are very fine girls and promise to be good and beautiful.

January 29th.

Met with Sharpe (William Sharpe, a Bradford surgeon from 1792 to 1833.) who was going to look for a hare with his greyhounds. We ranged the upper side of Heaton for about two hours but never found anything.

January 30th

At church this morning. Went up to Heaton to dine. Miss Marshall of Legrams dined with us - a maiden lady over fifty, celebrated as a pedestrian.

February 6th.

I went in the afternoon to see Field who has got a very bad cold, as have also the young ladies and Mrs. Field. I took tea there (The four colds developed into whooping cough that confined the whole family to the Hall for a month. Medicines being at that time of an uncertain quality, one of the Misses Field was "taken dangerously ill" but recovered quickly when the effect of the medication wore off!)

April 10th

I went up to Heaton for dinner, . . . took a bottle of claret, which certainly was most excellent . . . Mr. Field is very much inclined to go to the continent and would go if I would go with him. I wish it were in my power to do so . . .

(From April 17th to June 21st Mr. Field was away on business in London from whence he sent his daughters a "beautiful blood pony". Being a popular guest at the Hall Dr. Simpson continued to call for Sunday dinners).

May 15th

The Miss Fields were at church. I went and dined with them. In the afternoon Mr. Thompson (John Thompson, a partner with Samuel Hailstone, Mr. Field's solicitor.) came up to see them . . . We all took a walk, or rather a romp in the gardens, for the young ladies were in high spirits and delighted to have some visitors. They showed me several birds' nests and we had a game of hide and seek with the old gardener and Mr. Thompson.

The gardener's name is Moses. He is a Scotchman and above eighty years of age, and has been upwards of fifty years in his present situation. I was astonished and shocked on conversing with him today to find that he was a confirmed Skeptic on religious subjects, in fact little better than an Atheist. Miss Marshall came up to tea. The young ladies loaded me with roses and other flowers.

Poor old Mrs. Field is getting quite in her dotage. I am a great favourite with her, and she is always glad to see me. Poor thing! After dinner she watched her opportunity when the young ladies were out of the room and put a five pound bank note into my hand . . . Not to hurt her feelings I took the note but I shall return it to Mr. Field when I see him. . . . She brought her husband not less than £180,000.

May 28th

(Reference to "half a dozen games I have played with Mr. Field who has a very good billiard table").

May 29th

Mr. Field had a most excellent crop of grapes last year. (Apparently in a hothouse.)

June 8th

(Dr. Simpson was canvassing for support for a proposed newspaper, the Bradford Courier and West Riding Advertiser, in which he was a partner) . . "I had to go into the country, therefore got some names for the newspaper as I went along. I called at Heaton to see Mr. Field had got home." (i.e., from London; he returned by the Yorkshireman Steam Packet to Hull and thence by coach.)

(At Harewood Dr. Simpson bought a new house for which he " traded in" the pony called Weasel which he had bought from Mr. Henry Harris, the Bradford banker, and Mr. Field invited him to graze the horse in his park) . . .

July 3rd

"Mr. Field was not at church, being rather indisposed, but the young ladies were. I went home with them in the carriage to dinner . . . After dinner we all took a walk in the garden and then Field and I went into the park to look at my horse. . . . After tea we amused ourselves by looking over some new maps. I walked home in the evening."

July 18th

"Mine must be a very sagacious horse, for ever since the intensely hot weather set in (a few days later it reached 90-92°F in the shade.) he has in the day time gone into a fish pond and there remained in the water only with his head above water, until the heat having abated he was able to feed" (The fishpond appears to have been that at Heaton Hall, as the horse was still "at grass").

On the death of his uncle in July, 1825, Dr. Simpson promptly removed to Malton, but kept up his friendship with Mr. Field:-

"I remained at Mr. Teasdale's until the middle of September (1825) when I went to York to be present at the Musical Festival and where I had agreed to meet my friend Wilmer Field . . . On the Friday there was a grand Fancy-Ball . . . Field went in the character of a Spaniard, and with a piece of burnt cork I painted him a most handsome pair of mustachios. He looked very well, but I suppose in the ball room he forgot his mustachios and took some snuff, and in blowing his nose he spoil'd his mustachios and covered his face with the burnt cork, to the no small amusement of the spectators."

"Towards the latter end of November I went to visit Field at Heaton to have some shooting with him. I was most unlucky, for I was only out one day when in the evening I ran an oyster knife into my thumb joint which laid me up for a month, and I narrowly escaped having locked-jaw which would have killed me.

Whilst I was staying with Field in the early part of December there began the most tremendous panic in the money and commercial world (occasioned by the failure of Wentworth, Challoner and Rishworth's bank at Wakefield which had serious repercussions throughout Yorkshire.) which seemed as if the public credit was entirely put a stop to and the whole nation going to be ruined . . . .Field was in a great fright, for he was a partner in one of the Leeds banks. He vowed if only he could get out he would have nothing more to do with banking, and he has been as good as his word, for when things got quiet he retired as soon as he could." (The family firm of Wickham, Field and Cleaver 'Leeds New Bank' renamed Field, Greenwood & Co. in 1800, stopped payment in 1827.)

Again in the spring of 1826 Dr. Simpson spent five contented weeks at Heaton Hall:

March 1st, 1826 "Set off for Heaton from Malton to visit Wilmer Field" (it was a leisurely journey, with at least one night at York)

March 4th This day I got to Heaton.

March 5th I was up too late to get to church, but I spent the morning reading a pious book.

March 8th Went to Leeds to meet Field. He was busily engaged about the bank, so could not get to Heaton, (in fact he did not return to Heaton until March 13th 1826.)

March 28th Received a letter from Mr. Hustwick of Hull to say that my Stanhope gig is ready. I had the horse with me at Heaton that I had intended to run in the gig. Field was so good as to allow his Timothy Stocks to go to Hull for the gig; he therefore set off today on the horse, and I wrote to my servant John Skinner at Malton to meet Timothy at York on his return and come with him to Heaton.

March 29th At Bradford in the morning. Got my hair cut, for which I always pay a shilling.

April 1st Timothy and John arrived about dinner time with the Stanhope from Hull. . . .Heard this evening that Mr. Hodgson of Wheatley was just dead - one of the greatest misers in the county (i.e. the celebrated "Dicky Hodgson" of Whetley, Manningham, an incessant talker who reputedly spent only £200 a year out of an income of £8,000. The heirs to his Manningham (Clock House), Heaton and Chellow properties were initially his sister Mrs.

Mary Simes and ultimately his niece Miss. Jowett.)

April 3rd I drove Field over to Leeds in my new gig. We dined there. Field set off for London (where he had "particular business") and I returned to Heaton.

April 6th I left Heaton this morning

June 20th (at York for the election of Members of Parliament) Saw Field, Dr. Outhwaite and the Vicar of Bradford at the "Black Swan".

Dr. Simpson's visit in the autumn 1826 was particularly memorable for him.

October 21st Went from Leeds to Heaton and found my friend Field in a bad state of health and very much depressed in spirits.

October 22nd This was one of the most singular-looking days I have ever beheld. The morning was rather cloudy and looked like rain; therefore we did not go to church.

About 12 o'clock at noon it suddenly became so dark that we could scarcely see anything. I was sitting by the fire reading when it became so dark I could not see the print. I then went to the window, but even there I was not able to see the print distinctly.

The Heavens had a most singular appearance. It was not black that the cloud was, with which the whole firmament was obscured, but it had a most singular clay-coloured appearance, and towards the South the colour was a deep orange.

I was perfectly astonished at the wonderful phenomenon, and so was Field, and we looked at each other as if we expected some great convulsion of nature to take place, or that some hidden volcano was going to burst forth and overwhelm us, as in former times Herculaneum had been destroyed.

This very singular appearance continued for about fifteen minutes, when a most violent thunderstorm broke over our heads, and the rain came down in torrents. This continued for about half an hour, when the darkness gradually subsided, and in a little time the sun broke out of the dingy orange cloud and once more delighted us with his presence.

October 23rd/24th   I am shooting at Heaton. Had good sport, but Field did not come out with me, as he was indisposed.

October 28th.   Out shooting, and shot a fine Woodcock.

October 29th.   Field went today to London, and I left Heaton.

Dr. Simpson's last recorded visit took place shortly afterwards.

November 8th. "Went to Heaton in consequence of Job, Mrs Field's manservant, having robbed his Mrs. to a great amount. He had made his escape, but they are in pursuit of him."

November 11th. "Had a coursing meeting at Heaton. We had 13 runs; I killed 5 hares."

November 14th. "I was shooting at Heaton. I killed 3 hares, 2 woodcocks, 2 pheasants, 1 partridge and 1 rabbit, which was a very good day's sport. The partridges are so wild there is no getting near them."

With the revival of trade on 1827 a new joint-stock Bradford Banking Company was formed, with Mr. Field and his neighbour E. C. Lister of Manningham Hall among the first stock-holders. Shortly afterwards, however, Mr. Field purchased a London residence and thenceforth resided there with his family for the greater part of each year. Dr. Simpson's marriage soon afterwards put an end to carefree bachelor ways, and Mr. Field subsequently married Miss Isabella Helena Salter, daughter of Captain Salter, R. N., presumably in London.

The family's periodic returns to Heaton Hall were the occasion for celebrations. On October 30th, 1834, the press observed that,

"The neighbourhood of Heaton, near this town, has lately been the scene of such a round of festivities as have seldom, if ever, enlivened that quiet village, occasioned by the arrival of J. Wilmer Field, Esq., who is apparently disposed to establish his residence among his old acquaintances on a very friendly footing. Immediately on his arrival Mr. Field gave orders for the preparation of a fete, which was sustained throughout the whole of last week, on a scale of unusual extent and splendour, nearly all the fashion and respectability of the surrounding district, as well as many distinguished persons from a distance, having shared in the enjoyment. Among the visitors present we noticed John Hardy, Esq., M. P., and family, Miss Jowett, Matthew Thompson, Esq., Major Ferrand, Col. Richardson, Col. Wainman etc."

On these festive occasions the elegant furnishings of the Hall seldom failed to arouse admiration - the gilded alcoves, glittering looking-glasses, Queen Anne side-table, handsome ebony clock, antique Chinese bowl and vase and Wedgwood dinner service, the Queen Anne mirrors in the drawing-room to the left of the main entrance, and Mr. Field's library in the side wing, with its onlaid mahogany bookcases. Next day the "leavings" from the festivities doubtless gladdened many of the cottage tenants, and the long tradition of "a basin of dripping at the back door of the Hall" was remembered until recent years.

When Mr. Hardy was again returned as Member for the new parliamentary borough of Bradford, many well-known Bradford gentry of the Regency era such as J. G. Horsfall, C. H. Dawson (Low Moor), John Rand and Henry Harris (banker) held a celebratory dinner in January 1835, and Mr. Field replied to the jocular toast to "the strangers present". The wider world continued to beckon, however. The York Musical Festival in September - a brilliant county event - was attended by the Duchess of Kent, her daughter Princess Victoria and "Wilmer Field, Esq."

The removal of the Field family to the metropolis brought them into contact with high society, and soon the London papers were prophesying that "Lord Oxmantown, eldest son of the Earl of Rosse, is shortly to be united to Miss Field, the eldest daughter of Wilmer Field, Esq., of Heaton Hall in the County of York." The marriage duly took place on April 14th, 1836, at St. George's, Hanover Square, London, being performed by the Archbishop of Armagh. On May 5th Mr. Field and Mr. Hardy were presented at Queen Adelaide's Drawing Room, and soon afterwards Miss Delia Field married the Hon. Arthur Duncombe, younger son of Lord Feversham and a relative of William Duncombe, M. P., whose cause her father had so warmly espoused.

Mr. Field did not long survive these notable events, which had linked an old Heaton family with the peerage and introduced them to royal society. He died at his London home on January 11th, 1837, at the age of 61. Ten days later his remains were conveyed to Heaton in a hearse drawn by 6 black horses all splendidly decorated with the family arms in which Mr. Field had taken so much pride.

> "The funeral took place at Shipley church the Monday following (23rd)," the press related, "in a style probably never surpassed in this neighbourhood, and the solemnity of the scene on leaving Heaton Hall was very striking. The train,

which started at eleven o'clock, went in the following order: tenantry on horseback two abreast, then the body in the hearse, with six horses, followed by three mourning coaches each with four black horses, and next to them came sixteen private close carriages sent from the surrounding families . . . a number of gentlemen followed on horseback. The procession extended probably half a mile in length", being witnessed by thousands of spectators.

In August 1838, Lady Oxmantown and Mrs. Duncombe erected a monument in Shipley Church. "as a tribute to the justly cherished memory of a kind and indulgent father".

Meanwhile King William IV had passed away and the young Queen Victoria had been crowned. The fortunes of Heaton, too, were destined to be guided by a woman, as Mary, Lady Oxmantown, was now lady of the manor.

Monument to Mr. John Wilmer Field, St. Paul's Church, Shipley   (Copyright: Author)

With the death of Mr. Field some of the family spirit disappeared from the village, as although his widow, Mrs. Isabella Helena Field returned the use of part of the Hall until her death in 1842, the supervision of the estate was left wholly in the hands of the steward, Mr. Tim Stocks, and a portion of the mansion was leased to a Mr. Alfred Gerard Robinson.

Nevertheless family visits occurred from time to time. Lord and Lady Oxmantown spent a week at the Hall in September, 1837, whence they proceeded to Birr with the intention of returning within a month, and in October Captain and Mrs. Duncombe also sojourned at the Hall and worshipped at the Parish Church.

Inevitably, however, wider interests and responsibilities absorbed more of their time, especially when Lord Oxmantown succeeded his father as 3rd Earl of Rosse in 1841 and the Field estates were formally divided between the two sisters, Mrs. Duncombe inheriting the "York" (i.e., East Riding) portion and Lady Rosse the Heaton and Shipley manors. The new Earl was rapidly achieving a reputation as a distinguished scientist while his wife took a keen and capable interest in the new art of photography.

When John James wrote his "History of Bradford" in 1842 – the first serious attempt at a historical account of the parish – he summed up Heaton township in typically terse and authoritative words: -

"If I was asked what was the principal component of beautiful scenery or

Birr Castle, King's County (Co. Offaly), founded by the Earl of Rosse in the 17th century and still occupied by them. Family records and portraits have been housed there since Heaton Hall ceased to be owned by the Parsons family.   *(Copyright: author, courtesy of the Earl of Rosse)*

happy prospects, I should, to the question thrice repeated, answer – Wood – Wood – Wood. The lower part of the township or manor of Heaton is ornamented with several fine woods, and the undulating face of the country agreeably variegated with hawthorn fences sprinkled with timber trees – shewing that the former proprietors have neither been void of taste to plant and adorn their grounds, nor so needy as to be forced prematurely to apply the axe. The numerous stripped oak saplings, which constantly appear in various parts of the parish (i.e., Bradford) prove either need or avarice, and the rectilinear stone fences which are daily supplanting the winding quickwood hedges augur ill for the taste of the owners".

There were in fact more than 100 acres of woodland and copse in the township, chiefly on the Rosse and Jowett estates, and all were well maintained. In addition, there was an arboricultural curiosity of which Heatonians were proud – an oak and an ash apparently springing from a common root in Toller Lane near the "Hare and Hounds".

On the death of Mrs. Field and the departure of Mr. Robinson, the esteemed Bradford banker and family friend, Mr. Henry Harris became tenant of the main part of the Hall. The bank in which he was a partner had been formed in May, 1803, by Edmund and Joseph Peckover of Eastbrook House and their nephew Charles Harris under the name of Peckover, Harris and Co. All were descended from an old Norfolk family related to the Gurneys, bankers in Norwich, and all were Quakers, although Alfred Harris later became an Anglican. During the 1825 financial panic in Yorkshire (which caused so much alarm to John Wilmer Field) the businessmen of Bradford saved Harris and Co. by publicly expressing their confidence in the bank – a rare event in banking history.

A lifelong philanthropist, as early as 1826 Henry Harris had joined a committee which was finding work for unemployed men in Bradford, and was a regular subscriber to charitable causes such as the Bradford Infirmary for whom he later acted as treasurer. At Heaton Hall his favourite sitting-room was a small apartment on the left of the entrance; when the old bookcases were removed from it at a later date they were bought by his nephew Alfred Harris junr. for use at his new home at "Lunefield", Kirkby Lonsdale.

Mr. Harris always took a kindly interest in Heaton and its poorer inhabitants, and although a lifelong Quaker he assisted the Baptist and Wesleyan Chapels and, later, St. Barnabas parish church, by maintaining pews there, i.e., he paid

Henry Harris (1790-1872), the Quaker tenant of Heaton Hall from 1842 to 1869 and a good friend to the needy.
(Author's collection)

the pew rent but allowed others free use of them.

In July, 1838, Dumb Mill was sold by Joshua Field junior (brother of the late Wilmer Field and a popular figure at Heaton until his removal to London and death in 1863) and his partners H. W. Wickham of Low Moor and Alfred Harris (brother of Henry) to Joseph Wood and Joseph Hargreaves, cloth manufacturers, of Shipley Fields.

The mill had been empty since the departure of Jesse and David Oliver who had succeeded Matthew Phillip as millers. The premises included three cottages at Dumb Mill Place, a kiln, kilnhouse, stable, steam engine, boiler and cornmilling equipment, but within a year they were augmented by a new two and three storey mill, where the busy clacking of power looms soon replaced the leisurely rumble and plashing of the old waterwheel.

Although the old cottage trades were to persist in Heaton for another generation, the press soon prophesied that –

"– – – handloom weavers, combers and other kindred artisans and craftsmen
must be content to take their place with the shoebuckle makers, leather
breech makers, pigtail perruquiers and other divers artists of an age gone by."

Steam was to conquer all.

In Lister and Ingle's valuation of the township compiled in 1839, Heaton's industries were summarised as follows; –

Quarries

Owner	Tenant	Location	No. of getters	Area
Samuel Crabtree	Sowden	Heaton	2	1a 13r 10p
John Wood	Burnley	Heaton	2	1 0 29
Oxmantown	W. Greenwood	Heaton	2	
Oxmantown	Abm. Greenwood	Heaton	2	
Oxmantown	Milnes	Heaton	2	
	J. Greenwood	Chellow Height	?	
	Parkinson	High Park	2	

Colliery: Owner Lord Oxmantown, tenants James Hustler, at Toller Lane; area 30 perches, with pithill.

Comb Shops

Owner	Tenant	Location	Description
Jonas Greenwood	Combers	Small Tail	Wash houses
Hargreaves	James Lee	Frizinghall	Cottage & combshop
Lord Oxmantown	C. Greenwood	Heaton	35 $^1/_4$ sq.yd.
Lord Oxmantown	W. Murgatroyd	Heaton	Shop, enginehouse

Textile Mills

	Area	Location	Description
Owner Joseph Wood	162 $^3/_4$ sq.yd.	Dumb Mill	2 storey old mill
Owner Joseph Wood	396	Dumb Mill	3-4 storey new mill
Owner Joseph Wood	228 $^1/_2$	Dumb Mill	2 storey corn mill

Serenely indifferent to these human endeavours, the vagaries of the local climate continued to delight and alarm. In January 1838 the temperature plunged to 27 degrees (F) below freezing-point (the coldest for 23 years), while in June 1846 destructive thunderstorms lit up the interior of houses with their vivid lightnings. The momentous year of 1848 began pleasantly, with daisy-strewn pastures supplying lush fodder for grazing animals, but before January was ended, snow had obliterated all. In two successive winters,

1853 and 1854, it was reported that " – – – old inhabitants who complain that winters are not what they used to be have had their wishes granted – heavy snowfalls and chill winds have made the district impassable." Capricious storms in June, 1858, filled the dale bottom with a broad sheet of water, after which temperatures of over 100°F aroused a whirlwind which gathered up dust into a dense mist – but the hay harvest was excellent.

When the schoolroom at Paradise had been let to the Wesleyans by Joshua Field in 1815 there had been an understanding that if the Established Church should at any time desire the use of the premises, it would receive preference.

The understanding was invoked in 1840 in consequence of a letter to the Vicar of Bradford (Dr. Scoresby) from the Incumbent of Shipley-cum-Heaton.

Shipley, March 13, 1840

My dear Sir,

For the purpose of obtaining more efficient spiritual superintendence of the people in Heaton, I sometime ago applied to the Clerical Aid Society, but they are so tardy in their operation that I received no reply till you were on the point of coming into residence. Thinking that it was a matter in which it would be desirable for me to have your concurrence and approval I postponed any further negotiation in the business.

When I had the pleasure of calling upon you it was my intention to introduce the subject to you, but your engagements that morning prevented my call.

I assure you that I shall feel much grateful pleasure in co-operating with you in the plan you purpose, whereby Heaton may have a share of those pastoral services you are about to provide for Manningham. The schoolroom is tolerably commodious and may, I hope, be readily obtained. When the Curate arrives, I shall be happy to accompany you with him on his first introduction to the place, and shall be quite willing to render him any service in my power by becoming associated with him in holding weekly Lectures there.

Believe me, my dear Sir, yours faithfully,

T Newbery.

At first Lord Oxmantown demurred at Dr. Scoresby's application for the use of the schoolroom.

"The Wesleyans", he wrote, "have so long had the use of the schoolroom, and from what I have heard of the former neglected state of the parish were, I believe, so useful, and considering their friendly feelings towards the Established Church here, and the zealous support they have afforded it in Ireland, I should be unwilling to deprive them of the schoolroom."

But whereas in the days of Vicar Crosse (died 1819) and John Wesley there had been a friendly understanding between the two denominations, Dr. Scoresby disliked dissenters and they him. He promptly reminded Lord Oxmantown of the undertaking given 25 years earlier, and received an encouraging reply:

"I have had the opportunity of conferring with Mr. Stocks, "his Lordship wrote. "I find I was under an erroneous impression as to the circumstances attending the transfer to the Westleyans(sic), and I do not now think there can be any objection to its being immediately handed over to you for the use of your curate."

A letter from Dr. Scoresby to Mr. Newbery followed quickly.

"Field House, Manningham
May, 1840

Revd. Sir,

Some months ago a school room belonging to Lord Oxmantown at Heaton was mentioned to me as available for the use of a Curate I designed for Manningham and Heaton and for the furtherance of my objects, under the blessing of the great Head of the Church, of endeavouring to be useful to the needs of the extensive Parish of Bradford for which as far as in me lies, I feel myself responsible. Understanding that the Schoolroom in question was merely lent to the Wesleyans whilst the Church was not in a condition (beneficially to the People) to make use of it, I wrote to Lord Oxmantown to inform him that if it were his Lordship's wish to have the School employed under the instrumentality of the Church, I should shortly be in a condition to take charge of it. Circumstances occurred (and among them a conversation with Mr. W. Walker on the subject) which induced me to write to Lord Oxmantown so as to leave the application I had made on a different footing and, indeed, all but to withdraw it.

A recent letter however from Lord Oxmantown informed me that his Lordship purposed (as I understand his communication) to transfer the school room at Heaton to me for the use of my Curate. That I should accept his offer I can have no hesitation any more than I had that whilst the Church was unable to make use of it, it should be usefully employed by the Wesleyans.

I shall be obliged therefore by your communicating to the persons under whose charge the school now is, this decision of Lord Oxmantown, made, however, I am bound to say, with much consideration for those who have heretofore had it in charge – and that we should wish to enter upon the charge in the course of a month, notice of course being given to this officially under his Lordship's direction.

I remain,
Revd Sir,
Your faithful obedient Servt.
Wm Scoresby.

Copy to Wesleyans.

The Wesleyans accordingly resumed their former practice of holding Divine Worship in the upper room of a cottage where about 100 scholars were taught the Word of God every Sunday, being supported by proceeds of sermons at White Abbey Chapel, Manningham. In 1846 they bought a plot of land in Back Lane whereon they erected a square stone 120 seat chapel which they proudly named Ebenezer – "a strong rock"."

In the same year the Railway Age dawned in Heaton when the Leeds and Bradford line was laid via Shipley along the valley, passing to the west of Dumb Mill with a level crossing at Lane Side. Work on the section through Heaton township began in the autumn of 1845, claiming its first victim in February 1846, when James Hargreaves, (26), a labourer, attempted to climb aboard a wagon as the locomotive began to move; he was thrown out

Back Lane, 7 June 1970, following the demolition of the shop and house built by William Dawson at the corner of Quarry Street and Rossefield Road and later sold to J. S. Driver. The cleared site was converted into a car park for the 'Delvers' Arms'. On the right, the old Ebenezer Wesleyan chapel was converted into two houses about 1897, but the former pulpit steps are still in regular use in one of the houses. *(Copyright: author)*

and run over, the first Heaton man to be killed by machinery. On the afternoon of March 12th thousands of people gathered along the valley to behold the first railway train run into Bradford.

"It was a delightful evening, and all waited patiently for the approaching train. About half past three the railway whistle was heard sounding along the valley, and a few minutes after, the engine 'Stephenson' with 22 wagons behind it" passed by with a brass band on board. The public service commenced on July 1st, bringing with it a novel dilemma: the Meridian time observed by all clocks and timepieces in Bradford dale was $7^1/_2$ minutes behind the Greenwich mean time observed by the railways. Before long Greenwich time was universally adopted, but was the cry, "Give us back our seven minutes!" heard in Heaton or anywhere else?

Until the inauguration of the National Health Service in 1948, most people considered it prudent to insure against illness by making regular payments to Friendly Societies which gave financial assistance in time of need, thus avoiding the social disgrace and shame of "going on the town", i.e., seeking "parish relief" from the poor-law overseers and thereby rendering themselves liable to a means test.

The first reference to a Friendly Society in Heaton occurred in December, 1834, when there was a grand procession of the Independent Order of Oddfellows from Heaton to Shipley Church for the funeral of one of their number, with "a great concourse of people assembled to witness the scene." Then in June 1834, the Quarter Sessions ordered that,

> ". . . the Rules of the Economical and Philanthropical Friendly Society, Towler Lane, Heaton, be filed and confirmed."

Unfortunately they were not filed very well, as they are no longer to be found, but it is reasonable to assume that the society's officers met at the "Hare and Hounds" to transact their business.

The Ancient Order of Foresters was also active in the district from the 1850's, and the author's parents subscribed to it until its beneficial activities were superseded by National Insurance.

Parliamentary reform in 1832 resulted in a new Poor Law two years later, which swept away the old arrangements dating from the reign of Queen Elizabeth and replaced them with Poor Law Unions administered by elected Guardians to whom the Overseers were made responsible. A Bradford Union of 21 townships was therefore established in 1837, with workhouses at Barkerend and Thackley. Bradford, Heaton and Manningham constituted District No.5 with their own Medical Officer of Health – a part-time post filled by a local physician.

At first the new system encountered hostility and opposition. When Heaton's assistant overseer attempted to collect the first instalment of rates due to the Union, he was prevented from doing so by the threats of his angry townsmen and was duly summonsed for failure to execute his duties. Matters were smoothed over by Mr. Stocks, the manorial steward, and opposition melted away when the new ways were found to be better than the old: indeed, the local press hailed them as "the greatest boon ever conferred on the poor".

From that date all poor rates collected by the townships were paid into Union coffers, an inevitable source of discord, as the fast-growing, newly-industrialised town of Bradford soon absorbed a disproportionate share of the funds. When the four townships of Bradford, Bowling, Horton and Manningham became the new Borough of Bradford in 1847, the unfairness of the system was plain to see: –

Paid by the Union to the poor of the Borough	£ 990
Poor Rate collected from the Borough	249
Paid by the other 17 townships towards the Borough's poor	£ 741

Following heated disputes in which one of the Bradford Guardians was heard to express indifference as to whether the rural townships would "sink or swim", the Poor Law Board agreed that they should "go their separate ways". A separate North Bierley Union was therefore set up on November 9th, 1848, Heaton, now part of District No.8 along with Shipley, being allotted one Guardian, William Crabtree, with his son Samuel as Overseer and (concurrently) township constable.

Accompanying the Guardians on their first visit to the old (1765) Thackley workhouse, the press penned a dramatic picture of what they found there – " . . . a very cleanly appearance - not one in a thousand of our working population being as comfortable as they are . . . . as a refuge for the parish poor of a country district, it affords all the comforts that is expected or required," as the occupants were mostly old people, "some worn out by infirmity or age, but most helpless by reason of imbecility." In one room the old men were observed sitting motionless around the fire "like a picture in still life . . . reminding one of the stiffened corpses which, after Napoleon's retreat from Moscow, were sometimes found with their hands outstretched before the dying embers of a fire." The women's room, crowded with "forsaken wives and mothers never wed" as well as their children, presented a melancholy sight. An improved workhouse at Clayton Nab End was opened in 1858 and served until recent years as an old people's home under the name of "Thornton View".

Although the phrase, "cold as charity" probably applied to everyday life in the workhouse, the Guardians endeavoured to introduce an occasional note of cheer at their own expense; "Christmas Day at the Workhouse" in 1849 brought "a good dinner of Old English fare - roast beef and plum pudding" followed by "home brewed and a pipe" for the old and spice cake for the young, doubtless a welcome change from the daily diet of thick porridge, skimmed milk, bread, cheese, broth and "meat-and-potatoes", sometimes in a pie.

The children's welfare was not neglected, as their "school pence" were paid by the Union, and in 1864 they were taken on a day trip to Morecambe Bay, a pleasure which contemporary children in better circumstances rarely enjoyed. Happily, few Heatonians experienced workhouse fare; in 1878 the Clayton premises housed only five Heaton folk - one able-bodied man, two infirm, and a "lunatic" of each sex. "Outdoor relief" was being distributed to one married couple, two widows, ten children and six males and six females who were not able-bodied.

The census return for Heaton taken in April 1851, reflected the change and evolution taking place in the townships.

	Inhabited Houses	Uninhabited Houses	Male Residents	Female Residents	Total Residents
Sandy Lane,) Chellow &) Toller Lane.)	86	2	213	200	413
Heaton, Syke, Shay & N.Hall	153	–	390	404	794
Frizinghall	72	2	203	227	430
	311	4	806	831	1637

The majority of the "born and bred" Heatonians lived in Heaton village and its immediate surroundings; Sandy Lane Bottom had attracted many "off-comed 'uns" from Allerton and Wilsden, and apart from young people few Frizinghall residents were natives.

Most "Sandy Laners" were employed in textiles, both hand – and power-driven; in Heaton village farm workers, "mill hands", handloomweavers and delvers lived cheek by jowl, and all the fifteen distinct Greenwood households in the village were proud to claim Heaton as their birthplace. Six households had migrated from Southowram in 1845, the link between the two communities being the quarries. Others had migrated from distant rural areas, but the farthest-travelled were a few unmarried Irish labourers who had doubtless fled the Potato Famine. Only six persons were "in receipt of parish relief". The oldest person was John Hill of Paradise, born in Heaton in 1765 when King George III had been on the throne a mere 5 years; his rival the Old Pretender (born 1688) was still alive, and America was still a British colony.

Occupations were many and varied: -

Agriculture: farmers, yeoman, dairymaid, labourer, milkman.

Quarries: delver, stone-getter, flag-dresser, mason, stone-merchant.

Coal: collier, coal hurrier, banksman, pit lad, coalman.

Wool: sorter, carder, comber, drawer, rover, spinner, twister, winder, reeler, hanker, bobbin-layer, weaver (hand- and power-loom), shuttle-maker, overlooker, foreman, warehouseman, engineer and manufacturer, producing worsted, stuff and moreen, also warp-dresser and cotton warp-dresser.

Domestic: butler, domestic servant, housekeeper, maid, cook, gardener, charwoman, mangler, children's nurse, errand-girl.

Professional: banker, solicitor's clerk, book-keeper, collector of poor-rates, schoolmaster/mistress.

Railways: platelayer, gatekeeper.

Trades: maltster, cart-driver/waggoner, grocer, butcher, clogger, boot and shoemaker, carpenter, joiner, woodcutter, shipwright, boatman, cordwainer, tailor, dressmaker, bonnetmaker, gardener, mechanic, painter, blacksmith and blacksmith's striker, marble-cutter.

And: gentleman (which usually denoted "retired") and proprietors of houses.
Contrasts were revealing: –

William Laycock	Lane side	mill boy	aged 7
Mary Gill	Plantation	children's nurse	aged 8
Branwell Watmuff	Small Tail	woolcomber	aged 9
Mary Tillotson	Town Gate	dressmaker	aged 10
Richard Craven	Royds	pit lad	aged 10
Thompson Greenwood	Paradise	delver	aged 11
William Tetley	Chellow Height	scholar	aged 14
John Hollingworth	Syke	coal-cart driver	aged 15
William Waterhouse	Low Moor	handloom weaver	aged 73
Benjamin Haigh	Cross Hill Head	farm labourer	aged 73.

As the old folk insisted,"Hard work never killed anybody". Thompson Greenwood (see above), later a farmer, died peacefully in his bed in 1927 aged 87.

With the gradual spread of education the old forms of patronymic names were slowly dying out; one of the last recorded instances occurred in 1817 when Thomas Craven and Samuel Firth, the overseers, made a payment of 6s 2d for "Sal a Nat's childer", i.e., the children of Sally daughter of Nathaniel. Similarly, "Sammy Isaac" and "Sally Isaac" were the children of Isaac Broadley. Nevertheless as late as 1876 William Cudworth noted that nicknames were used as a method of distinguishing members of the same family. Thus, in the numerous Greenwood family, "Joseph at Lillams" was the tenant of Leylands Homestead, "Jim at t'Steps" the occupant of a cottage which currently forms part of Clark's restaurant in Highgate, "Jonas at Whitley's" was presumably a servant of the Whitleys, whilst "Dan lad" was doubtless Daniel Greenwood of Garter Row.

The descendants of Joseph and Mary Greenwood of Heaton, photographed in July 1980, on the steps of Heaton Baptist Chapel. *(Copyright: Telegraph & Argus)*

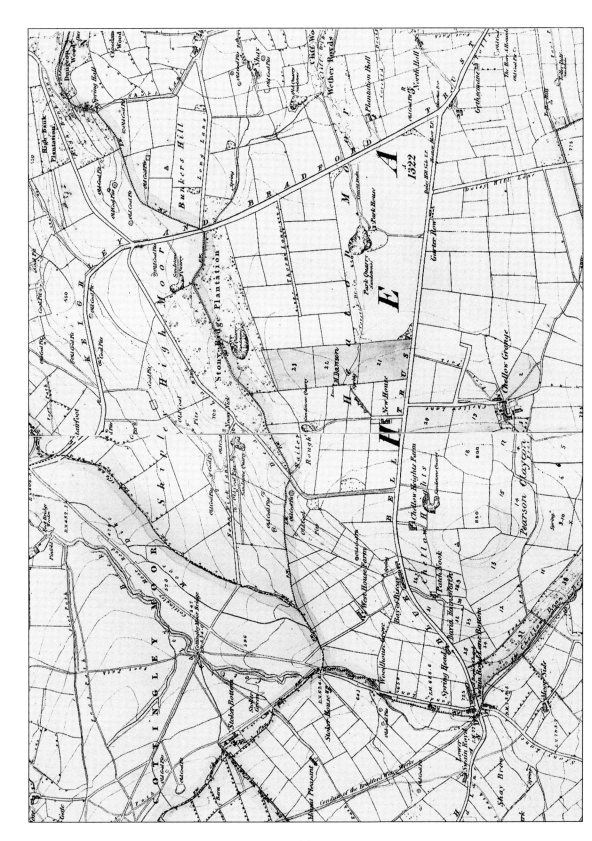

96

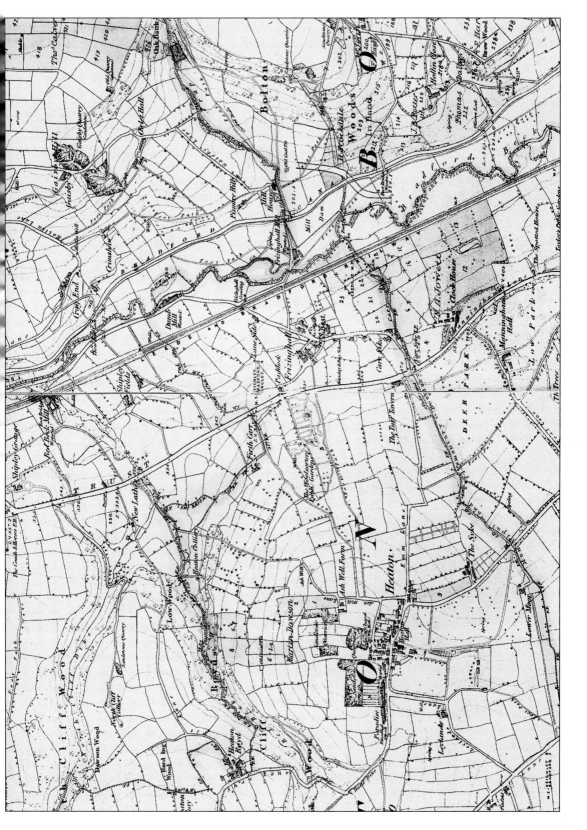

97

Chapter 15 — Crime and Constables

In a quiet rural district such as Heaton problems of lawlessness were rare, and only in the lonely parts of the township such as New Road could danger lurk for unwary travellers.

A few days before Christmas, 1841, Joseph Lister, a Baildon woolcomber, was robbed of 17/- (probably his week's wage) by three men at Carr Syke. Three years later Samuel Sharp, a Keighley comb-maker, was knocked down and robbed at the same place; his assailants fled when the lights of a gig were seen. In 1855 a young man named Shackleton, pleasantly happy after having imbibed four pints of beer and 1¹/₂d worth of whisky was deprived of his watch on leaving the "Craven Heifer", and in 1857 Patrick Ryan of Bradford was committed for trial at the Assizes on a charge of stealing 8/2d from Sophia Gott, a weaver at Listers' "Lillycroft Mill" who was on her way home with her wages in a basin when she was stopped between the Turf Tavern and the Woolsorters' Gardens.

Not all the victims needed the assistance of the law. When Nathan Firth of the "Hare and Hounds" was set upon by three men near the "Upper Globe", Manningham, he seized one of them, "knocked the wind out of him, laid him on one side" and went after his companions, who fled. A month in Wakefield Gaol as "a rogue and vagabond" awaited the would-be assailant when he recovered consciousness.

During the troubled years of the Chartist agitations the magistrates appointed special constables to protect the Queen's Peace. Thus in May, 1839, no fewer than 1,835 "specials" were enrolled for Bradford Parish, but Heaton's contingent of 37 volunteers found that its services were rarely called for, except presumably in August, 1842, when a riotous mob said to number almost 10,000 men set out from Bradford to bring local industry to a halt. Finding Lillycroft Mill well defended by the 17th Lancers, they proceeded to Frizinghall where they intimidated Hargreaves' woolcombers. On their return by way of Bingley and Wilsden they were intercepted in Toller Lane by the military, who promptly dispersed them. Among those arrested was Samuel Tillotson, a Frizinghall comber, who, having used considerable violence during the disturbance, was sentenced to channelling his energies into enforced hard labour for a period of six months.

Normal processes of law and order were performed in early Victorian times as in previous centuries by the elected Constable and his Deputies. Their nomination at the annual Town's Meeting was automatically confirmed at the October session of the Court Leet in Bradford, the Leet jury comprising one man from each of the 19 townships, Samuel Crabtree being the Heaton juror in 1840.

Most of the constables were farmers, John Andrew (blacksmith) and John Binns (handloom-weaver) being rare exceptions. Benjamin Silson (born 1813) of Toller Lane Farm often combined constabulary duties with the less demanding tasks of byelaw-man and pinder - indeed, the pinfold adjoined his house. His services were required one Sunday night in December, 1857, when a drunken fight erupted outside his house between three revellers who had spent the evening in the nearby "Hare and Hounds". As the contestants were a constable, a deputy constable and the schoolmaster, the affair caused much gossip and scandal in the village - and, no doubt, secret laughter in the schoolroom!

Many infringements of the law were of a non-violent nature. In June, 1851, two men were discovered gambling on the Sabbath, an offence considered to be "demoralising to the

.... labouring classes as well as productive of loss and ruin among them." They lost the gamble and spent a month in gaol, while in April, 1864, a £2 fine was imposed on Thomas Morey and John Firth Smith when they were accused of having driven a cow through Heaton village without a licence. Thomas, aged 14, protested that he did not know what the word "licence" meant, and Mr. Smith pleaded ignorance of the law, which, as everyone knows, is never a valid excuse!

On the passing of the 1842 Police Act the West Riding magistrates began to issue yearly precepts to the Town's Meeting for the appointment of Parochial Constables. Heaton with 1,573 inhabitants was allowed 5 (later 6) such constables, and the ratepayers' choice fell upon Mr. Silson, Jonas Sunderland (Frizinghall), William Taylor (Frizinghall), Thomas Thompson Hudson (Heaton) and John Gill (Chellow Heights) - all farmers - who were duly sworn in at the West Riding Court House, Bradford, where the magistrates informed them that they could "act outside their township if they liked, but they need not without they liked!" Mr. Silson as senior was empowered to serve precepts or summonses.

All able-bodied men aged between 25 and 55 were liable to serve as Parochial Constables if they occupied property of at least £4 rateable value, and received fees of 2/6d for attending magistrates and Sessions, 2/- for executing warrants and apprehending miscreants and 3d per mile travelling expenses.

In some townships there was rivalry between Leet and parochial constables: not so in Heaton where the two offices were usually combined in one person despite differences between the dates of the appointments - parochial in April and Leet in October. Complications arose in 1846 when parochial nominations were declared invalid because the Overseers had omitted to sign them, whilst at the Leet Mr. Silson declined to pay the Court fees until threatened with an action, on the grounds that the ratepayers would not reimburse him. Both types of constable were answerable to the Superintendent Constable of the East Division of Morley, a paid officer of the Riding authority.

The end of the old, easy-going order was foreshadowed in July, 1856, when a Bill for a regular County Constabulary was enacted. Col. Cobbe, the first Chief Constable of the new West Riding force, appointed 500 county constables, all of whom had to be at least 5'8½" tall and under 40 years of age; they received uniforms and regular wages ranging from 2/7d a day for a third-class constable to 23/- a week for a sergeant. They took up their duties on January 1st, 1857, when Heaton's own County Constable began patrolling the lanes and roads of the township. Old habits died hard, however; when Irish "navvies" caused uproar at the Turf Tavern it was the Overseer (Mr. William Booth) who was called in to restore order by the landlady, Mrs. Hunter.

For some years the magistrates continued to insist that ratepayers should still nominate parochial constables, now condescendingly dubbed "the Dogberries of former days". However the office finally lapsed in 1872, after which parochial officers could no longer be appointed unless Quarter Sessions thought them necessary, which they did not.

One of the last of Heaton's parochial constables received a friendly tribute on his retirement.

> "On Friday last, 1st May (1857), a dinner took place at .... the Hare and Hounds, Heaton, prior to a presentation to Mr. Joseph Murgatroyd, the late precept-constable of that township. After dinner, which was most ably served up by the worthy host (Mr. Nathan Firth), the chair was taken by Mr. William Murgatroyd, the inspector of the reservoirs, and the vice-chair by Mr. William

Booth, overseer, and the testimonial, which consisted of a purse, well-filled, was delivered to Mr. Joseph Murgatroyd with an appropriate address by Mr. William Cox. Mr. Murgatroyd briefly responded, and the remainder of the evening was very pleasantly passed with toasts, sentiments etc."

Mr. Murgatroyd retired to more tranquil pursuits; in August he took second prize for verbenas at the Bradford Floral and Horticultural Show held "in the fields opposite Trafalgar Street, Manningham Lane", and first prize for heathers and light geraniums at the Airedale Show, Shipley.

The Leet constables faded away after 1866, when the ratepayers declined to pay heed any longer to the Court's ancient but outworn summons. Undaunted, the Leet officials continued to make nominal appointments from the ranks of their own cronies until 1926, but none of these irregular nominees ever ventured out on patrol.

As Dr. Simpson had discovered some years previously, the woods and becks of Heaton and Chellow abounded in game and trout, which were a source of temptation despite severe penalties for trespass and poaching. When Andrew Jennings and John Magson of Wilsden were discovered poaching by night in Lord Oxmantown's woods in 1837 they were sentenced to two months hard labour and, upon release, to find sureties for good behaviour as well as a bond of £20. Similarly, John Jennings of Shipley spent three months in the House of Correction in 1844 after having been caught with a gun at midnight by Battye, Lord Rosse's gamekeeper.

About 1857, Mary, Countess of Rosse, photographed two of her sons with a young lady, probably the Hon. Mary Ward. The eldest son, Lawrence, Lord Oxmantown, succeeded his father as Earl of Rosse in 1867 and died in 1908, whilst his younger brother, Randal, later took Holy Orders and is commemorated in Randall Place, Heaton.

(Copyright: the Birr Scientific Heritage Foundation)

The killing of a hare on the Rosse estate cost Thomas Moseley £3-2-6d in 1853, but Tom Smith of Heaton and Joseph Hill of Manningham were more fortunate, as their employer, Mr. Atkinson Jowett of Clock House, paid their fines when they were apprehended with dogs and nets in Lord Rosse's wood at Chellow Dene. Mr. Jowett's heir and successor, Mr. George Baron, was less tolerant when John Leeming shot a pheasant on the Jowett estate: he had to pay his own fine.

Gamekeeping was a hazardous occupation, especially when poachers went out in gangs. At the West Riding Court in 1855, five Heaton men - Thomas Binns, Thomas Collins, George Copley, John Greenwood and Jonathan Jackson - were each fined 5s plus costs, but Samuel Ibbetson was gaoled for having absconded ("been out of the way") when apprehended nine months previously, and when George Copley assaulted the keeper he was fined £2 with costs or two months in gaol in default.

The occasional "thrill of the chase" aroused much excitement, Whenever the Clayton Subscription Harriers passed through Heaton "the sound of the horn" attracted men, women and children to enjoy the sport, although Mr. Lister forbade the hunters to disturb the deer in the Heaton section of his park, and Col. Joseph Hirst, the master of hounds, was fined £2 with costs in 1856 for having trespassed on Lord Rosse's land at Chellow Grange despite having been "warned off" three years earier by the farmer, William Tetley.

The phenomenon of back-to-back housing, so prevalent in West Riding towns in the 19th century, made its first appearance in Heaton in 1855/6 when William Sugden and Thomas Thompson ("Tommy") Hudson bought the lower end of the Crosshillhead Farm croft. Mr. Sugden erected a beerhouse (later called "The Fountain Inn") with a brewhouse, ten "back-to-backs"alongside Crosshill and nine at the edge of the cart track leading to the Syke cottages. Each house comprised a living room, bedroom, attic and cellar with a "cellarhead kitchen" devoid of light or ventilation; all had shared privies (earth-closets) and ashpits (where ash from domestic fires was thrown) in a common yard. Six similar but larger cottages were built by Mr. Hudson at the northern end of the plot, with individual gardens and privies and a communal wash-house for domestic laundry. Water was carried in pails and

Heaton Syke viewed from Heaton Road in 1958.   *(Copyright: author)*

flagons from Syke Well and Middle Well, although when "muck-spreading" took place in Heaton Hall Park, the housewives had to venue further afield in search of purer supplies.

Other similar developments followed during the next three decades at Sandy Lane Bottom, Toller Lane End, Heights Lane and Heaton village, and although the principle of "back-to-back" dwellings has often been criticised, it should be remembered that for the early occupants the new houses were usually preferable to those in which they had dwelt previously.

In these small, close communities, relationships with neighbours regulated daily living. When lines of washing had to be pegged out across streets or yards, good neighbours refrained from shaking rugs or beating mats, and when children were being born or old folk nearing the end of life's journey, kindly neighbours helped to cook, wash and care for their families. Immorality incurred disapproval; women who were "no better than they ought to be" had to endure the clashing of pans and buckets when they ventured forth, and errant menfolk were shunned. News spread quickly - women (and occasionally men) leaned over garden gates to "kall" (exchange gossip) while others were fond of "neighbouring", i.e., paying visits.

To modern eyes, living conditions were spartan and cramped. One of the two-bedroomed Paradise cottages sheltered nine adults - parents, five daughters and two sons, while the nine cottages in Stocks Yard (later Hammond Square) housed 42 people. Self-respect triumphed nevertheless. In one of the tiny Syke "back-to-backs" there dwelt a married couple, an aged aunt and five small children, all of whom were immaculately attired ("like royalty") for their Sunday strolls - "a lovely family".

Since 1847 the adjacent township of Manningham had formed part of the new borough of Bradford, whose need for a supply of fresh, clean water was desperate. The Bradford Waterworks Company had therefore obtained parliamentary powers to tap Manywells Springs at Cullingworth and convey its waters to reservoirs to be constructed on land which they had purchased at Chellow Dene, on the Heaton/Allerton boundary. Work was in progress by July, 1844, as the local press approvingly reported: -

> "A beautiful dell it is, this Chellow Dene! One of those quiet, sequestered English nooks in which solitude and silence have held converse with great Nature from the beginning until now (n.b., evidently they were unaware of poachers or mediaeval herds of swine in those solitudes!). But see now how its trees are felled, its solitude teems with human life, its silence is put to flight by the sounds of hard and harsh labour. Pickaxe, mattock, shovel and sledgehammer are being plied by rustic strength, and slowly but surely are changing Chellow Dene from a thing of natural beauty to the less dazzling beauties of utilitarianism. Our heartfelt blessing on these rough working Saxons with their huge limbs and sandy hair who are . . . lifting the murmuring stream from its old bed deep in the dell."

When complete, the upper of the two reservoirs covered eight acres and held 50,000,000 gallons at an altitude of 691 feet above sea level, while the lower level contained 28,000,000 gallons. The finished works were viewed by the Earl and Countess of Rosse (formerly Lord and Lady Oxmantown until the death of the 2nd Earl in 1841) and their young family, who in August 1849 were staying at Heaton Hall; they "expressed themselves highly gratified at the improved appearance of this pretty little glen."

Two years later Bradford Corporation were empowered to purchase the Company, construct new reservoirs at Barden in Wharfedale and at Heaton Syke, and exercise monopoly water rights not only in their own borough but also in the unsuspecting townships of Allerton, Wilsden, Heaton, Clayton, Shipley and Idle. The new Heaton Reservoir, built by Messrs. Duckett and Stead astride the Manningham boundary, received its 31,000,000 gallons from a conduit which passed under the Keighley turnpike to skirt Northcliffe Woods and the brickworks near Firth Carr. The contract was let in April, 1856, and was near completion eighteen months later. Early visitors "were struck during one of the late hot days by the delightfully sweet and cool air which can be enjoyed from its lofty (39 foot) embankment and by the charming views of Bolton Woods."

The interfering hand of authority attempted to mar the innocent pleasure which families derived from their visits to the reservoirs. In July, 1858, the Bradford Corporation Watch Committee forebade the Chellow Dene reservoir keeper to augment his income through sales of ginger-beer and dishes of fruit, even though the committee were exceeding their powers, the reservoirs being outside their borough.

As the Industrial Revolution became firmly established, most of the Turnpike Trusts enjoyed a brief season of prosperity. Each year the privilege of collecting the tolls was let by auction to the highest bidder, subject to a month's rent in advance, and security for the remainder. In this way the Keighley and Bradford Trust accepted bids varying from £2,350 in 1824, and £3,150 in 1844.

The quieter Haworth and Bluebell road with its tollbars at Two Laws, Stanbury, West Lane (Haworth), Hewenden Bridge, Hewenden Brow, Lingbob, Swain Royd and Heaton Moor (Heights Lane bottom) achieved a modest profit of £355 in 1855. The Heaton Moor bar was "manned" in 1851 by Elizabeth Tetley, assisted no doubt by her sons Ezra (aged 11) and William (9). In May, 1855, Heaton acquired two additional tollbars when the old bar house at Little Lane, Manningham, was dismantled and rebuilt at the junction of Toller Lane and Leylands Lane, while the Carr Syke bar was merely moved across the boundary, the Trustees being determined to escape Borough rates and interference!

The quaint Toller Lane barhouse was the scene of a violent assault in 1866 when Robert Patterson of Bingley, returning home one windy night with two friends asked leave to step inside to relight his pipe. The toll collector, Mr. Mercer, gave him a candle, but Joshua Hirst, quarryman, and James Hird and John Greenwood, cart drivers, all of Heaton, knocked the pipe out of his hand, blew out the candle, assaulted him and kicked one of his friends unconscious when he intervened. Five witnesses who were also in the house testified against the ruffians, each of whom was fined £2 - 10 - 0d (about two weeks' wages).

But tolls and turnpikes had had their brief day. The impoverished Bluebell Trust was wound up in October, 1858, while the Keighley and Bradford Trust collected its last tolls on October 31st, 1868, after which the property and implements (shovels, scrapers, carts and weighing-machines) were sold.

> "This will be a great saving and convenience to vehicles which will be able
> to pass to and fro without interruption", the press observed. "The removing
> of the great gates which have been the means of causing more than one death
> will be a source of satisfaction to some and grief to others."

In all probability the deaths referred to were those of young gentlemen unwilling to pay the tolls, who urged their steeds to jump over the gates and broke their necks in the ensuing fall. Equally unwilling was a drover who in 1841 set his dog on his flock of sheep, thereby

The Keighley and Bradford Turnpike Trust's tollbar at the junction of Leylands Lane (left) and Toller Lane. When it was sold by the Trust in 1868, it served as a small shop until its much regretted demolition in 1951. *(Copyright: Keighley News)*

causing them to flee through Carr Syke gate so quickly that the tollkeeper could not count them. He was fined 18s 6d for his initiative.

The persons aggrieved by the abolition of the tolls were, of course, the township ratepayers on whom the whole burden of highway upkeep now fell. In 1878, however, the former turnpikes in Heaton were accepted as Main Roads by the West Riding authority, which thenceforth bore half the cost.

Although the Carr Syke and Heaton Moor tollbars were soon pulled down, the Toller Lane barhouse was bought by Lady Rosse for £80 in November, 1868; it served as a cottage and sweetshop tenanted by the Shoesmith family until its regretted demolition in 1951. A toll board rescued from Swain Royd barhouse and now on display at Bradford Industrial Museum lists charges varying from 8d for every horse or beast drawing a coach, carriage or hearse, 1s 8d a score for a drove of oxen and 10d a score for a drove of calves, sheep, lambs or swine.

When the Bradford Temperance Society held its Whitsuntide gala in Manningham Park in 1848 by courtesy of Mr.Lister, the event was well attended, although the abstemious entertainments "bore but a faint resemblance to the old sports and pastimes of Merrie England." Unfortunately, not all those who attended were free from the influence of alcohol. Scorning the official entrances at Oak Lane and Carr Syke, a gang of Heaton quarrymen scaled the walls, trampled through the shrubs, overturned benches, tables and fences, broke down the booths and partly demolished the bandstand. Then, coarsely insulting every member of the sedate assembly they met with, they escaped back over the wall before the borough police could be summoned.

An ever less pleasing picture was revealed a few years later in a letter published in the press entitled,

"THE UNCULTIVATED HORDES AROUND BRADFORD."

"As a stranger to the town I have always been pleased to observe ... the cordial co-operation of all right-minded Bradfordians in the laudable desire to elevate their fellow-townsmen, as is evidenced by . . . the various societies and institutions established in Bradford and the neighbourhood. It might naturally be expected that they would exhibit outward and visible signs of religious, moral, social, intellectual and healthful improvement.

Being fond of skating, fortune led me (as I thought) to the reservoir which is in course of formation at Heaton, and there, on a small sheet of frozen water, I hoped to enjoy that healthful sport in peace and quietness, free from the bustle and smoke of the town. But alas! I had reckoned without my hosts, for no sooner had I whirled on to the ice than I was saluted with a volley of stones accompanied by curses and denunciations both loud and deep, from a number of young men and boys who were "slurring" on a portion of the ice. Somewhat astonished at finding myself in a hornet's nest, I rushed among them to inquire the reason for their unwelcome demonstration, and was told among sundry oaths, 'Ye mun goa, for we'll hev noa skatin' atop o' this hice – we doan't want skatin' here, an' ye mun goa!' I expostulated with them, endeavouring to show that there was enough ice for all, but in vain, for they only answered me with oaths and curses. Finding fair means were of no avail, I was compelled to call in the aid of my walking-stick, a temperate display of which kept the unmannerly rascals at bay and left me in undisturbed possession of a beautiful piece of the virgin ice. I shall not attempt to pourtray the remainder of their proceedings for the rest of the afternoon, for grosser, filthier and more obscene language I have never heard than that which they used among themselves . . . not only the young men but little boys, mere children, cursed and swore like their elders. I took several of the little fellows to task for using foul language, but when they again went into the midst of their companions I heard them exclaim, "Whooa's yond? Whooa the divil cares for him?"

. . . I have visited on foot the interesting and beautiful tracts in the locality, among the coal miners of Wibsey and Gildersome, the quarrymen of Haworth, Allerton and Idle, in districts where the inhabitants are rough and unpolished, yet it was never my misfortune to be molested or insulted save by the Heaton roughs. I understand it is the intention of some benevolent gentlemen to establish a Mechanics' Institute at Heaton. The above plain, unvarnished statement shows that there is plenty of scope for its operation."

Such uncouth behaviour was in fact by no means unknown in other Yorkshire villages where strangers were viewed with suspicion and their personal appearance was commented upon with forthright frankness. Indeed, John James in his "History of Bradford" in 1841 wrote that,

"It is a rare occurrence that a stranger can pass a group of loungers who may be loitering in any of the surrounding villages without being grossly insulted."

Fortunately, help was at hand. By 1852 a Yorkshire Union of Mechanics' Institutes was in being and in a position to promote the formation of village libraries, stressing that,

"Within distances varying from three to eight miles from Bradford . . . are populous localities lingering a whole generation behind the townspeople of their vicinage - their education neglected, their manners brutal, even their dialect so dissimilar as to suggest the idea of some hundred or two miles of interval."

The Union undertook that if a group of twenty-five penny subscribers could be formed in a village, it would receive a loan of fifty books which would be exchanged half-yearly, or oftener if required. This offer was taken up in 1863 by a committee of Heaton folk, headed by the curate, who set up a Heaton Mechanics' Institute complete with library, periodicals, chess and draughts available every evening in the little schoolroom, and commenced a series of "popular readings" at an admission charge of one penny.

The second "Penny Reading" of the 1867 winter session was vividly described. A "goodly gathering of gay and glowing-checked maidens with a full complement of admiring swains" heard Mr. Mitton recite Tom Brown's description of an Oxford Boat Race, followed by the "Squire's Story" read by Mr. Hardwick. A "good-natured, ruddy-faced agricultural person" read "Mary Queen of Scots" as well as "Th'way Billy Armitage gat a neet's lodging", which aroused almost as much mirth as a Lancashire dialect poem which followed. Others recited "Besom Ben" and selections from "Twelfth Night", whilst the church choir which was "just blushing into bloom, burst into harmony and song between each reading," although the few "nigger minstrel songs" in their programme were deemed inferior to "compositions of the best masters" which would help the choristers to "cultivate their musical taste." Despite the "smothering" atmosphere in the little room, the sessions were hugely popular, and optimism was expressed that Heaton would soon have "a new school suitable to the growing wants and intelligence of the villagers" - a need made more urgent by the passing of W. E. Forster's Education Act in 1870.

A pleasing account of life at this period was provided by Mr. John Lee (1844 - 1931) in his reminiscences published in 1928: -

JOHN LEE'S REMINISCENCES

"About 1850 Heaton was an isolated little village with no vehicular help for those of its inhabitants who needed to go to Bradford, and a considerable number of householders went once a week, and of course had to walk both ways, carrying their purchases of groceries, etc., home with them.

At that time the population might be divided broadly into four classes-farmers, quarrymen,-hand combers, and handloom weavers. Quarry-men had more or less fixed hours of labour, but combers and weavers could work as they liked. Both combers and weavers had a "carrying-in day" once a week, when the completed materials were returned to the employers (Titus Salt being one of these), and a fresh supply of wool, warp, and weft were brought back-the pieces woven being known as "Moreens." This was a red-letter day for the children, who were occasionally allowed to ride in the carriers carts to see the sights of Bradford and to bring home a packet of Old Judy Barrett's humbugs, which were not unacceptable to older folks. It may readily be imagined that the weavers at any rate, by reason of their daily operating the treadles of their looms, would be kept in good walking trim. As an illustration of this I may mention the case of a man whom I knew well, a man who was not only strong on his feet but equally strong in his religious opinions, walking from Heaton to Harewood and back once or twice in the course of a summer, and taking two or three of his children with him, to hear the Vicar preach on Calvinistic doctrine.

At some of the small quarries there were no mechanical means of raising the stone to the surface, not even a "gin," so that the work of the "getters" and "huggers" was very arduous. A well packed leather saddle was strapped to the hugger's back, and the man bent forward so that his hands rested just above his knees, and the stone was then placed on the saddle, and with a man on either side to steady him, the hugger struggled up the rough winding track to the delph hill. Some of the men could carry tremendous weights in this manner, but none but the strongest could endure such a strain

Sporting instincts were common to all the villagers and much indulged.

Football was much favoured, but of a type neither Soccer nor Rugby. No ground was set apart for the game, and there was neither touchline nor goal posts. The course was usually across two or three pastures and over intervening walls to the fence decided upon as the goal. It depended upon the place chosen as to the length of the course. There were few rules and consequently no referees, which gave considerable liberty to the players. The ball itself was, of course, not the finished article of to-day, the air chamber being an ox bladder blown up by the players through a pipe stem. Sometimes on account of defective tying up, the ball became deflated and the game was stopped until it was blown up again. Cricket was the favourite summer pastime and was played on the recreation ground then called Quarry Hill. Bowling was underhand; consequently wides were unknown and leg-byes few. The expert bowlers of their day bore the family names of Broadley, Pickard, Bennett, Greenwood, and Spence. The first time I saw round arm bowling was on Heaton Hill. It was introduced by Jim Broadley and played havoc with the opposing team. Where Jim had picked it up I don't know, but he developed it with considerable success. Knur and spell, drive knur (much on the lines of hockey, minus its refinements), arrow-throwing and slinging had many followers, and some of them could sling and throw very long distances. Snowballing matches were often indulged in and frequently developed into a very rough and tumble game.

(Running was also popular. When a "foot race" from Wilsden to Manningham was arranged in June 1840, for a prize of £5, the contestants were "Naylor of Heaton" and "Whitaker of Derby". The satisfying outcome was that "Derby lacked speed and stamina, and Naylor won by 150 yards").

The village maintained two blacksmiths who found their time fully occupied in shoeing horses, repairing carts and waggons, hooping cartwheels, and sharpening picks, shovels, etc.; for farmers and quarrymen.

The village boasted two bootmakers, a clogger, a shuttlemaker, two tailors, and two or three dressmakers, so that as regards clothing the villagers were to a considerable extent provided for.

One of the first classes formed in Bradford district for the purpose of teaching Curwen's tonic sol fa was established at Heaton by Mr. T. K. Longbottom who, I believe, came from London to one of the Bradford warehouses. This was a source of great pleasure to the members, who met once a week in the vestry of the old Baptist Chapel. Since then there have always been villagers keenly interested in music.

Taking them all together I should say the villagers were a hardy lot, notwithstanding, perhaps indeed in consequence of, their food being of a very simple character. With few exceptions flesh meat would not be available in many cases on more than one day a week, Sunday. Those who had small gardens attached to their cottages had a limited supply of potatoes, apples, pears, and gooseberries. Imported fresh fruit was a very scarce article. The brewing of "small beer" was not an uncommon practice. A walk through the village often revealed beer tubs standing at the cottage doors, each with a sieve over it in which the scalded malt and hops were left to "sile," while the beer underwent its cooling process. This small beer was looked upon as a wholesome beverage and was occasionally taken in place of milk with a dish of porridge. Some villagers kept a pig or two, and those of their neighbours who were unable to do the same contributed their scraps to the swilltub.

Pig-killing was a notable event, and most of the housewives could make a very tasty dish of the offal, combined with a savoury pudding, portions of which it was customary to distribute amongst their relatives, neighbours, and friends. The story goes that on one occasion a man who had killed his pig was met by a friend, who remarked, "Well, ah suppose tha's sent yahr Jack a bit o' summat," to which the sarcastic reply was "Nay, lad, tha knaws ahr Jack nivver kills a pig." Another story runs that one who had overlooked his obligation to a neighbour found the following rhyme chalked on his swilltub-

Tha villain o' villains
Ah've gien tha mi swillins,
Tha's hed 'em both rough, smooth and fine,
But tha's neglected, what I fully expected,
Tha's nawther sent sparrib ner chine.

This was the time of transition from cottage industries to mill work. Those workers who were capable of making the change found employment in the following mills- Manningham, Frizinghall, "Dumb," and Shipley. There were, of course, elderly people who could not adapt themselves to the new form of employment, and consequently suffered great hardships. The mill hours were long, beginning at six in the morning and finishing about six at night, except on Saturday, when work ceased at two o'clock. "Short-timers" were allowed to work at eight years of age. So when they were on the morning turn and had to walk to the mills furthest away, they, along with their elders, needed to be astir very early, about 4.30. a.m.

In my very early days local races were run on the public highway, the mile course being from the milestone (near the electric transforming station in ToIler Lane recently built by the Bradford Corporation) to the top of Shay Lane. About two or three hundred yards from here there is a deep hollow running parallel with the road, High Bank, leading down to Saltaire. This hollow was the site of many prize fights. The ring was formed on the flat portion, while the spectators occupied the slopes on either side. No gloves were used, and if my memory serves me right the fight was always to a finish, either by one of the pugilists acknowledging his defeat, or by being so battered that he could continue the contest no longer. These contests were terrible to watch, but they drew large crowds of men, women, and children from Bradford, some coming through the village, where their numbers were considerably increased, and others by way of White Abbey and ToIler Lane. After the fight the pugilists presented most unsightly objects, sometimes their faces being so scarred as to be unrecognisable by their best friends. The site referred to was just outside the parish of Heaton, but these encounters had their effect on the life of the village, where it became a common practice to settle differences which mainly came to a head in the public houses, by a resort to fisticuffs. How the supporters of these prizefights managed to elude the vigilance of the parish constable, or to prevent his interference, I know not, but they did."

(But not always! On December 5th, 1857, the West Riding constabulary intervened as Hugh Gordon and Larry Nicholson stripped off for a contest, at Stoney Ridge, attended by a large crowd. Nicholson "beat the officers with great violence and escaped," but his adversary was apprehended and fined £5.)

"There was one characteristic which I imagine would appeal to the present generation, that is the freedom to work or play as one felt disposed, in relation to the state of the larder.

It seems to me that the immense developments of the last seventy years, to go no further back, have placed within the reach of industrious thrifty working men, greater comforts, conveniences, and pleasures, both material and intellectual, than were possible to some of the landed gentry at an earlier date.

In conclusion, I should say that few persons with experience would care to go back to the "good old days" I have endeavoured to describe."

Chapter 16 — The Age of Improvement

That most genial of English institutions, the village hostelry, had long been established in the township. Within its unpretentious walls the menfolk sat in contemplation over a gill of "homebrewed" while they smoked their clay pipes and "put the world to rights."

The "Black Swan" and "Ned Brook's" seem to have been the earliest in the field. Once kept by "Mally Rhodes", the local midwife, the former, jocularly termed "'t Mucky Duck", was sold by auction on September 10th, 1770, as "a messuage, being the sign of the Black Swan." Perched on a knoll overlooking the highway (Frizinghall Road) it accumulated a group of tidy cottages collectively called Swan Hill. Francis Rhodes, victualler and landlord in 1822, was followed by James Rhodes, Tate Ambler, James Oddy and John Harrison, and by 1881 when Henry Walker held the licence, the old building had become a local hostelry rather than a wayside inn.

Up in Heaton village the original inn, familiarly known as "Ned Brook's" in honour of Edward Brook the innkeeper stood opposite the top of Cross Hill (Crossilleead). The premises were first mentioned in township records of 1768, as the town's officers congregated there to discuss public affairs over a gill of beer and a pipe of tobacco, and occasionally "Ned" would be paid to provide a meal for a destitute person, i.e., a pauper who was "on the town".

After "Ned's" death in 1789 the inn fell into disrepair, and when it was demolished (the site is now occupied by no.6, Highgate) the licence was transferred by his sister-in-law, Sarah, to Garth House under the jolly title of the "Punch Bowl". Shortly afterwards she was

Old Frizinghall, photographed on 5 April 1980. 'Rookery Nook', Frizinghall Road.

(Copyright: author)

succeeded as licensee by Solomon Clark whose descendant John Clark was tenant of the same property in 1911 and was long remembered as a Heaton "character". On being widowed in 1814 Mrs. Elizabeth (Betty) Clark took over the licence, transferring it about 1823 a little further down Town Street to Bell Cony under the new name of the "Masons Arms" in honour of the quarrymasons who "slecked" their thirst there.

When Betty retired to Low Moor Farm in 1833 Peter Laycock took over the tenancy with William Greenwood as licensee, paying a yearly rent of £12-16-0d to Mr. Field and £4 for the licence. The little inn comprised a taproom, back room, kitchen, three bedrooms and a "fair cellar". About 1830 the more splendid title of the "King's Arms" was assumed, no doubt to celebrate the accession of the popular William IV.

A shortlived hostelry existed under the name of "Shoulder of Mutton" at Leylands Homestead about 1808; predictably Richard Greenwood, the tenant, was a butcher, and two well-known Heatonians of a later generation, William Clark (1820-1883) and William Crabtree (1806-1891) learned their trade from him.

The "Delvers' Arms" in Lambert Fold was probably so named by its first owner and licensee, Joseph Kay, a stone getter, on its completion about 1852, while nearby in Back Lane John Slingsby and his sister Betty kept a beerhouse in their cottage for a few years.

By mid-century the stone quarries and other workings had extended their operations from Emm Field and the lower end of Roydscliffe Woods to Chellow Heights. Many sites were already exhausted, and more than two dozen crop-bearing fields bore traces of old spoil heaps, pit hills, shafts and trial bores. In 1869 Messrs. Smith & Gotthardt, Lady Rosse's agents, listed sixteen workings:-

(1)   Messrs. J. and S. Ackroyd and T. Lambert, on Silson's farm at Westfield, Chellow, opened 1867

(2)   Messrs. J. Gray (Allerton) and Thos. Cockroft (Sandy Lane Bottom) on James Tetley's farm at Westfield, Chellow, opened April 1868; depth of stone 4 feet to 27 feet; steam crane.

(3)   Mr. William Greenwood, Plantation (Bingley Road), trial about 1829, opened 1866; depth of stone 3 feet.

(4)   Messrs. Ledgard and Hainsworth, Chellow Heights Quarry, opened 1849; 7 ton steam crane.

(5)   Messrs. A. & T. Hill, Chellow Quarry at Well Close; depth of stone 36 feet; hand and steam cranes; water leaking in from Park Quarry.

(6)   Roper & Co., (formerly A. & T. Hill), Heaton Park Quarry; "untidy".

(7)   Dyson & Tetley (formerly A. & T. Hill), Heaton Park Lower Quarry; one horse-gin.

(8)   Tomlinsons (formerly A. & T. Hill), Heaton Park Lower Quarry; one steam crane; "tipping too high".

(9)   Messrs. James Fyfe, Weather Royd Quarry, opened about 1848 by T. Tilney and sold to Fyfe 1863; engine out of use.

(10) John, James and Kitching Greebwood and their brother-in-law Joseph Kay of the "Delvers' Arms", Victoria Quarry at Weather Royd, opened 1859; horse-gin and hand-crane.

(11) Messrs. Turner and Brook (formerly A. & T. Hill), Back Lane Quarry; flags and wallstones; hand-crane.

(12) William and Joseph Greenwood and Wilkinson Patefield, Chellow Road Quarry; 7 foot delfstone.

Dyson's Quarry, with Emanuel Dyson, quarrymaster (left); the author's grandfather, John Edward Hornsby (back row, second from right, with hand in pocket) and 59 other stalwart delvers from Heaton and district. Photographed on 8 December 1899, by William Mann of East Bierley.

(Author's collection)

(13) William Tetley of Manningham and Henry Toothill; Moor Close Quarry, opened 1864; 3 foot delfstone.

(14) Joseph Cliff and Son (manager Squire Brook), North Cliffe Colliery; fireclay and hard and soft bed coal.

(15) Messrs. Beck and Ellis, High Bank Colliery, now worked out.

(16) Taffymire Clay Works (lower end of Roydscliffe Wood); fireclay and common clay; coal both hard and soft bed; $18^1/_2$ yard shaft to low bed; a dayhole to the hard bed; three kilns; brickmaking shed; 8 h.p. engine and 6 h.p. pit engine.

In addition, trial boreholes had been sunk in 1864/5 at Chellow Dene and Hazelhurst Brow, between 18 and 88 yards in depth. In almost every hole bands of "Four Lane Ends Better Bed Coal" 26 inches thick were found, and it was calculated that the bed extended to 30/40 acres.

Competition for labour was so strong that in 1866 there was a distinct scarcity of delvers. Messrs. A. & T. Hill who employed over 400 men had therefore erected a new stone-polishing plant incorporating four machines powered by a 20 h.p. engine for the production of flagstones, steps and landings. Activity in the quarries reached its peak in 1875, as demonstrated by the Rosse estate annual rentals: –

1870	1875	1880	1885	1890	1895	1900	1905	1908
£1,917	£2,653	£1,082	£880	£946	£657	£628	£534	£330

The last of the blacksmiths at Heaton Syke was John Dewhurst about 1832, but by 1839 "his fires were spent". Benjamin Beanland continued to strike sparks at the Carr Syke smithy until about 1848, being followed in his profession by John Slingsby of Low Lane and John Slingsby of Lane Side. Dumb Mill also employed two smiths.

The Eden smithy prospered to such a degree that "Jack" Andrew relinquished the workshop at Back Lane, which by 1851 was employing no fewer than three smiths - Benjamin Bennett, aged 19, Thomas Gott, 20, and William Robinson, 31. Thirty years later Mr. Bennett, then living at 16, Quarry Street, next to his "shop", was as much a "village institution" as his partner Bill Robinson, who was universally spoken of as "Billy Blacksmith". Both smithies, John Lee recalled, were fully occupied in shoeing horses, repairing carts and wagons, hooping cartwheels and sharpening picks, shovels etc. for farmers and quarrymen. They possessed "a great attraction for boys, especially in wild wintry weather, and a great privilege it was to be allowed to blow the bellows".

When "Jack Andrew" retired about 1870, a shortlived smithy was set up alongside the then "King's Arms", while between about 1850 and 1882 John Holroyd occupied a cottage and smithy owned by Bairstow Mortimer at no.9, Toller Lane End. Round the corner in Haworth Road Seth Robinson ("Billy Blacksmith's" son?) laboured in a small "shop" conveniently adjoining Bill Chadwick's wheelwright's hut. Meanwhile at Bay of Biscay William Rawnsley was combining two useful skills as smith and publican at the "Blacksmith's Arms".

A period of severe trade depression in the early 1840s prompted Bradford's Amicable and Brotherly Society of Woolsorters to devise alternative employment for its workless members. The cultivation and sale of vegetables and plants seemed to offer a prospect of success, and in August, 1844, Mr. James Beanland of Firth Carr agreed to lease nine acres of land for transformation into what the press termed "a pretty Eden-spot" for public gardens and recreation. The land comprised four closes - Upper and Lower High Green, Flatt Close and Four Days Work - adjoining New Road.

Farsightedly the "Woolsorters' Gardens" provided not only garden plots but also public baths, tea rooms and lawns, facilities hitherto unknown in Bradford dale. "Then for a glorious, refreshing plunge!" exulted a correspondent. "A luxury, which will be new to our ill-watered locality."

No fewer than 1,700 people flocked to the formal opening on May 20th, 1846, when they were allowed to marvel at the warm Bath House (said to "resemble a seraglio at Constantinople" despite the absence of nymphs), a Chinese pavilion, verdant lawns, a concealed open-air pool fed from the Ash Well and other springs, and "moss cottages" for private parties. Royalty, nobility and local businessmen generously donated money, plants, furniture and exotic birds such as a stork, a Chinese golden pheasant and, less pleasantly, a vulture.

The yearly programme of events followed a regular pattern between Whitsuntide and autumn - brass bands, strawberry fairs, skittles, tea on the terrace, dancing on the greensward, strolls around the gardens and swimming in the pools (men and boys only in the open-air pool, as no lady could have entertained the prospect of disporting herself in public). Band concerts attracted up to 6,000 visitors on Sundays; trains from Bradford, Keighley and Leeds made special halts at the Frizinghall level crossing, and sometimes a pig was offered as a raffle prize although the joy of winning it may have been tempered by the difficulty of transporting it!

The "Old Year" of 1854 was blown away by a destructive gale which sounded like gunfire at Heaton. Also blown away were the pavilion and the cold frames in the Gardens. The woolsorters' honest endeavours had sometimes been compromised by the foolish activities of others, particularly in the pools where dogs, nude bathers and visitors armed with bars of soap were allegedly seen. Being "too far out in the country", the Gardens could not compete with the public parks within the borough, and the agricultural venture failed through inexperience. The 1864 season was, sadly, their last. Mr. Beanland had already sold the land, "situate near to Frizingley" and attractively "free from the Borough Rates of Bradford", and when the woolsorters disposed of their bedding-plants and shrubs in May, 1865, the brave venture was ended.

The "Hungry Fifties", a decade of bad trade and uncertainty were over at last, and, unknowingly, Heaton was about to enter upon an era of irrevocable change which was to transform it from a placid farming, delving and mining district into a prosperous, desirable suburb of a great city.

Symbolic of the impending changes was the small schoolroom, filled every day of the week by Heatonians young and old, engaged in scholastic studies or Church devotions. Until about 1856 the schoolmaster was Robert Clough, assisted by his wife Nancy, whose combined qualities ensured that a rival "dame school" set up in a cottage at Bell Cony enjoyed but a brief existence. New pupils were given an arithmetical test in culinary terms: -

"Nah then, what's two-thirds of three-quarters of a round apple pudding the length of my arm?" - to which, the answer was, of course, a half!

Further competition arose in the form of a new "dame school" at Back Lane, but whereas the dame, Miss Beaumont, charged 3d a week, Mr. Lee's fee was a mere penny. Being a single-storey edifice, his school was a paradise for pranksters - a slate placed over the chimney pot to fill the rooms with billowing smoke, and illicit late-night tolling of the school bell in its little turret; no wonder that years later, former pupils admitted having been glad that Mr. Lee had a wooden leg, otherwise "they would have had many a tanning!"

Not surprisingly, moves were made for the raising of funds towards improvements to the school. In September 1857, the Rev. Welbury Mitton, incumbent of Manningham, and Mr. Porter, curate of Shipley-cum-Heaton, led services at which hymns and psalms were sung by an amateur choir coached by Mr. John Binns Hammond, son-in-law of Lord and Lady Rosse's steward, Timothy Stocks. In November the choir attempted "a portion of the liturgy, with excellent effect", at a "tea festival" held in aid of Church Pastoral Aid Funds. A noble army of ladies provided ample provisions which the villagers heartily devoured, but little money was raised.

Happily, the pace quickened when the incumbent of Shipley-cum-Heaton, Mr. Kelly, appointed as full-time curate at Heaton Mr. Welbury Mitton's son, the Rev. Henry Arthur Mitton, who took lodgings at Garth House with Tom Greenwood, the gardener at the Hall, and soon became a familiar figure in the district. His labours often took a practical form. A recently-widowed lady was struggling to make a living out of a small cottage-shop, and "as regularly as the week came round, Mr. Mitton called on a Friday evening to help her make up her accounts until she was able to manage herself."

When a scheme for the erection of ten new churches in Bradford Parish was formulated in 1859, it was agreed that the eighth church should be sited at Heaton, and in August, 1863, Lord and Lady Rosse donated part of the Half Acres at the corner of Ashwell Lane and Whiteley Lane. Messrs. Mallinson and Healey of Bradford were appointed architects, and

when the foundation-stone was laid on September 26th, a well attended tea party was held to swell the funds.

In its original form the church, dedicated to St. Barnabas, comprised nave, south aisle, chancel, apse and an organ-loft adjoining a tower and sturdy steeple containing a single bell, the architectural style being French 13th century Gothic. Gifts from benefactors such as Lord Rosse and Benjamin Wood (owner of Dumb Mill) ensured that within two months only £700 of the total cost of £2,800 was still owing. Enthusiasm was such that when the pillars for the nave arches were being chiselled, the masons' wives volunteered to smooth them by hand. Not surprisingly the church was completed in only thirteen months, being consecrated by the Bishop of

St Barnabas' Church in its original condition, photographed before 1896 and possibly as early as 1868. The large vicarage (right) was let out to tenants until the church finances were placed on a sound footing by the Rev. G. B. Flynn, vicar from 1891 to 1917. *(Courtesy of Mr H. Cheetham)*

Ripon on October 28th, 1864, with the Rev. H. A. Mitton as perpetual curate or incumbent. The district assigned to the church was co-terminous with Heaton township. The initial congregation contained several former Baptist adherents, but as St. Barnabas' has never possessed a burial-ground, patriotic Heaton Anglicans desiring interment in their native soil have always had to choose between the two Baptist graveyards at Town End or Sandy Lane Bottom!

A revival of the Baptist cause had begun somewhat earlier. On March 2nd, 1862, the little-used chapel in Town Street was re-opened "as a Christian Church holding the principles of the Particular Baptist denomination and holding the doctrines commonly called Calvinistic." Samuel Gill of Chellow Style Farm was "set apart . . . to the office of deacon," with a body of trustees which included Mr. John Crabtree, woolstapler, who had recently built a large and comfortable residence at Well Springs - the first of the many "woolmen's villas" to adorn Heaton's landscape. The Rev. George Brockway officiated as pastor from 1865 to 1873, during which time a substantial Sunday School building was erected alongside the cemetery. Subsequently lay preachers and ordained ministers conducted the services alternately, William Dawson of Back Lane providing them with Sunday dinner and tea at a cost of two shillings.

The Sandy Lane Baptists were also progressing strongly, especially during the ministry of the Rev. W. E. Winks, a man of "strong faith and unquenchable zeal", whose prayers were considered "unforgettable". Among the great occasions of the year was the Chapel Anniversary with its eagerly anticipated "Treat" which was usually held in Mr. Miles Gawthorpe's fields at West House Farm. In 1868 the Whit Monday Treat provided coffee, buns, rural sports and "the ascent of several balloons", while a few weeks later the Sandy Lane Bottom Band of Hope and Temperance Society paraded their banners before a 400-strong choir accompanied by the band of the Second West Yorkshire Artillery. The band failed to match the vigorous pace of the temperance hymns, but fared somewhat better with the more familiar strains of "All Hail the Power of Jesu's Name!"

The Wesleyans were sharing in the revival too. In 1869 the renovation of Ebenezer Chapel in Back Lane was celebrated with the customary tea and a prayer meeting addressed by the leading Bradford industrialist Mr. Angus Holden (Mayor of Bradford 1878-1881 and 1887-1888). Their Frizinghall brethren were more ambitious – a stately new 450-seat chapel in Frizinghall Road costing £3,000 was formally approved in May, 1871 and opened in 1878.

Heaton was fortunate in acquiring one of the earliest public recreation grounds in the district. Quarrying operations at the rear of the village had thrown up a considerable spoil heap adjoining Nog Lane, and when the quarry closed about 1843 the villagers obtained permission from Lord Rosse to partially level and grass it, thereby transforming it into a favourite promenade and playground from whose summit wide vistas could be surveyed and "Morecambe air" inhaled. Unfortunately the unruly activities of a few spoiled the enjoyment of the many. When local farmers complained of trespass and damage to their fields, "Quarry Hill" was briefly closed by Lord Rosse's steward (Timothy Stocks), but when a committee of 58 local men offered to manage the grounds, they were reopened on October 9th, 1869 amid great rejoicings and lively music played by the Heaton Brass Band.

The earliest reference to the Brass Band occurred in April, 1855, when its eighteen musicians led by John Fawcett Lister competed in a Grand Brass Band Concert at Headingley but failed to gain a prize. Success eluded them again a month later, when they achieved eighth (and last!) place in a similar competition. Possibly their talents were more appreciated on their native hill-top. When the Crimean War ended in 1856, Heaton folk organised a full day of festivities in which the Band featured prominently. In the morning it led a procession of locals - in carriages, carts or on the backs of horses or donkeys - from the assembly point at Haworth Lane Bottom, through the village, down to "Frizingley" and thence to Bradford, "to the great astonishment of the inhabitants" of that place. Returning via Heaton Hall Park, the band played the National Anthem on Heaton Hill, and returned in the evening to accompany open-air dancing.

Mr. John Lee recalled that the band met once a week in a "comb-shop" at Heaton Syke under the baton of a Frenchman named Montague. "The shop would not be more than 18 feet square", he added. "I think that few people will be able to imagine what the rendering of a double-forte passage was like when the band was at full strength and the roof held on!"

In 1857 the Heaton, Clayton, Low Moor and other bands accompanied the Bradford Festival Choral Society (then in its first year of existence) and the Bradford Choral Union in a grand concert which culminated in the "Hallelujah Chorus". Events such as this must have improved the techniques of the Heaton instrumentalists, as they gained second prize at a later contest. Brass bands are, of course, dependent on the availability of their members. In August, 1858, the Heaton Band, led by B. Bennett, were unable to join thirteen others at a contest in Peel Park. Was the "test piece" (if there was one) beyond their powers, or had their "better halves" "put their foot down" on that occasion? History is silent.

Who was B. Bennett the bandleader? Could he have been Benjamin Bennett, the Quarry Street blacksmith? Could it be that the hands which beat Heaton's horseshoes into shape also welded Heaton's musicians into a harmonious whole?

At Heaton the popular wedding of Albert Edward, Prince of Wales, and Princess Alexandra of Denmark in March, 1863, was celebrated "with great spirit" at Heaton through the generosity of Henry Harris, the tenant of Heaton Hall, almost every person in the village being enabled to enjoy the festivities. At the schoolroom 200 parents of Sunday scholars and members of the Church congregation ate a hearty breakfast at 8.30; the 120 scholars ate afterwards, each receiving a medal with rosette and a couple of oranges. Similar feastings took place at the Baptist and Wesleyan chapels, and at 2pm Messrs. Hill, quarry owners, paid for dinners for their 200 delvers at the public houses. In Bradford the Mayor and Corporation, together with the local yeomanry, fire brigade, thirteen brass bands and 15,000 revellers formed a monster procession; in the interests of sanity the bands were spaced at regular intervals along the column, and the Heaton Band marched behind the Shipley and Saltaire fire brigades.

The last known appearance of the Band was at the re-opening of Heaton ("Quarry") Hill in 1869, but a year previously, in May 9th, 1868, it had "played lively tunes all afternoon" outside the schoolroom and headed a procession to the Hall on the occasion of the celebrated "Old Folk's Gathering". Longevity in Heaton had often been the subject of comment. On June 8th, 1865, the press noted that at a dinner at the "Hare and Hounds" Mr. Samuel Stead of Garter Row had celebrated his golden wedding anniversary in the company of his father, William Stead, aged 92, his children, grand-children and great-grandchildren, a total of fifty persons. Mr. Nathan Firth, "mine host", "fully maintained his credit as a first-rate caterer", and the novelty of the event excited great interest. The topic recurred three years later when three sisters aged over 70 met in Heaton. "There is a saying at Heaton", the press commented, "that its inhabitants can live as long as they like, and there appears to be a moiety of truth in it. There are several persons alive in that salubrious village who are above 80, and some almost 90 years of age."

A gathering of old folk was accordingly arranged by Joseph Lee the schoolmaster and Isaac Broadley (Heaton Syke); Henry Harris,(Heaton Hall) John Crabtree (Well Springs), Benjamin Wood (Dumb Mills), Robert Kell (Heaton Mount) and Nathan Firth (Hare and Hounds) paid for meals and presents, and the forty-six elders of the township, aged between 70 and 94, were entertained by song, music and speeches before being photographed with Mr. Harris "in front of the venerable old Hall" where long ago the Misses Field "had played and romped when young in these beautiful grounds under the shade of the noble trees which looked so grand and proudly down on the forefathers and foremothers of the village." Those present judged it to be "one of the pleasantest sights ever seen in the quaint and salubrious village of Heaton."

The Rt. Honble. William Parsons, 3rd Earl of Rosse, died on October 31st, 1867, after a protracted illness. Born at York in 1800, he was the worthy heir of a family which had been established at Birr in King's County, Ireland, since 1620 and which through its progressive policies had earned a lasting reputation as enlightened and liberal landlords. He has been described as "the Tubal Cain of the Irish peerage, a smith and an astronomer equally at home in the forge or among the stars. If his father had worn a blacksmith's apron instead of ermine

The 'Old Folks' Gathering' photographed at the front (east) entrance to Heaton Hall on 9 May 1868. Of the forty-three persons present, only two are identifiable – Mr Henry Harris (front row, extreme left) and Mr Joseph Broadley (1782-1870) of Heaton Syke (front row, sixth from left, with hands resting on his walking stick). *(Courtesy "Heaton Review")*

and sable, his son would still have risen from the cinders to become a Stephenson or a Herschel."

In his earlier days as Lord Oxmantown he had served as M.P. for King's County, 1821 – 1834, while qualifying for a First Class Honours degree in Mathematics at Magdalen College, Oxford. In 1828 he decided to design and build a giant telescope, a project which was to last seventeen years and cost £20,000; the vast speculum with a surface of 5,184 square inches was cast at Birr Castle and left for sixteen weeks to cool, but when finished it enabled its creator to make "marvellous discoveries" in the heavens, particularly the Crab Nebula and hitherto unknown features of Jupiter. Honours were heaped upon him: Lord Lieutenant of King's County (1831) and Colonel of the county militia (1834), Representative Peer of Ireland (1845), President of The Royal Society (1848-1854), member of the St. Petersburg Imperial Academy, the French Legion of Honour, a Commissioner of the Great Exhibition (1851) and Chancellor of Dublin University (1862). Local distinctions proliferated too - honorary membership of the Bradford Philosophical Society (1840), patron of Bradford Mechanics' Institute (1853) and, jointly with Henry Harris, patron of the Bradford School of Design (1857).

During the Irish Potato Famine he devoted all the income from his estates to provide work for the people of Birr, and ensured that his farm tenants were able to prosper. His sons inherited his many talents - Lawrence, the 4th Earl (1840-1908), became a distinguished astronomer and the first man to measure the heat of the moon; Clere (d.1923) pioneered railway construction in South America; Charles (d.1931) invented the steam turbine at his Heaton Works on Tyneside and was honoured as Sir C. A. Parsons, O.M., K.C.B., F.R.S., while the other surviving son became the Hon. and Rev.Randall Parsons, Rector of Sandhurst.

His widow Mary, herself a pioneer photographer of great distinction, took on the direction of her Heaton and Shipley estates. She was "of a very kindly disposition," and took a lively interest in family matters; a true nineteenth-century romantic, she would often stay out late to watch the hay-harvest by moonlight. Lady Rosse took pride in the fact that her native township had not succumbed to the industrialisation which had overwhelmed much of Bradford Dale, even though the stately chimney of Sam Lister's Manningham Mills could now be glimpsed from the windows of the Hall beyond the timbered parkland. Nevertheless within the township boundaries only Dumb Mill and Sowden's Mill could be said to represent the Machine Age.

Portrait of Mary, Countess of Rosse, who was born at Heaton Hall in 1813 and died in 1885. A pioneer photographer, she cherished her connections with her old family home at Heaton.

(Copyright: author, courtesy of the Earl of Rosse.)

Following her death on July 22nd, 1885, three stained-glass windows commemorating her life were presented to St. Barnabas' Church by her family, and a century later her great-great grandson the 7th Earl attended the Bradford Photographic Museum on the opening of the exhibition, "Impressions of an Irish Countess", organised to mark her pioneering achievements.

By mid-century the traditional, easygoing forms of public administration by elected amateurs were increasingly seen as obsolete, especially in matters of highways and health, although in fairness it could be said that in Heaton the town's officers had in 1833 removed their deliberations from the cosy convivialitity of hostelries to the more austere ambience of the Baptist Chapel vestry and in 1851 had appointed a paid Surveyor in the person of Benjamin Silson. The Public Health Act of 1848 had empowered townships to elect Local Boards with a paid staff, but ratepayers were wary, fearing increased rates. At Idle in June 1863 the townsfolk overwhelmingly rejected change, thereby incurring a wrathful comment from the "Bradford Observer" that "perhaps the next generation will learn that the Act is less expensive and burdensome than scarlet fever and cholera."

However, a further Act in 1858 empowered the Home Office to compulsorily amalgamate sparsely-populated townships, and it may have been the fear of merger with Shipley or Allerton that prompted Mr. J. B. Hammond, Mr. Stocks' son-in-law, to induce twenty Heaton ratepayers to request the convening of a public meeting by the Overseer. Chaired by Mr. Hammond, the meeting was held about May, 1863, when a petition in favour of a Local Board was forwarded to the Home Secretary, receiving official approval on August 13th.

A flurry of election fever then ensued, resulting in nominations from (inter alia) four farmers - William Crabtree, also a butcher, (Heaton), James Clark, (Low Moor), Edward Bilton, (Chellow Grange) and Bairstow Mortimer (Spring Head, Sandy Lane Bottom), two publicans - William Bakes, ("King's Arms") and Nathan Firth ("Hare and Hounds"), John Crabtree of Heaton Villa (i.e., Well Springs, a woolstapler), John and Abraham Hill (quarrymaster and stone merchant), Isaac Broadley of Heaton Syke (tailor), Benjamin Wood of Dumb Mill (manufacturer), Lister Hargreaves of Frizinghall (shopkeeper) and Timothy Stocks (Heaton Hall) land agent. The successful candidates appear to have been Messrs. Broadley, Mortimer, Wood, J. Hill, W. Crabtree and one other, and at its first meeting on Wednesday, September 30th, 1863, the members of the new Heaton Local Board solemnly foregathered at 7 p.m. in the little Baptist chapel vestry where by the yellow light of an oil lamp they appointed a Clerk and a Treasurer, adopted 94 byelaws and standing

Mr John Crabtree, woolstapler, of 'Well Springs' (originally known as 'Heaton Villa'), Chairman of Heaton Local Board 1875-1882, and until his early death in 1884, a Borough Councillor.

(Copyright: Mr John Raw)

orders for their future conduct, and took the existing Highways Surveyor (and his tools) into their employ.

At first the Board's jurisdiction was restricted to highways, public health and general improvements, as the Overseers were responsible to the North Bierley Poor Law Union formed in 1848, while the constabulary was answerable to the West Riding authority. Fortunately, several Board members simultaneously served as overseers or poor-law guardians, thereby providing a useful liaison. From 1872 the Board received additional powers to construct public sewers.

For the Board's annual elections the law was simple and robust: those who paid more rates qualified for more votes than those who paid little, and those who did not trouble to pay at all were passed by when the voting papers were distributed from door to door and collected three days later.

In 1872 the meetings were transferred to the new Baptist Sunday School in Paradise Road, from where the Board kept a watch on local happenings. Tommy Hudson was ordered to replace paving flags broken by him at Paradise Hill, while on the advice of Bob Isles, who was now combining the offices of surveyor and inspector of nuisances, William Marvel at the Heaton Syke beerhouse was notified to "put a door on his ash place and keep his privies clean and respectable", and quarry owners were warned to cease excavating beneath the highways. Plans for new buildings were usually approved if drainage arrangements were satisfactory, and flagged causeways and paved crossings were laid down to protect pedestrians from the worst effects of the muddy highways. Twice a year the Board members set out on foot to inspect the whole of their township.

The gradual introduction of modern improvements began when the Shipley Gas Light Co. obtained powers in 1870 to provide Heaton with a gas supply. Not possessing financial resources for a widespread street lighting scheme, the Local Board reacted cautiously. In November they voted to instal four street lamps in the township, i.e., at the top of Small Tail and at the bottom of Leylands, Jer and Church Lanes respectively; then, with increasing enthusiasm, they erected three additional lamps at Frizinghall, Carr Syke and Heaton Syke and moved the Church Lane lamp to Cross Hill Top.

At first the street lamps were lighted only in the winter months (but not until after the first full moon!), in the evening and early morning only, and when Spring returned, James Dunn the lamplighter was ordered to remove the glass lanterns and store them until they were needed again. From 1877 they remained lit all night, and their numbers were allowed to multiply. However "to the old folk who had been accustomed to go about with (paraffin) lanterns the street lamps were a great nuisance, as the lamps were so far apart that they got lost in the darkness between!" Even as late as 1896 there were only three lamps in Haworth Road between Toller Lane end and Chellow Heights.

To householders the ability to light their houses with gas was a wonderful boon, although outlying farms were excluded from the scheme, and the cost, always higher than in Bradford, was a source of discontent, the reason being of course the sparseness of population and the distance from the gasworks at Dockfield, Shipley. Nevertheless, within nine years (1871-1880) Heaton's consumption increased from 3,283,100 cubic units to 11,219,100 or 1/7th of the total output. Sandy Lane Bottom and Bay of Biscay were allowed to take their supplies from the more convenient Clayton, Allerton and Thornton Gas Co. mains.

The sanitary condition of the township improved considerably when Dr. Philip E.

Cogan of Allerton was appointed Medical Officer of Health in 1873 at a yearly salary of £20. Plans for a public water supply were hampered by the monopoly powers which Bradford Corporation had secured twenty years earlier, as although the Local Board could collect water from springs and quarries, they could not charge for supplying it to householders. The need for piped water was very real, as the manuring of the fields did little for the purity of the local springs, and in February, 1876, it was reported that "the three watercourses supplying the village at Heaton were all foul by operation of the quarries."

The only option, therefore, was to buy water in bulk from the Corporation at whatever price it decided to impose. At Frizinghall the supply was piped via a meter near Carr Syke tollbar from the nearest Bradford main, whilst the remainder of the township received a metered supply from the Chellow reservoir. In order to avoid summer shortages, the Board built a storage reservoir at the summit of Heights Lane on land bought from Lady Rosse in May, 1876, Mr. James Lumley being the contractor. Unfortunately the reservoir was never wholly watertight, and when it was first connected to the Corporation's mains and tested in 1878, surplus water flowed down Heights Lane and filled all the cellars at West View, whose occupants "made great complaint thereof." Having borrowed £8,900 for its construction, the Board were adamant that the public should derive some form of benefit from it, and when it froze over in 1881 it was opened for skating, the proceeds being distributed among the poor.

The problem of sanitation and what was euphemistically termed "nightsoil" was becoming increasingly urgent. In former days when population was sparse and scattered, the contents of domestic dunghills, "muck-heaps" and "muck-middens" could safely be dispersed over the fields, but now that the link between unclean privies and infectious diseases had been realised, closely-packed yards and folds were seen as sources of fever and diphtheria.

Nevertheless plans for public drains and sewers were often fiercely resisted unless there was a prospect of treating the sewage, which would otherwise flow undiluted into the watercourses. Across the valley from Heaton, the beleaguered residents of Idle whose shores were lapped by the increasingly-befouled waters of the Bradford Beck and the River Aire, wanted none of it. "That grand mark and evidence of advanced civilisation, the water-closet nuisance, has gained but a slight footing in Idle," they thundered, adding that "refuse should be kept by those who create it, not despatched on to someone else's property!"

Accordingly, most of Heaton's refuse found its way into disused quarries, with layers of ash from domestic ashpits to cover and seal it. But the refuse still had to be collected and carted, a process not without mishaps. In 1872 the Board were obliged to order that "no Night Soil be allowed to be laid in the Highways", and, more pointedly, they resolved a year later to warn Bradford Corporation against its insanitary habit of leaving nightsoil on Heaton's highways "without first obtaining the consent of the Board." (!). Bradford retaliated by objecting to an open sewer being dug across Heaton Reservoir grounds from the Syke to Emm Lane, and bewailed the fouling of the new Lister Park lake by the tainted stream which flowed down from Heaton.

The laying of public sewers in Frizinghall and Heaton began in 1877, but when Bradford declined to allow Heaton's sewage to be processed at the Corporation's not-too-successful sewage works, the outfall was fed directly into the Bradford Beck, to the displeasure of those further downstream. No sewers were laid at Sandy Lane Bottom, as the proposed outfall arrangements did not meet the Local Government Board's requirements.

The Heaton Local Board offices at no.70 (originally no.55) Highgate were built on the site of a previous cottage and, after incorporation with Bradford in 1882, served for many years as a police station. Photographed by the author on 6 April 1958.

In the same year most houses received numbers for the first time, and three new street names - Highgate (between Cross Hill Top and Eden), Ashwell Road and Cottingley Road - replaced time-honoured "Town Gate" (alias Town Street and originally Town Lane), the more recent "Church Lane" and quaint "Small Tail Road".

A modest surge of civic pride entered the Board's proceedings in May, 1876. Following animated debate on Nancy Lambert's lead piping, Murgatroyd's pigsty, Wadsworth's drain, improvements to the railway bridge and the iniquities of the Shipley Gas Co.'s charges, the nine members decided to buy James Briggs' cottage at Paradise for £150 (plus 30s for tenant's fittings) as well as the land at the rear for a staith. The cottage was demolished and replaced by a tall office emblazoned with the proud title, "HEATON LOCAL BOARD, 1876", wherein the ground floor served as the Clerk's headquarters and rate office, leaving the upper floor for the Boardroom. A vacancy in the membership having arisen, the Board expressed a wish to recruit a member from Sandy Lane Bottom, but acknowledging that no one from that remote area would attend during the winter months, they co-opted Heber Duckworth, butcher, from Highgate, instead, although in the event Messrs. Charles Sowden and John Greenwood from "Sandy Loin" joined the Board shortly afterwards.

A programme of highway improvements brought about the partial widening of Leylands Lane where John Midgley received £10 for the loss of his strawberry bed, and when the surface of Heights Lane was levelled, ratepayers were allowed to "work their rates out" by performing an equivalent amount of manual labour. The short length of Gazeby Lane (Mill Lane) within the township boundary at Frizinghall received a solid stone sett surface, and Emm Lane was widened and remodelled: the lower portion was absorbed into Manningham Park as a carriage drive and replaced by a new section outside the park wall with a connecting link to North Park Road, Manningham, along the line of the old Kirk

Steelhole - the mediaeval church stile.

These works were largely inspired by the sudden and rapid transformation of Frizinghall into a desirable middle-class residential area, a process which began in July, 1863, when Mr. Robert Kell, a Bradford merchant, and subsequently a founder of the Bradford Girls' Grammar School, bought two fields on rising ground and erected thereon a large, imposing Italianate mansion named Heaton Mount, overlooking the valley. Designed by Mr. J. T. Fairbank, architect, it was the first local house to be glazed with plate glass. Two years later his brother, Mr. Samuel C. Kell, bought the old Woolsorters' Garden, demolished the "Craven Heifer" and engaged Messrs. Andrews and Pepper to plan an estate of semi-detached "Swiss Chalets" or villas, which he named "Heaton Grove". East of New Road rows of stone-built terrace houses sprang up, commencing with Aireville and Granville Roads in 1875 and extending to Midland Road and Terrace within four years, at which time the Park Grove estate was being laid out by Mr. John Ambler to the design of H. & E. Marten.

The new, sumptuous "villas" provided new sources of employment for milkmen, coalmen, butchers, chimney sweeps and domestic servants - maids with a flutter of frilled caps and starched white aprons, gardeners with green baize aprons to trim the laurel hedges, tend the flowers and mow the emerald lawns, "odd-job men" to black the boots, carry the coals and stoke the boiler, and housekeepers ("maids-of-all-work") who cleaned, cooked, baked and looked after children. It was soon noticed that the women servants quickly established their own role in society, marrying not the milkman or the butcher's boy but the farmer himself, and then managing his finances in a way which he might not have chosen!

In Emm Lane land opposite the Park had been bought by the Congregational Church, who employed Messrs. Lockwood and Mawson to erect a stately training college, which, when it opened in June, 1877, superseded the original Airedale College at Undercliffe. When a sister college at Rotherham closed in 1888, the two institutions combined at Emm Lane as the Yorkshire United Independent College, with Dr. Fielding as Principal in succession to Dr. Fairbairn. The Countess of Rosse was induced by her agents, Messrs.

The United Independent College, Emm Lane, photographed about 1903. The premises are now owned by the Bradford University Management Centre. *(Author's collection)*

An 1896 view of West Bank, which was built in 1874 and occupied by subscribers to the West Bank Building Society.
(Courtesy of the late Miss Binns)

Smith, Gotthardt & Co., to release several fields adjoining the College for an estate to be called "Park Drive", the first plots being sold in December, 1874.

All these promising developments encouraged the Midland Railway Company to open a station at Frizinghall in February 1875. The old level-crossing near Lane Side was replaced by an overbridge surmounted by a booking office; spacious waiting-rooms were built on the long platforms, and goods sidings, complete with hen-huts, pigsties, stone staiths and a 16-lever signal-box, were installed. Now easily accessible from Bradford and beyond the reach of its borough rates, Frizinghall became popular with merchants and bankers who were wishful "to exchange the hurly-burly of town life for the serener atmosphere of the country".

In Heaton village two rows of "back-to-back" and "through-light" cottages had been built about 1866 on Backside Close; one of the builders, Mr. J. Hill, wished the new street to bear his name, but when his rivals W. Lambert and Joseph Kay demurred, the name "Quarry Street" was agreed upon. At Paradise the West Bank Building Club built a terrace of spacious houses with fine views across the countryside; their first occupants included Fred Jowett, clerk to the Local Board, and John Lee, one of the Board members. Rural sounds and scents were never far away, however; cattle passed through the streets on their slow journey to and from the mistal and horses left rich deposits for collection by sharp-eyed gardeners - but times were changing, and when Tom Tetley installed a piggery at Bell Coney, Highgate, he was promptly ordered to remove it elsewhere.

The tiny hamlet of Sandy Lane Bottom entered upon a period of expansion and prosperity in December, 1871, when Mr. Charles Sowden of Wilsden (1828-1901) purchased from Mr. Bairstow Mortimer, farmer, part of the Low Field on which he had already erected Springfield Mill, comprising a three-storey spinning block, a weaving shed and engine-house, with the help of a loan from the Bingley and Morton Building Society. On July 12th, 1872, Hannah Denby, weaver and William Hudson, warp dresser, produced the mill's first consignment of cloth, and at a later date the company specialised in wool worsted goods such as men's suitings, flannels, gabardines, serges, ladies' dress and costume cloth and tropicals. A native of Wibsey and brother of David Sowden, loom maker, and Isaac Sowden of Globe Mills, Manningham, Mr. Sowden built Springhead House (no.15, Sandy Lane) and began a long and fruitful association with the Baptist chapel.

Charles Sowden (1828-1901), builder of Sowden's Mill at Sandy Lane Bottom in 1872, a member of Heaton Local Board 1876-1882 and subsequently a borough councillor. *(Courtesy of Messrs. C. Sowden Ltd.)*

The need for shopping facilities for the growing population was supplied in 1876 by the little Allerton Co-operative Society established eight years previously, who purchased a cottage in Cottingley Road opposite "Wonderful".

In Heaton village the tiny, overcrowded school at Paradise had at last reached the end of its days. On September 28th, 1870, the Local Board happily agreed that, "The plans submitted by Messrs. Healey for the erection of the New School be passed", Lady Rosse having given 1,200 square yards of land opposite the Church for educational purposes.

Financed by the National Society and built of local stone with a Westmorland slate roof, the building work progressed so rapidly that the new schoolmaster, Mr. Taylor, was able to open the doors on April 17th, 1871. In the logbook two days later he recorded that he had,

"Examined the several standards . . . most of the I Standard deficient in writing and arithmetic, six having no notion of writing and twelve unable to work an addition sum, . . . the reading . . . was moderately fair."

Fortunately Standards II and III fared much better, but discipline was hard to achieve, as most parents considered homework unnecessary, and some pupils arrived at school without slates or books. Nevertheless, corporal punishment was was not used except for insolence or lying.

Within a year there were 159 pupils, although the Frizinghall children left in August, 1875, to attend a temporary school alongside Dumb Mill. Attendances were not affected by poverty, as the North Bierley Poor Law Union paid the school pence for fatherless or orphaned children, but the lure of the "great outdoors" was never far away - the hay harvest, a gypsy encampment or news of a cow or sheep to be butchered in "t'bull'oil" (Heber Duckworth's slaughterhouse — village children were not squeamish) often proved a greater attraction than "the three Rs".

Not until April, 1893, when the still-remembered disciplinarian James Harvey Wilkinson was appointed head teacher did standards begin to improve. Before long, the school achieved "utmost credit" and a "very praiseworthy condition of general efficiency", together with a sound musical tradition.

The onward march of improvement also began to affect the southern fringes of Heaton, where, to quote William Cudworth's appreciative description,

> "The Syke occupies a beautiful position on the sunny side of the hill on the Heaton road." For generations it had housed "its own distinctive colony of Broadleys, Normingtons and others who had been 'bred and browt up' there and who cultivated garden plots as a source of real pleasure. There was little to attract the passer-by, however, beyond the privilege of inspecting enormous 'berries', or it might be of tasting the flavour of real Heaton 'peys'." (peas) . . .
> "In the olden days, and not long ago either, gardens and green pastures sloped towards the (present-day) reservoir, among the former being Poulter's Garden with its collection of old-fashioned flowers and bed of watercress at the bottom."

The imminence of change was realised in 1878 when as part of Messrs. Smith & Gotthardt's scheme for residential development on Lady Rosse's lands east of the village, a

A snowy day at Heaton Syke in February, 1960. Seen left to right is the tall, three-windowed building formerly used by the Broadleys as a tailor's and grocer's shop, the block of 'back-to backs' attached to the 'Fountain Inn', and nos. 23/25 Syke Road, built by Richard and Mary Thompson in 1734.

(Copyright: author)

new thoroughfare linking Emm Lane with highways under construction in Manningham was laid out and named Wilmer Road in honour of her Ladyship's late father. By agreement with Mr. William Firth, owner of the row of post-1781 cottages at Heaton Syke, the original pre-1734 dwellings and smithy were demolished to make way for a new paved street called Syke Road, constructed over the watercourse and superseding the old cart track, while a parallel street named Firth Road was created alongside the allotment gardens. Richard Thompson's old farm where Jonathan Long had lately kept four horses and two cows was converted into two dwellings numbered 23/25, and Mr. Firth's property was bought by one of his tenants, Mr. Isaac Broadley, who engaged Mr. W. C. Atkinson, architect, to enlarge and improve most of the cottages by the addition of a kitchen with bedroom over it, and a neat garden.

Isaac Broadley (died 1883, formerly an industrious member of the Local Board) was content to inhabit the house later known as no.3, Garden Terrace, where his wife Sarah presided over the homely grocer's shop while he laboured upstairs with needle and thread (Sam Lister of Manningham Mills bought suits from him), but his son Rhodes Broadley (1849-1939), a small, dapper gentleman, occupied the new and more stately "big house" (no.17) which was soon overflowed by his wife, five sons and two daughters.

The construction of a Bradford Provident Industrial Society store (Co-op branch no.26) in 1894 at the top of Firth Road provided unwelcome competition for the shop, and "superior villas" in Wilmer Road (Belvoir Terrace) and Randall Place ended the isolation of the Syke. Happily, hints of its old-world charm linger to this day, and older inhabitants still use the phrase,"Going up (to) Heaton" when planning an expedition to Heaton village, a few hundred yards distant!

In December, 1865, there occurred an event which aroused considerable interest and had unexpected consequences. At a lecture delivered at St. George's Hall, Bradford, Dr. Parker of Manchester, a Baptist divine, examined the then-topical question of "Nonconformity in relation to the Book of Common Prayer," praising the devotional aspects of the book but condemning its Anglican services of burial and baptism. Chancing to be in the audience, Mr. Mitton, the vicar of Heaton, asked leave to reply, whereupon Dr. Parker courteously lent him his manuscript for study and analysis.

A month later in the same venue Mr. Mitton vigorously explained the viewpoint of evangelical clergymen such as himself, and describing himself as "not one of the milk-and-water brethren", he refuted Dr.Parker's controversial assertion that Anglican doctrines were virtually identical with those of Rome. If they were, he asked, "Had the noble army of martyrs in the days of Mary Tudor died for doctrines differing only in name?" He

The Rev. Henry Arthur Mitton, first incumbent of Heaton (St Barnabas') Parish Church, 1864-1868.

(Courtesy: St Barnabas' Church)

concluded with St. Augustine's wise advice:

"In essentials unity, in doubtful parts liberty, in all things charity."

The fame of his lecture spread far beyond the bounds of Bradford. Many months later the Bishop of Durham travelled incognito to Heaton to see and hear for himself, and unhesitatingly offered Mr. Mitton the vacant living of Bishop Auckland. "An offer so graciously made was in due time accepted", and at his leave-taking in March, 1868, Mr. Mitton received presentations from his congregation and also from his successor, the Rev. Thomas Miller, who won warm applause from his hearers for his denunciation of the novel notion of ritualism and for his determination to live by the scriptural precepts of Romans vi v.2 and Corinthians ii v.2.

Sadly and sensationally, Mr. Miller failed to live up to his high ideals, and his association with the wife of the schoolmaster, Mr. Matthew Tait, caused a section of his flock to boycott his services and worship in a cottage at Paradise. Worse was to follow. In December, 1875, the vicar and his son ejected the schoolmaster without prior notice, and but for the intervention of the constable and the superintendent of the Shipley police division would have thrown him over the wall. After Christmas, in the presence of a shocked and scandalised crowd, he refused to allow the master to re-open the school. Next, late at night, he evicted the verger and his wife who had been his housekeepers, obliging them to seek shelter at the "King's Arms". The wronged parties, together with Miss Mary Ann Swailes, the Frizinghall schoolmistress, successfully sued him for damages and costs. Finally, after a stormy church vestry meeting, he left Heaton, never to return, but as he could not be compelled to resign, he employed a series of curates who succeeded in maintaining a level of church life in the district.

More happily, in the same year of 1877, the Heaton Baptists embarked on a new era of forty halcyon years under the inspired pastorate of the Rev. Richard Howarth. Within a few years membership trebled, and fees from the extensive graveyard were used to pay for improvements.

The year 1879 opened with a severe frost which halted work in the quarries. Lady Rosse found work for many of the "idle hands" by arranging for the levelling of old quarry hills at Back Lane, while the employers dispensed relief-tickets and carted coal to those in need. Not that the quarrymen were always "deserving causes": many of them were wont to patronise the "Delvers' Arms" and "go on the rant" until the money ran out. Their employers knew them well. Surveying his workforce each morning, Emmanuel Dyson was heard to say, "Ye wi' t'gooid booits - dahn i' t' wet 'oil! An' ye wi' t' bad booits - likewise!"

On a cultural level, Bradford Corporation had for some time been discussing the establishment of a public library and art gallery in their borough, but before their plans reached fruition an outstanding art exhibition had already taken place in the humble surroundings of Heaton's Mechanics' Institute. The aim of the exhibition was the liquidation of a £30 deficit, and the President, Mr. W. H. Townend, a woolstapler, used his commercial connections to obtain the loan of over 150 paintings as well as scientific apparatus and birds both living and preserved. Thus the pleasant tinkling of a fountain (supplied from the Local Board's mains at a cost of 10s) blended with the lively twittering of nightingales, finches, "parroquets" and cardinal and weaver birds.

Of especial interest to Heatonians were W. O. Geller's portrait of "Blind Jimmy" Mortimer of Heaton and the clarionets which he once used while begging in the streets of Bradford. The squires of Heaton - no doubt to their surprise - gazed down upon the assembly, Mr. Townend having lent the old Field family portraits from the Hall, the other paintings being mostly of the "modern" school. An unexpectedly large attendance, assisted by a service of horse-drawn buses which must have been the first (and last) ever to make the ascent to Heaton, enabled the exhibition to make a £100 profit and remain open for a fortnight. The Borough's art gallery in the new Central Library opened on May 28th, 1879 – but Heaton had "stolen their thunder", even if only by a month!

Until the advent of the "Universal Penny Post" in Britain in 1841, mail was delivered to recognised collection points and not conveyed to specific addresses unless the addressee paid an additional fee. Joshua Field used a private box at Bradford Post Office, but gave it up in January, 1805. "when he intended to discontinue going to York."

By 1835 local carriers and milkmen were taking letters out to the villages, and within ten years, when the delivery charge from Bradford to Heaton was ½d per letter, the appointment of a daily messenger to Heaton was under discussion. In addition, a "light, 4-inside Post Coach" called the "Rob Roy" left Bradford daily at 10.15a.m. and passed through Frizinghall to connect with the Skipton coach at Keighley. The earliest surviving Heaton postmark bears the date "14-11-1857", but for some time previously a daily delivery (Sundays excepted) had been made at 7-30 a.m. from Bradford.

Heaton's first "receiving-house" or sub-post office was in the cottage of Jonas Rhodes at Paradise, from whence local deliveries commenced at 7a.m.; the post-box closed at 6.5p.m., and its contents were despatched to Bradford five minutes later. Money orders could be purchased at Shipley or Bradford. Mr. John Lee recalled those early days –

> "At one time the village postman could not read, and his wife used to arrange the letters between his fingers in the order of delivery, telling him which houses the letters were for. I think he must have had a good memory, as I never heard of a wrong delivery.
>
> In the very early days of post cards he met a neighbour one morning with the amusing remark - "Here's a postcard for tha', Ah don't knaw what it's abaht!"
>
> In this connection I may mention another incident which might have had serious consequences, but fortunately only resulted in a certain amount of annoyance. One of the villagers was expecting from his uncle who lived at a distance, a letter containing important documents for his perusal, and suggesting an interview for their discussion. As this letter did not arrive, the nephew communicated with his uncle who assured him that it had been sent, and advised him to make inquiry at the village post office. This he did, when the wife of the postman just mentioned, made the astounding statement that as he had had a good deal of trouble lately, and as the large envelope looked like that of a lawyer, she had put it under the sofa cushion to save him further trouble! She immediately produced the missing document."

By 1879 the sub-postmaster was Richard Robinson, boot-and shoemaker, at no.7, Back Lane, but within a year or two he had removed to more spacious premises at no.3, Lambert Fold (nowadays known as 37, Rossefield Road). The growing influence of businessmen in the area brought about the establishment of centralised deliveries and collections based on Bradford, as confirmed on October 25th, 1879, by the Secretary of the G. P. O. in London to Fred Jowett, the clerk to the Local Board: -

> "With reference to your letter of August last, I beg leave to acquaint you, for

the information of the Heaton Local Board, that an agreement has been sanctioned for the establishment of a Day Mail to and from Heaton, and directions will be given for Wall Letter Boxes to be fixed at Reservoir and at Sandy Lane Bottom."

Seventy years later another generation of Heaton businessmen complained that the Reservoir (Emm Lane) box was too small for modern packages, and it was replaced by a second-hand George V box, but boxes bearing the royal cyphers of Queen Victoria and Edward VII can still be seen at Paradise and Toller Lane respectively.

Sadly, all was not well in public affairs. The "off-comed 'uns" who had settled in the new villas in Heaton Grove and Frizinghall to enjoy lower rates and rural surroundings soon began to miss the urban amenities they had left behind, particularly street lighting and good roads. Perversely, when the Local Board agreed to provide sewerage, waterworks and highway improvements,and to raise loans to pay for them, the resultant increase in Heaton's rates aroused great discontent among the newcomers, and their leaders, Messrs. J. E. Bonville, W. Gilyard and G. H. Rushworth, vociferously contested the Board elections in 1880, although they were defeated by Mr. John Crabtree (the chairman), Mr. Charles Sowden of Sandy Lane and Mr. William Crabtree, a native of Frizinghall.

Agitation continued, however, animosities being sharpened by the proximity of a General Election, and there was dismay in the Board's offices when three valued members – Heber Duckworth the butcher, Bairstow Mortimer, farmer, from Sandy Lane Bottom and old Isaac Broadley, the tailor from Heaton Syke — were replaced at the March, 1880, election by men such as Mr. Gilyard from no.19, Aireville Terrace.

Events then moved rapidly. On receipt of a formal petition from Frizinghall signed by the requisite number of ratepayers, the Board were compelled to summon a public meeting at the Baptist Sunday School on June 22nd, 1880, for the purpose of discussing incorporation with Bradford. Forthright argument raged. Ratepayers were warned that under Corporation rule water charges would be halved but rateable values doubled; Bradford's much-vaunted sewage works had been professionally described as "neither a success nor a failure", and Heaton's affairs would be much better run by nine local Board members than by an arbitrary, political Corporation.

The Local Board placed the issue before the public at a ratepayers' poll in July, 1880, when the following results were declared: -

	FOR INCORPORATION		AGAINST INCORPORATION	
Heaton	41	(26.5%)	114	(73.5%)
Frizinghall	174	(84.4%)	32	(15.53%)
Sandy Lane Bottom	51	(37.7%)	84	(62.2%)
	266	(53.6%)	230	(46.3%)

Majority: 36; 53 neutral votes cast; 4 spoilt papers.

The Local Board accordingly approached Bradford Corporation, and the enlargement of the Borough was authorised by the Bradford Corporation Act 1881.

Ironically, although Mr. Gilyard and his colleagues welcomed the advent of municipal government, their welcome for the industry which could be expected to follow it was a little less enthusiastic, and when Messrs. North and Ackroyd announced their intention of constructing a dyeworks at the top of Aireville Road, they busied themselves with another petition. Although not legally empowered to prevent the scheme, the Board successfully persuaded the promoters that the drainage problems were insuperable, and no more was heard of the plan.

The Heaton Local Board met for the last time on April 29th, 1882, when the members approved plans for housing in Spring Gardens Road, Carlton Drive and Wilmer Road, shook hands and parted. In his valedictory report the Medical Officer pronounced Heaton to be a very healthy place: in his view no other township within a radius of several miles was so salubrious. At midnight on April 30th , 1882, the West Riding constabulary withdrew from Heaton, and the Borough police entered upon their new beats, using the redundant Board offices as a new "Heaton Police Station". P. C. Stephen Ponton, who had previously watched over Heaton village from his cottage at no.35 (later renumbered 534) Heaton Road, was "posted" to Shipley and his Sandy Lane Bottom colleague P. C. Scott to Windhill.

The demise of the Board was soon followed by that of the Mechanics' Institute which since 1872 had been based in the Baptist schoolroom; its evening classes and reading room gave way to the brisker professionalism of the Bradford School Board, who within a few years also established regular day-schools in rooms leased from the Wesleyan Methodists in Frizinghall Road and Bairstow Street, Sandy Lane Bottom.

In August, 1836, the "Bradford Observer" had commented on

" . . . the universal observance in every township, hamlet, chapelry etc. of keeping tides or feasts which are looked-forward to with great anticipation and for which great preparations are made - thorough brushing and whitening of walls and plentiful ablutions of the furniture with soap and water. When Sunday comes (for most tides begin on a Sunday) they are donned in their finest. All our relations and particular friends within the distance of at least ten miles are confidently expected to dinner. It is rare that they disappoint. Ale is then imbibed in dreadful quantities, not only on the Sabbath but for the whole of the following week, which is called a spree. For what purposes tides were instituted no one knows. They have always been kept, and the present generation are resolved to keep them."

By tradition Heaton Tide (or Feast) began on the first Sunday after October 11th - the week following Wibsey Horse fair - when the custom of open-house hospitality was cheerfully observed ("Ee, Ah'm reight glad ta see thi; Ah thowt tha worn't bahn ta come!" would be a regular greeting). As recently as 1990 Mrs. Maud Halliday (1897-1999), daughter of Dan Craven of Chellow Grange Farm, recalled that her mother always had a 20lb piece of beef ready for visitors; it was roasted very slowly on a jack over a large open fire for a whole week - "and the beef dripping tasted wonderful!"

In his logbook for 1871 the schoolmaster recorded that

"The children had holiday this afternoon (Friday, October 6th) and from October 9th to 16th for Heaton Feast."

And in 1876 several children were "kept in" for late arrival, their heartfelt excuse being "that they had been to see the slaughtering of the Tid❋ oxen."

Other townships' feasts were enjoyed also, sometimes excessively so. In August, 1837, John Pate, Light Harrison and John Binns, all of Heaton, were fined 12s each for having demolished a stall at Shipley Tide fair and assaulted its owner, a travelling hawker, whilst in a state of drunkenness.

As the years passed, other more sophisticated entertainments beckoned - Barnum and Bailey's circus in Bradford, Gunpowder Plot, the Queen's Birthday and the Relief

Highgate in 1883, showing the original 'King's Arms' in the foreground and its successor in course of erection. Mr William Bakes (1818-1894), landlord, and his wife Zillah (1833-1905) are standing near the doorway in company with a venerable and bewhiskered Heatonian.

(Courtesy of Mr F. D. Richardson)

of Mafeking — so that by October, 1893, Heaton Tide merited no more than a mere half-day holiday for the schoolchildren. In its latter years the feast was enlivened by a funfair in the paddock behind the "King's Arms", but it was a small affair in comparison with the mighty fair at Manningham, whose condescending residents sometimes visited Heaton with a candle, pretending to "look fer t' Tide". All that they found was a collection of stalls and sideshows and a hand-operated roundabout.

The last funfair was held on Heaton Hill about 1897/8, when wild autumn gales blew down the tents and extinguished the feast forever.

One of the last street improvements carried out by the Local Board prior to its dissolution was a partial widening of Highgate, which at its narrowest point where it squeezed between the cottages and the park wall was a mere 16 feet in breadth. The principal victim was "Billy Bakes' Brewery", the "King's Arms", which, though little changed during its long life, had accepted a water supply from the town's mains in 1876, a move which doubtless prompted the regulars to grumble that "t'ale's noan what it ewsed ter be sin' Billy stopped fetchin' t'watter fra t'well!" Lady Rosse agreed to construct a new public house nearby, and when the old premises were demolished in 1883, Mr. and Mrs. Bakes retired to no.25, Ashwell Road, part of a block of "back-to-backs" recently built by Emmanuel and Henry Dyson. John Clough, the new landlord, also had building interests; he and his wife Ann bought part of the Bull Croft and erected a few houses in "Crofton Road".

The original Turf Tavern, Frizinghall, photographed about 1879. The horse-drawn cart glimpsed on the right is laden with bales of wool. *(Author's collection)*

When the old "Turf Tavern" passed into history in 1893/4, it became evident that the licensees had never entrusted their takings to banks, as sovereigns were found in every nook and cranny, and by the time that the constabulary had been summoned, most of the hoard had been pocketed by the "navvies". More than ninety years later the palatial new premises were insensitively renamed "The Park".

An ever-increasing demand for water induced Bradford Corporation to enlarge Heaton Reservoir to a new minimum depth of 6 feet and to construct a pumping house connected by a 24" main to the high-level reservoir at Horton Bank Top. When fully commissioned in 1890 the pumps were capable of raising a million gallons in 24 hours to a height of 484 feet. The imposing, Italianate pumping house included a 180 foot high brick chimney, but when the residents of Heaton Syke criticised its stark ugliness, it was encased in good Yorkshire stone.

The coming of age of Lord Oxmantown, eldest son of the 4th Earl of Rosse, was splendidly celebrated and long remembered in Heaton. On the evening of October 9th, 1894, about 130 Heaton and Shipley tenants, with several invited guests, dined at the school in the presence of Lord and Lady Rosse, Lord Oxmantown and his younger brother the Hon. Geoffrey Lawrence Parsons.

Presenting an illuminated address and timepiece on behalf of the tenantry, Mr. W. H. Townend spoke proudly of Heaton and its valued connections with the Parsons family, expressing the hope that in due course Lord Oxmantown would show himself worthy of his forebears. Somewhat nervous of the occasion, the young nobleman replied briefly, and suitable speeches were made by the Rev. G. B. Flynn (vicar), Mr. Emmanuel Dyson (quarrymaster), Mr. J. H. Wade, J. P. (tenant of Heaton Gardens, Joshua Field's old

The illuminated address presented to Lord Oxmantown (later the 5th Earl of Rosse) on his coming-of-age in 1894.
(Photo: author, courtesy of the Earl of Rosse)

kitchen-garden), Mr. C. J. Vint and Mr. Wheater Smith (solicitor and agent to the estate respectively). Next evening the cottage tenants, numbering about ninety, were entertained to tea, speeches and song at the new "King's Arms".

While professing pretended surprise that an Earl and Countess should deign to visit the Bradford area, the local press had to admit that the proceedings had been "of a hearty and simple kind", with "a creditable absence of condescension on the one hand or fulsome flattery on the other". More importantly, long after the newspaper had been more appropriately used for the lighting of domestic fires, the villagers recalled "the good sit-down meal" served by butlers, the champagne, liqueurs and "silver cutlery from Spinks". And the illuminated address still hangs to this day at Birr Castle.

A religious census taken on December 11th, 1881, had shown what seemed to be an encouraging position:

	Seating	Morning Attendance	Evening Attendance
St. Barnabas	520	135	114
Heaton Baptists	325	193	223
Sandy Lane Baptists	300	130	155
Heaton Wesleyans	120	89	35
Frizinghall Wesleyans	450	207	139

Nevertheless, the Anglicans and Baptists were dissatisfied, and blamed bad weather for poor attendance! Better days lay ahead.

St. Barnabas' Church was beginning to recover from Mr. Miller's scandalous behaviour and non-residence. The immediate impetus came from the appointment of his last curate, the Rev. G. B. Flynn (1856-1917) in 1883. Within five years the Easter communicants had increased from 43 to 143, with corresponding growth in weekly congregations. In 1885 he re-opened the Frizinghall school at St. John's Mission Room for evening services after a nine year interval, and from 1888 it was served by his assistant, the Rev. J. W. Hind, who many years later (1905) became the first vicar of Frizinghall. When Mr. Miller was persuaded to resign in 1891, Mr. Flynn succeeded him, and local people responded with characteristic generosity. Mr. Frederick Illingworth of "Heather Bank" (now "Beechcliffe") paid for a new organ, vestry, lectern, oak choir stalls, reredos, peal of bells and a complete North aisle, while Messrs. W. N. Aykroyd and W. Martello Gray provided pine pews and Mr. W. H. Townend, a Wesleyan, gave a stained-glass window.

At Sandy Lane Bottom an impressive, classical-style Baptist Chapel seating 500 worshippers replaced the original building in 1884 at a cost of £1,500, and three years later there began the impressive ministry of the Rev. Walter Wynn, who was once described as "the man who struck twelve all at once." Many years after his subsequent departure his doctor advised twelve months' rest and a change of air, and, sensibly, he returned to peaceful Sandy Lane Bottom where, during his stay, long queues formed each Sunday outside the chapel. Three thousand people attended his open-air farewell service.

Among the "off-comed'uns" who had settled at "Sandy" following the building of its two mills were several Wesleyan Methodists who about 1875 began to hold preaching services in their homes. A formal Methodist society meeting at no.11, Stone Street, was organised in November, 1880, transferring three years later to a rented cottage at no.55, Cottingley Road. Quickly outgrowing their homely premises, the congregation opened a spacious chapel in Bairstow Street on November 6th, 1886, with seating for 200 members. In the same way that the nearby Baptist chapel owed much to the generosity of successive generations of Sowdens at "t'bottom mill", the Methodists benefited from the patronage of Mr. S. P. Myers and his successor Alderman David Wade, owners of "t'top mill".

Under the inspiring leadership of Mr. Howarth the Heaton Baptists were experiencing a similar need to "arise and build". A building fund was set up in 1890; in September, 1893, the chapel was demolished and its site quarried for the materials needed for the construction of a new chapel to be built on a corner of the Bullcroft which had been bought from Lord Rosse. Prominent among the builders was Benjamin Patefield, a former Local Board member, who at great personal loss undertook the masonry work including a magnificent flight of stone steps, formed in blocks each 13½ feet wide, mounting upwards to a large and handsome chapel. The opening service on October 1st, 1896, was followed a few days later by a tea-party for 1,400 people and two bazaars which raised over £1,000. A three manual organ was added in 1902 and a substantial manse three years later.

The little Methodist chapel in Back Lane had led a stuggling existence since the opening of the beautiful St. John's chapel in Wilmer Road, Manningham. Its baptismal name of Ebenezer - the strong rock - having proved ironic when quarrying operations undermined it, the members transferred to St. John's about 1890 and Lord Rosse bought the building in 1897 for conversion into two cottages. Mr. A. V. Gott who died in 1966 aged 93 recalled that the chapel had often been spoken of as "The Old Body" in connection with its adherence to the "old original" Wesleyan sector of the Methodist persuasion, and dry Heaton humour sometimes applied the same name to old Mrs. Martindale who resided there in later years!

In 1896 William Cudworth published his popular "Manningham, Heaton and Allerton", a genial expansion of part of his "Round about Bradford" written twenty years earlier, in which Heaton was seen as a quiet, healthy and serene village and township, bound municipally to Bradford but still an individual district well endowed with natural beauty and an abundance of "characters".

A year later, Mr. Townend gave up his tenancy of the Hall and retired to Rosse Mount, Emm Lane, where he died on September 9th, 1902, aged 71, after more than thirty years

Heaton Baptist Chapel, photographed about 1908 from the immaculately tended graveyard, with the newly built terraced houses in Leylands Lane on the right. The memorial stones of the chapel were ceremonially laid on 18 May 1895 by the pastor, deacons and congregation.

(Author's collection)

The Binns family of West Bank, 1896.   *(Courtesy of the late Miss Binns)*

Mr William Henry Townend, a Bradford woolstapler, was tenant of Heaton Hall, president of Heaton Cricket Club and a member of Heaton Local Board from 1872 to 1876. After vacating the Hall he resided at 78 Emm Lane until his death on 9 September 1902.

(Courtesy of the late Mr Arnold Pickles)

Emanuel Dyson (1839-1902) of Paradise and (later) Randall House, quarrymaster, builder, member of Heaton Local Board 1878-1882 and Poor Law Guardian 1898-1902.

(Courtesy of Mrs Mary Barrie)

devoted service to his adopted village and the trade of Bradford. A woolstapler specialising in English wool, he was a founder member of the Bradford Liberal Club and a good friend to the Infirmary. At Heaton he served on the Local Board from 1872 to 1876, and after incorporation he was a Heaton councillor between 1889 and 1895. His "quiet geniality, perfect loyalty and friendship" were greatly valued in the village. Each Whitsuntide he welcomed the Sunday scholars to his park and thanked them for their simple hymns, while at Christmas the old folk gathered for a meal in the large, old-fashioned kitchen - "an event long looked-forward to and longer kept in memory". His widow, Mrs. Helen Townend, "a good, kind soul", survived until 1907, when she quietly passed away at the age of 72.

In commemoration of Queen Victoria's Diamond Jubilee in 1897 the Borough of Bradford was elevated to city status, and in the following year Heaton ceased to be a separate poor-law township when the whole of the new city was consolidated into one township whose Guardians were appointed by the Council. One of these was Emmanuel Dyson, quarrymaster and former Local Board member, who served conscientiously until his death in 1902. A much-needed school was opened in Cottingley Road, Sandy Lane Bottom, by the Bradford School Board in September, 1898, in replacement of the cramped facilities provided since about 1883 in the Baptist School, Stony Lane, Allerton.

Some parents preferred a private education for their offspring. In 1901 a Mr. Macfarlane was administering a shortlived boarding-school in the old Chellow Grange farmhouse, while in 1898 Rossefield School was founded by Miss Gregson of Girton College Cambridge and Miss Rendall. From modest accommodation in "Penrhyn", Emm Lane, the two partners expanded into Rossefield Hall which had originally served as a Quaker Sunday School, before erecting the present-day purpose-built school in Parsons Road in 1908. In 1924 they bought a preparatory school in Lynton Drive which had been established by Miss E.W. Riley and named "Netherleigh" in honour of the book of the same name written by her well-known brother William Riley, author of "Windyridge".

The century was drawing to a close - a century of unimaginable change and unprecedented progress. When it began, Heaton was a sparsely-populated country district often threatened by poverty, scarcity of food and Napoleonic invasion, its only motive power that of the horse. Now, at the extremities of its boundaries steam-powered looms and spindles clacked and whirred; mighty locomotives drew "long-linked trains" to faraway places and the humbler steam-tram puffed and jolted along the old turnpike on its way to Saltaire. Where rushlight and lantern had once glimmered, gaslight now spread its brighter glow; the novelty of electricity was being enjoyed by a few Park Drive residents, and telephone wires already stretched a few tentative tentacles along the highways.

More prosaically, the onward march of the water-closet was beginning at last to disperse the stenches of privies, muck-middens and the night-soil carts which rumbled through the streets under cover of darkness. Convention and good manners had largely subdued the uncouth boisterous roughness of former years; church, chapel and school had instilled their beneficial influences - a process not unaided by the schoolteachers' cane!

Frizinghall was still growing. Only in the fields south of Frizinghall Road could cattle still be seen grazing; elsewhere long streets of prim terrace houses stood in dignified ranks between Keighley Road and the railway - respectable residences of managers, bank officials and commercial travellers, secure behind their plush curtains and aspidistras. Higher up the hillside, Heaton Grove was still incomplete, but its street lamps were slightly more profuse than in the days of G. H. Rushworth and his fellow malcontents.

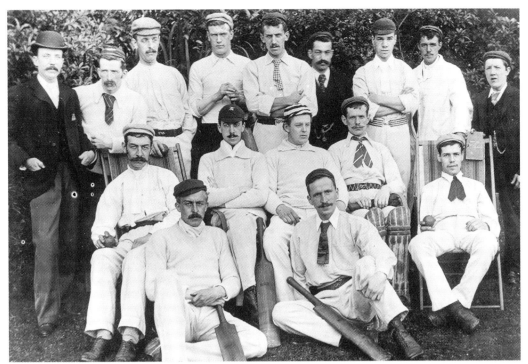

Heaton Cricket Club, 1895, photographed in the grounds of Heaton Hall.

(Courtesy of the late Mr Arnold Pickles)

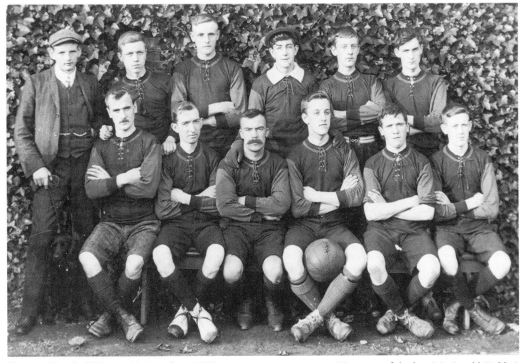

Heaton Football Team, 10 October, 1898.

(Courtesy of the late Mr Arnold Pickles)

The Co-operative Store in Heaton Road, opened in 1894 and photographed by the author at its closure on 6 July 1968.

The ascent to Heaton was impressive and stately in a late-Victorian manner. Flanked by the new "Turf Tavern" and the solid Norman Arch erected to mark the visit of the Prince and Princess of Wales (later King Edward VII and Queen Alexandra) in 1882, tree-lined Emm Lane climbed steeply past the United College whose Gothic elegance could be espied at the end of a long carriage-drive. Higher still the clear waters of Heaton Reservoir sparkled in their calm setting of trim lawns, ornamental bushes and a neat keeper's lodge, against a background of stone-built villas, the soaring spire of St. John's and the chimney and towers of Lister's Mill on the Manningham side of the lake.

On the opposite side of Emm Lane, comfortably situated among abundant trees and shrubberies stood the affluent residences of Park Drive, Carlton Drive and Parsons Road, whose owners' names were pre-eminent in the trade and commerce of their great city. A random sample may suffice: -

Emm Lane:	Heaton Rise	James Gordon, manager, Bradford Old Bank
	Rosse-Erne	Jacob P. Sichel, wool merchant (Mahler, Sichel & Co.)
Carlton Drive:	Aston Mount	Henry Muff, draper (Brown, Muff & Co.)
	Rocklands	Thomas Pratt, cabinetmaker (Christopher Pratt & Sons)
	Glenroyd	Eustace H. Illingworth, spinner (Daniel Illingworth & Sons)
	West Holt	Sam Ambler, mohair and worsted spinner (Jeremiah Ambler & Sons)

Parsons Road:	The Cottage	James Ledingham (1840-1926) FRIBA, architect
	Lark Hill	William B. Gordon, solicitor
	Myrtle Bank	Joseph J. Booth, worsted manufacturer
	Fern Bank	Joseph Whittingham, woolstapler
		(now Greystones)
Park Drive:	Maylands	Lady Hannah Cass
	Foxwell Grange	Adolph Reiche, wool top, noil and yarn merchant
	No.10	James Watson, waterworks engineer
	No.12 (Rye Hill)	Samuel Drummond (James Drummond & Sons)
	No.16	Frederick Illingworth, commission comber
	(Heather Bank)	
	Sefton Lodge	W. Martello Gray, chartered accountant
Heaton Grove:	No.8	James Metcalfe, M.D., L.R.C.P., surgeon
	Thornfield	Harry Behrens, stuff merchant (Sir Jacob Behrens & Sons)
Wilmer Drive:	Wilmer Grange	James Freeman, solicitor
Wilmer Road:	No.153	J. Charlesworth, orchid importer

Several of the above-named gentlemen were active in Heaton affairs as well as in the wider concerns of the city. Messrs. Whittingham and Freeman served as Heaton representatives on the City Council, while Mr. Frederick Illingworth was the leading benefactor at St. Barnabas'. Most of the owners of these opulent abodes were self-made men who did not forget their humble origins. Billy Bulmer (of Bulmer and Lumb) never forsook his native bluntness, even when making a proposal of marriage to his housekeeper. "Can ta cook?" he enquired. "Ay", came the frank reply, "Ah can cook owt tha's likely to buy!"

A vista of late-Victorian Heaton at the junction of North Park Road and Emm Lane, 27 April 1958.
(Copyright: author)

At the summit of Emm Lane lay the quaint huddle of cottages which constituted Hammond Square (late Low Fold) adjacent to old Crosshill Head Farm owned by the Jowett estate. Highgate, quaint and homely, had changed little since the modest widening schemes of 1883 and 1891; the hedged garden of Holly House above Bell Cony with its summer-house and "monkey-puzzle" tree still retained its original dimensions, to the discontent of carters and "carriage folk" who had to squeeze through the "bottleneck" which it presented. Where the highway curved sharply around the high boundary wall outside Heaton Hall, stately trees separated Highgate from Lambert Fold (later absorbed into Rossefield Road). Tom Hagyard's greengrocery shop adjoining the "Delvers' Arms" faced the entrance to the Hall stables, and opposite the rear of ancient Garth House a row of eighteenth-century cottages flanked the cemetery.

In the hollow beyond lay the woods. Traditionally, the public were allowed access to Weather Royds and Cliffe Woods (collectively known as "the Old Wood"), but Roydscliffe ("the New Wood"), Dungeon, Northcliffe and the more distant High Park and Stony Ridge woods were private game-reserves. The head gamekeeper, Tom Firth, was paid £1 per week to look after the woods and plantations, lop and trim trees, plant saplings, repair fences and gates and prevent trespass and illegal gambling on Sundays. His assistants Tom Smith and Edward Pallant each received 5s for Sunday work, and Pallant also watched the 43 acres of woodland west of Bingley Road and Toller Lane. Their vigilance was sometimes rewarded – in November, 1901, William Sutcliffe of Bowling was obliged to visit the agents' office to pay 2s 6d to Pallant and apologise for poaching.

Not that the keepers themselves were always beyond reproach: in July, 1903, Firth had to be instructed not to "cultivate" pheasants and partridges, to kill the rabbits which were plaguing the farms and to cease inviting his friends for "a shoot". The shooting rights, a manorial asset, were leased out periodically; Mr. Cutcliffe Hyne of "Heaton Lodge", the celebrated author of "Captain Kettle", paid £5 for licence to shoot in the woods from October 1st, 1909, to February 1st, 1910.

Beyond the woods lay well tended farms – North Hall and Plantation hemmed in by the quarries with their gaunt cranes and shrill steam whistles; quaint, mullioned Royds Hall; Shay and Stubbing Farms flanked by pastures reclaimed from the old collieries, and Shay Grange in the middle of the fields. Prosperous High Park Farm with its noisy rookeries was home to the Misses Kay, whose cowman, Burgess, maintained a cordial understanding with the farm bull, Billy. Whereas the other farmhands viewed the animal warily, from the other end of a pitchfork, every evening Burgess calmly led the bull into its stall with the reassuring words, "Good neet, Billy - Ah'll see thee in t'morning", and never experienced any kind of difficulty. The Misses Kay's brother, Sam, tenant of High Park Quarry, was once tossed out of his horse-drawn trap by a gross irregularity in the surface of Heights Lane. Being a practical man, he had himself elected to the City Council, whereupon the "rough places" were quickly "made smooth!"

At the foot of Heights Lane there stood a picturesque cottage through whose garden the stream from Chellow Wells flowed on its way to the woods, and whose tenant was in the habit of tying tomatoes to the trusses of his tomato plants to make them appear homegrown, fresh and saleable. Nearby, Sam and Mary Pickles lived in quaint, timbered "Swiss Cottage" which in later years was bought and demolished by Mr. Crowley, vendor of pots and pans, who erected an unusually narrow house at the corner of Neville Avenue and proudly named it "Caroline Cottage". The more observant local lads preferred to call it "t'Sliced Loaf!"

Higher up Haworth Road lay a profusion of dairy farms - Westfield alongside Naylor Rough pond, ancient Chellow Grange and Chellow Style, Chellow Heights perched 850 feet above sea level, and Pyke Nook, West House and Spring Head on the western hillside above Sandy Lane Bottom with its prominent chapel and smoke-plumed chimneys.

Such was Heaton at the dawn of the twentieth century. Previously described as an "extremely poor district" when still a purely rural area, it now ranked as the most affluent suburb of a world-renowned city.

'Snow Scene, Heaton', photographed about 1904 from North Hall. On the left, Heaton Hill flanks West Bank; in the centre Highgate and Shay Lane descend towards the woods, while Heaton Baptist Chapel and newly erected houses in Crofton Road and Leylands Lane (right) complete the scene.

(Courtesy of Mr Graham Hall)

Chapter 18 – Characters and Pranksters

Heaton's characters were greatly enjoyed during their lifetime and fondly remembered long after they had passed on.

The most celebrated was Ont (Aunt) Betty (Elizabeth Hudson, nee Greenwood, 1807-1892) who in her younger days shared a cottage at Paradise with her sister Mary, the fiancée of Tommy (Thomas Thompson) Hudson (1804-1880). Chancing to call on his "intended" one day at dusk, Tommy saw her light a candle, throw the spent match into the fire and walk out of the room with the candle. Before she returned, Betty performed a similar action, but carefully blew out the match and put it aside for further use. "By gow," Tommy mused to himself, "If she lewks after her own brass lahke that, she'll likely lewk after mine!", whereupon he switched his affections. They married on New Year's Day, 1835.

The bridegroom's fortunes never looked back. Betty, it was said, "would cut a currant in half" to save money. Indeed, it was alleged that "if she had two warts she would'nt give one away", and the phrase "as near (tightfisted) as Ont Betty" came into regular use. Often when Tommy, a farmer, was delivering milk in the village, customers would give him stale bread for his horse, little dreaming that Betty would deem it "tew gooid for t'hoss" and serve it up in the form of a bread pudding!

It could be said that her economies were fairly shared out. Itinerant Irish labourers who were hired for the harvesting often observed that their ale was less strong at the end of the day than at its beginning, and when the farm goat fell into the "licking" (a mixture of oats, turnips, barley meal, molasses and hot water used as winter fodder for cattle), she dragged it out and dropped it on a heap of bran with the words "There, that'll do thee four days!" Neighbours pointed out the unwisdom of "laying up treasure on earth."- "Nay, Mrs. Hudson," they urged, "Money's made round to go round!"-"Nowt o't sooart," came the prompt reply. "It's med flat to pile!"

Unknown to everyone, her frugalities had a purpose. When snowfalls isolated Heaton Royds she valiantly struggled through on horseback with bags of flour for her eldest brother and his

'Ont Betty' – Mrs Elizabeth Hudson, the author's great great aunt (1807-1892). *(Author's collection)*

family, and several of the houses built by "Tommy" at the Syke were occupied at low rents by her relatives. As recently as 1980 a nephew remembered her having left sovereigns in the crevice of a wall at Frizinghall for her youngest brother to collect secretly. As she was childless, relatives strove to "keep in her good books". On the day of her death excited villagers ran from door to door enquiring hopefully, "Art tha aught akin to Ont Betty?" as relatives flocked from far and wide. "Apronfuls of gold sovereigns" were reputedly spirited away, and when her late husband's old farm was demolished to make way for Dawson's new shop (the site of today's "Delvers' Arms" carpark), more bullion was found concealed in the stonework.

The more open-handed ambition of her nephew "Brazzen Harry" (Henry Greenwood, 1852-1936) was "to live till all t'hard work's done and all t'owd ale's supped." His working life was spent in the quarries, where, if a large flagstone needed to be loaded on to a cart in the absence of a crane, the cry went up, "Fetch Harry!" – and the job was done. If fights erupted at the hostelries, Harry could always separate the contestants by wrenching them apart with both hands. Most of his earnings were invested in drink, and having observed him being conveyed up "Syke Hill" in a wheelbarrow (with many a spill) by local youths, his exasperated relatives begged him to "do his drinking at t'top o' t'hill" so that he could stagger home unaided! His wedding gift to his second wife was a mangle, which enabled her to take in other folk's washing and "keep him in comfort!"

Equally intemperate and improvident was "Brass Jack" (John Broadbelt, 1846-1933) who, following a long session at the "Turf Tavern" was seen by the Baptist minister leaning on a wall in Emm Lane, unable to proceed further. "I'm very sorry to see you in this condition, John," said the minister. "Can I give you a hand?" – "Nay, Mr. Robinson," came the slurred reply. "Don't mind me - Ah'll be alreight. T'Lord allus lewks after His own!"

Rawson Broadley (1854-1930) of the Syke was dedicated to lethargy. His sister Martha kept the old-fashioned shop at no.3, Garden Terrace, wherein she sold goods and groceries ranging from ham and flour to currants and treacle, all of which had to be weighed and dispensed by hand. Rawson usually avoided the sticky task of decanting the treacle, knowing that his sister would rescue him. "Martha!" he would call out. "Wheer's t'spooin?" And long-suffering Martha would quickly find the spoon which had never really been lost. But even so, her patience was sorely tried when Rawson, temporarily tired of living, attempted to drown himself in a bucket.

Arthur Richardson (1872-1956), builder of many good stone houses in Ashwell Road, Rossefield Road, Highgate, Heights Lane and elsewhere, practised a down-to-earth creed:

"He who would thrive must rise at five,
And he who has thriven can rise at seven!"

True to his word, he once paid a holiday visit to Buckfast Abbey, where he espied a monk quietly engaged in the building of a stone wall. Having observed his actions for several minutes, he could not resist exclaiming, "By gum, lad, tha'd hev to frame thissen if tha worked for me!"

Hudson Greenwood (1862-1941) of Garth House Farm, not the most energetic of men, was always the last to mow fields or gather crops. If cows had to be taken to the bull, the task was usually delegated to his daughter with the jocular advice not to "let t'bull have more than one look!"

Before the days of organised entertainment, practical jokes were always popular with the young men, with Ben Tetley, butcher (1877-1951) and Milton Dyson, quarrymaster

Ben Tetley, butcher, photographed about 1903 with an appreciative customer.

(Courtesy of the late Mr and Mrs J. T. Tetley)

(1875-1948) usually to the fore. Arrayed in white sheets and armed with broomsticks they "haunted" Heaton Woods, to the indignation of "courting couples". On one occasion Milton, a burly, ruddy-faced individual, donned his wife's clothing and called on Edwin Tetley at Plantation Hall farm. Mrs. Tetley who opened the door in response to his knock was surprised to find a strange woman enquiring for her husband. Surprise turned to annoyance when they entered the barn together and she discovered them apparently in an embrace. Explanations having been made, Milton and Edwin next tried their luck at the "Hare and Hounds". "I'll have a pint", said Edwin. "Ay, and I'll have a pint an'all!" said Milton. "No you won't!" exclaimed the scandalised landlady. "I don't serve pints to women!"

Modern Heatonians suffering from a surfeit of car radios and mobile phones may find difficulty in imagining the atmosphere of tranquil peace which prevailed sixty or seventy years ago, when the unaided human voice could be heard over long distances. The tenants of North Hall Farm (at the top of present-day Roydscliffe Drive) had a daughter who regularly visited friends in Heaton village. When it was time for her to return home, her mother would open the farmhouse door and shout her name, a device which never failed to produce the desired result. When Mrs. Waterhouse (nee Hollingworth) at the Syke issued forth periodically to summon her four children for meals or bedtime, her voice resounded far and wide, to the amusement of neighbours. "Hilda, Edith, Ina and Will-ee!" she called.

The forerunner of the new twentieth century was undoubtedly the motor-car. The first such vehicle to reach Heaton managed to struggle northwards over the unpaved roads which constituted the King's Highway from London, but lost heart when confronted by steep Emm Lane and had to be hauled ignominiously to its new home by Heaton horses. Its unceremonious arrival gave no hint of the changes which "horseless carriages" were to bring, and the conversion of stables into motor garages was to be a leisurely process.

For the majority of Heaton folk including the affluent dwellers in Wilmer Drive and Emm Lane, the most useful form of transport was the tramcar. Since 1882/3 those who wished to travel to Bradford in comfort had used either the sedate horse-tram which lurked at the foot of Victor Road, Manningham, or the noisy steam-tram which rumbled along Keighley Road, but in 1902 these were superseded by modern electric tramcars. A shortlived service from Bradford to North Park Road was extended to Heaton via Wilmer

Heaton Hall, south and east fronts, and (left) the servants' wing, photographed in 1911 by Hood & Larkin, London. *(Author's collection)*

Road and Emm Lane, to the bewilderment of a venerable Garden Terrace resident who could not comprehend the notion of vehicles propelled by electricity drawn from an overhead wire. On the opening day, December 23rd, 1902, the whole village assembled to view the first tram, and free travel was allowed. Local children soon acquired a new pastime: they foregathered at the terminus at the "King's Arms" for the privilege of swinging the reversible seat backs to face the direction of travel or to alter the destination indicator from "Heaton" to "Forster Square" or wherever the vehicle was destined to visit. And when Allerton trams established a terminus in Prune Park Lane on October 12th, 1904, the good folk of Sandy Lane Bottom and Chellow were able at last to escape from their long isolation, although for several years visits to Bradford were considered "a treat".

Not everyone was pleased, however; Heber Duckworth of Highgate was compelled to sacrifice his beloved holly garden in the name of progress, to the satisfaction of the Vicar who had long complained of "the disgraceful and dangerous entrance to the village". At the same time the Shipley and Clayton gas supplies in the township were taken over by Bradford Corporation, thereby reducing gas charges by 10d per 1,000 cubic feet.

The magnificent Bradford Exhibition held in Lister Park in the hot summer of 1904 gave much pleasure to local people, but when it ended, a period of trade depression set in, and every penny of the church Poor Funds had to be spent. A few winters later Mr. Albert H. Illingworth, tenant of Heaton Hall since 1897, gave handsome donations for Christmas dinners, groceries and coal for those deprived of work by the bitter weather.

Heaton Tram Terminus, 1903. Tramcar no. 212 rests outside the 'King's Arms' after having been driven from Bradford by the author's grandfather, Mr J. E. Hornsby (standing next to the tram). Heaton Hall is glimpsed mistily behind the park wall (left), and the cottages and gardens of Frankland Fold are sandwiched between 'Bell Cony' (centre) and the hostelry.

(Author's collection)

Lawrence, 4th Earl of Rosse, 1840-1908.

(Photo: Rosemont, Rawson Square, Bradford, courtesy the Earl of Rosse.)

Tidings of the death of Lawrence, 4th Earl of Rosse, on August 29th, 1908, provided a reminder that nothing is permanent. As distinguished as his parents, Lord Rosse had served as Chancellor of Trinity College, Dublin, President of the Royal Dublin Society, the Royal Irish Academy, the Heaton Church Cricket Club and Bradford Amateur Rowing Club. A plaque commemorating his achievements was placed in the St. Patrick's Hall of Dublin Castle. "We had no idea that so great a loss would so suddenly befall us", wrote the Vicar, his chaplain, "and can only add a respectful tribute of regard. As Lord of the Manor of Heaton the late Earl has always displayed a most generous and kindly regard . . . a noble friend and supporter of church work and a generous employer." His title and landed property passed to his eldest son William Edward, but significantly the revenues of the Heaton and Shipley estates comprising a net rental of £3,000 per annum were charged with the payment of £10,000 to the younger children

Displaying an interest in his English estates of which his grandmother would have approved, the new Earl visited Heaton almost immediately, on September 10th, 1908, then for five days in June, 1909 and subsequently on August 11th, 1910. In 1905 he had married Frances Lois, daughter of Sir Cecil and Lady Lister-Kaye of Denby Grange, near Wakefield, and their son Michael, who had now become Lord Oxmantown, was born on September 28th, 1906.

Very regrettably, Lord Rosse's visits were not unconnected with the untoward effect of death duties. His last purchase of land in Heaton was made in December 1909, and the "Bradford Daily Argus" of July 25th, 1911, bore the unwelcome news that the Heaton and Shipley estates were to be disposed of. The word spread quickly, bringing with it a realisation that life was about to change for ever, not perhaps immediately, but certainly within a lifetime.

A long farewell, then, to old associations, to dusty roads and laden haycarts, slow herds winding their evening way to mistal and milking shed, to rooks and rookeries, peewits and larks in the empty places, cuckoos, hares, trout and wild hyacinths, hips and haws in the hedgerows and mushrooms on misty September mornings. Stone, slate and cement would eventually cover much of the landscape, and the day would come when a man would not know his neighbours.

But first the mechanics of the divorce had to be enacted. When the initial rush of enquiries and private purchases had subsided, Lord Rosse offered the estates for auction at Bradford Mechanics' Institute on November 28th-30th, 1911, stressing his hope that tenants would be able to buy their houses and lands. As a parting gift to the village he presented Heaton Hill recreation ground to the Corporation and

William Edward, 5th Earl of Rosse, who succeeded to the title in 1908 and auctioned his estates in 1911. *(Photo: author, courtesy of the Earl of Rosse)*

allowed them to buy the valuable Heaton Woods at a greatly reduced value.

The auction realised £33,180, but 600 acres remained unsold, and private transactions were resumed. Heaton Hall together with the manorial rights was offered at £10,000, and lower bids from the Lord Mayor (Ald. Jacob Moser) and Mr. William Greaves of "Bankfield", Toller Lane (clerk to the Justices and deputy steward of the Bradford manor; died January 31st, 1919) were declined. The manorial rights, together with 69 acres of land at High Park, were therefore sold to Mr. Jonas Whitley, a former chairman of Allerton Local Board and Mayor of Bradford in 1893-4. Son of David Whitley and his wife Martha, daughter of Solomon and Betty Clark (see above) he was born on April 30th, 1834, and devoted his energies to the Bradford wool trade from the age of nine. Sadly, the new lord of the manor had little time to enjoy his acquisitions, as he died soon afterwards, on July 2nd, 1912, at his Allerton home.

Meanwhile the changes brought about by the auction were beginning to take effect. On the expiry of their lease of Heaton Hall in June, 1912, Mr. and Mrs. Illingworth removed to Denton near Ilkley. With their departure from Heaton the Hall fell silent. No more congenial social gatherings (and "ha'porths of dripping" at the kitchen door next day); no more new pennies at the Whitsuntide "treats"; no employment for butlers, housemaids, lodge-keepers, chauffeurs, handymen or local traders. Darkened windows stared emptily across the deserted gardens; unchecked ivy crept over the old walls.

As the solicitors busied themselves with title deeds, conveyances and all the other accoutrements of property sales, the new owners took possession of their assorted purchases and began to plan for the future. The way was open now for large-scale development: Bradford could burst its bonds.

Fortunately the process was destined to last several decades, as the demand for housing was uncertain, and in any case widespread development - rare in that era - would have necessitated heavy expenditure on public services such as highways, drainage, gas, electricity, water and tramways, none of which was contemplated by the Corporation.

The first visible sign of changing times was the demolition of old-world Frankland Fold with its cottage gardens and trellised roses. Soon a yawning chasm engulfed the site, as the underlying bed of stone was far more valuable than the dwellings, and where old Phoebe Parker had previously shaken her rugs and gossiped with her neighbours, Michael Duxbury's steam crane could soon be seen busily hoisting hefty slabs of good Yorkshire sandstone to the surface.

Between the new "delf" and Bell Cony a tall house and shop arose, modestly emblazoned with the date "1912". Originally a men's outfitter's and ladies' drapery, it was opened by Freddy Smith whose "Eat-on" toffee and sweet business was already established next door in Bell Cony.

The normal routines of everyday life continued as before, the dawning of each new working day being unpleasantly announced by the strident hootings of mill "buzzers" and quarry whistles, the staccato clatter of clogs and boots on cold causeways and the rumble of

Hudson Greenwood's cows wend their way 'down the Cliffe' (lower Highgate) after milking-time, about 1908.   *(Courtesy of C.H. Wood, Bradford)*

the first tram. Later, after milking-time, milk-floats made their leisurely way from door to door as children walked, skipped or ran to school. Mid-morning visits to shops provided opportunities for the exchange of news and gossip, but door-to-door deliveries were commonplace, not only at the "big houses". In Highgate, Charles and Nellie George administered the post office and also employed errand boys to distribute fish, fruit and vegetables. Ben Tetley sallied forth with choice cuts of well-hung meat while Tom Hagyard and Arthur Greenwood set out with their horse-drawn carts to deliver groceries and greengroceries, their customers' children sometimes being rewarded with a cherry or similar inducement.

In that sedate world simple pleasures were enjoyed to the full. Hopscotch, hide and seek, piggy in the middle, rounders, "pies-ball", conkers and whip-and-top kept the children "out of mischief", or so their parents hoped. "Playing out" was discouraged on Sundays, as the Sabbath was reserved for Sunday School at church or chapel followed by Sunday Dinner and a decorous, fully-dressed walk with parents and relations "through the Woods", "to the Park" or "round the Shay" in the afternoon. Heaton Woods and the more remote Dungeon Woods were now open to the public from end to end, being reached by new paths - the "snicket" from Heaton Shay Farm and the Cat Steps (so called because their precipitous ascents were more suited to felines than humans) from Nog Lane and Quarry Street. Of the wide vistas available from the summit of the Steps it was claimed that they could not be excelled anywhere else in the city suburbs, and that the beautiful viewpoint needed "to be guarded like the frontiers of Eden, by an angel with flaming sword, otherwise the speculators will get it!" Generations of Heatonians have endorsed that claim. Below, wild orchids, primroses and darting trout could be glimpsed in the deep cloughs, although their profusion diminished as the popularity of the woods increased. The best bluebells were to be found in Dungeon Woods, and picnics at Chellow Dene could be enlivened by jugs of tea or gingerbeer from the reservoir keeper's lodge.

The first faint impact of sophistication was felt in 1914 when the former horse tram depot in Manningham was converted into the Oak Lane Picture House (later the Oriental Cinema), but for many years the flickering delights offered there were considered to be "treats" rather than everyday fare; indeed, the author's grandmother Mrs. Ellen Hornsby, having been induced to attend the opening performance, was perfectly content never to repeat the experience.

Newspaper reports of troubles in Zululand, outrages in the Balkans or the Kaiser's latest bombasts were of little more than passing interest to families who were more sensibly concerned with the normal practicalities of life, such as paying the rent, "saving up" for gas bills and rates, providing good food for the table, coal in the grate and warm clothes on their backs.

Some events more startling than others did however provide occasional sensations and "nine day wonders." The awesome tidings of the sinking of the Titanic circulated in hushed whispers, unlike the activities of Dr. Crippen which were hailed in gleeful rhyme by the schoolchildren:-

"Crippen i-addi i-ay, i-ay, Crippen i-addi i-ay,
To France he went with Ethel le Neve,
Dressed in men's breeches right up to her knees . . ."

Less well-mannered children daringly ventured to mock some of their elders. Observing the approach of his relation, "Ca'line"-ruddy-featured Mrs. Caroline Cromack of Back Lane, bedecked with bombazine and jet jewellery - George Greenwood of the "Delvers' Arms" evoked the memory of another Caroline - George IV's wayward wife - in bold and much resented song:-

> "Queen, Queen Caroline, washed her face in turpentine,
> Turpentine made it shine, Queen, Queen Caroline!" -

and then smartly took to his heels.

The assassination of a distant archduke in unknown Sarajevo produced no local reaction whatever, and it was not until a full month later, at the beginning of August 1914, that Heaton, like the rest of the country, found itself on the brink of an unexpected European war - not, this time, against French or Spaniards but the faintly ridiculous figure of "Kaiser Bill" whose armies were greeting the long-awaited arrival of "Der Tag" with an invasion of unsuspecting Belgium.

As the local volunteers of the "Territorials" and the "Bradford Pals" marched confidently away to the Western Front in the expectation of an early return, a stream of Belgian refugees crossed the Channel in search of a safe haven. At Heaton tram terminus on October 15th, 1914, a fascinated throng of Heaton folk witnessed the arrival of their own contingent - about half-a-dozen families carrying their few belongings into the nearby Hall which had been commandeered as a wartime billet. There they remained while the tide of war ebbed and flowed across their ravaged homeland. Kindly villagers lent them a gramophone and records of brass bands and other music to which they danced on Saturdays and Sundays until midnight, at which hour they solemnly played the national anthems.

Some of the young Belgians found local employment, such as Maurice Clibeau who worked as a "bobbin-ligger" at Listers'. Meanwhile in a corner of the Hall's cavernous kitchen a wrinkled old woman sat day by day smoking a clay pipe and watching a large flake of distemper (ceiling paint) which held a superstitious significance for her. "When it falls," she intoned, "the war will end." The same hope was inspired by a shell-damaged statue in a Belgian town, but optimism waned as the casualty lists lengthened. Seventy years later elderly Heaton ladies were still treasuring faded photographs of husbands whose brief married life had been cut short by machine-gun fire in Flanders.

In wartime Heaton, life became increasingly difficult. Quarries and mills were short of men; half completed "semi-detached" houses flanked Leylands Lane, and a partial "blackout" was imposed when German Zeppelin airships unexpectedly launched nocturnal raids on other parts of the North. Sights and sounds of warfare had been absent from Heaton since the Civil War, but now the night hours were filled with a greater sense of unease than the old boggarts and guytrashes had ever achieved. Nevertheless, patriotic fervour continued undiminished, and much interest was aroused in July, 1915, when Lady Jellicoe, wife of the Admiral of the Grand Fleet, stayed overnight with Sir Arthur and Lady Godwin in their home at "Emm Royd" prior to opening the Khaki Club in Bradford.

By 1917 food shortages were widespread, and Heaton families were reduced to spreading unpalatable lard on their bread and queueing at John Smith's factory at Windhill in the hope of a jar of jam, even though the sight of cartloads of turnips passing through the factory gates removed any optimism as to the quality of their purchase. A national system of food rationing staved off actual starvation.

The vicar, the Rev. G. B. Flynn, died on November 11th, 1917, after 35 years of service to St. Barnabas'. The village children had always held him in awe as he rode by in his carriage, resplendent in frock coat and silk top hat; indeed, the Baptist children thought he was God and instinctively stepped off the pavement at his approach. Gratifyingly, the Anglican children held the same exalted opinion of Mr. Howarth, the Baptist minister, on account of his neat white beard. To the great sorrow of his flock Mr. Howarth left Heaton in 1919.

A late casualty of the war, shortly before the Armistice in November, 1918, was the 45-year old Earl of Rosse, who as Lord Oxmantown had celebrated his coming of age at Heaton in what now seemed a different age. Convalescing after grave injuries on active service as a Major with the Irish Guards, he had recently visited the Lord Mayor to outline plans for housing development in the grounds of Heaton Hall, which still remained unsold.

The Governors of Bradford Grammar School were also considering the Hall and Park as the site for a new school, but decided to purchase the larger Clock House estate instead, with the result that on the departure of the Belgian refugees on May 15th, 1919, the trustees of the 12 year old 6th Earl leased the Hall and grounds to St. Bede's Roman Catholic Grammar School of Drewton Street, Bradford, who subsequently purchased the property in 1920.

The purchase was a distinct shock to the villagers, who feared for their long-enjoyed peace and quiet. Gloomily surveying attempts by the schoolboys to overturn a tramcar by dint of concerted swaying, Amos Beanland the postmaster commented that, "Heaton was becoming the capital of Ireland." Suspicions were mutual. A recent copy of the school's magazine had impolitely disparaged the links between many old-established schools and "the poor patronage of a Protestant King", on which its own pupils would not have to rely.

Happily unaware of their elders' antagonisms, the pupils explored their new surroundings - the hollow oak, the old stables, the attics and echoing cellars - a boys'

Heaton Hall and rear entrance gates seen from the bottom of Hilda Street about 1904. The Hall displays signs of previous alterations, with three blocked-up top storey windows on the west front (right) and one tall blocked-up first floor window (extreme left).   *(Courtesy of Mr Graham Hall)*

paradise. But the school's hopes of preserving the old Hall and constructing a new extension behind it were doomed from the outset, as the unsentimental Corporation decreed in 1920 that eventually the Hall would be demolished for road-widening. Barely twenty feet wide as it squeezed between the Hall's boundary wall and the houses opposite, Highgate was becoming inadequate for the Jowett and Austin cars now appearing spasmodically and fitfully on the highways.

Motor-cars were destined to change the face of Heaton in many ways. Whereas the newer thoroughfares such as Quarry Street, Milford Place, Rossefield Road and West Bank were solidly paved with local stone setts, and Keighley Road, Wilmer Road, upper Emm Lane and lower Highgate with granite paving at the expense of the Tramways Department, most other highways were still in a state of nature, with limestone or sandstone macadam, muddy or dusty according to the weather. A policy of tar-spraying about 1928 converted them into roads fit for motors, and Toller Lane, Bingley Road and parts of Leylands Lane and Haworth Road were considerably widened.

It was soon evident that much of the tranquil innocence of prewar life had vanished forever. Four years of trench warfare had created much disillusionment, and at Heaton Baptist Chapel the Rev. A. E. Robinson mourned the lads who had never returned from Flanders as well as those who had survived but never resumed their old religious practices. "It has been relentlessly borne in upon us all," observed the curate of St. Barnabas', "that the war altered many things and that the world we live in has greatly changed. Points of view have changed; people are less fixed in their abode, outlooks have broadened."

Confidence in the future had been shaken too. On Advent Sunday, 1919, the new vicar, the Rev. Richard Whincup, M.C., M.A., preached on the theme, "It is high time to wake out of sleep". Mr. Winston S. Churchill, M.P., had warned that the Peace was merely a peace of exhaustion, and that once the nations had recovered, they would be at war again. No one was more distressed than the vicar when the prophecy came true twenty years later.

Sedate "Conversaziones" and social gatherings at church and chapel were facing new competition in the form of wireless and mass entertainment. When B.B.C. 2LO commenced broadcasting in 1922, the strains of the "Savoy Orpheans" and Henry Hall's Band were miraculously coaxed out of the air by crystal sets assembled for a few shillings by enterprising Heaton boys. In the city centre, new dance-halls

The Rev. Richard Whincup, MC, MA, Vicar of Heaton.
(Author's collection)

St Barnabas' Hall (Whitehead Memorial) Rossefield Road.   *(Copyright: author)*

such as Barraclough's and Gledhill's were throbbing to the alluring rhythms of foxtrot, quickstep, waltz and tango, not to mention the "Charleston" and "Black Bottom", and young men and maidens who had worked since dawn in mill or milking-shed were blissfully happy to dance the night away, even at the risk of missing the last tram home.

Nevertheless, village life was prepared to fight back strongly, assisted greatly by the splendid Whitehead Memorial Hall - St. Barnabas' Hall in Rossefield Road - presented by Sir Henry and Lady Whitehead and opened in September, 1924, by General Sir Charles Harrington, head of Northern Command. With billiard and function rooms, kitchen and a maple-floored hall and stage, it was in great demand for concerts, dances, prizegivings, Whitsuntide fetes and wedding receptions; a bazaar held there soon after its opening raised the impressive sum of £2,300, and in 1930 the new Heaton (Church) Operatic and Dramatic Society began a successful run of popular musicals such as "Lilac Domino" and "Quaker Girl". The levelling of the old quarry ground at the rear of the Hall facilitated the laying out of playing fields, tennis courts and a bowling-green.

Tennis courts destined for national acclaim were opened in 1928 on Bull Croft by the Heaton Tennis Club, an amalgamation of an earlier club of the same name which had used the private court at Parkside Farm for over thirty years, with a sister organisation from Cunliffe Road, Manningham. The popularity of the new club was such that within a year eleven courts were in use; a pavilion was erected in 1930, and competitions were being staged by 1934.

The completion of a tunnel from Gaisby Lane to Esholt in 1923 enabled the Corporation to close its Frizinghall sewage works on the site of the present-day King George V Playing Fields in Bolton township - to the great relief of local residents. A heatwave in June, 1911, had caused them to protest that,

St Barnabas' School, Ashwell Road, built in 1871 and enlarged several times. The St Barnabas' Village Hall has occupied the site since 1965. *(Copyright: author)*

"The stench regularly pervades the valley from Frizinghall to Belle Vue and sometimes up to Heaton. Last week when it should have been a pleasure to live outdoors we were forced inside and compelled to close doors and windows, and even then could not escape the vile odour. The Post Office cadets have stayed only a week at their Frizinghall camp - had they stayed longer they might all have been smothered in their beds!"

At Heaton school the retirement of the Victorian head teacher J. H. Wilkinson (died 1946) and the vigorous policies of his successor, Harold S. Coward (from 1926) inspired Mr. George Green to express sentiments felt by generations of scholars: -

"Cold, grey-black stones that wall our school!
No stately pile nor steeple proud;
No monument to builder's skill
Or edifice to draw the crowd -
But round your walls there sweetly clings
The memories of childhood's joys.
We dream again of happy days
Spent in your rooms as girls and boys."

The demolition of the now-disused pumping station and chimney at Heaton Reservoir on February 5th, 1926, removed a familiar though incongruous landmark. The steeplejacks, Messrs. C. V. Barber, of Windhill, found their initial efforts frustrated by the locals' earlier insistence that the brick chimney stack should be concealed by an additional casing of stone. 14lb of gelignite, "more than enough to wreck the Town Hall", had to be used before it consented to fall. Reflections by a local poet revealed the chimney's

The demolition of Heaton waterworks chimney on 5 February 1926, was photographed from the safe vantage point of Heaton Road. Also visible are the pumping station (bottom left), the reservoir (centre) and Co-operative Store (right). *(Author's collection)*

innermost feelings in verse: -

> "This afternoon the Lord Mayor and
> His councillors imposing
> Came up to see the final blasts
> And me on ground reposing -
> But still I stand! though much I fear
> To-morrow's blasts will break me;
> The crowds will hear my crashing fall,
> My mighty strength forsake me."

One of the best-known figures of Heaton village at that period was Thompson Greenwood, a dairy farmer who rented part of Ashwell Farm. Normally a steady, sober individual, he was overcome from time to time with an urge to "throw over the traces" at the local hostelries, when his neighbours had to be summoned to attend his cows at milking-time. Possibly the same urge brought about the last recorded use of the township pinfold in 1905, when he had to pay 4s 6d for the release of his horses which had been found straying in the village. His garden contained succulent gooseberries which were illicitly appreciated by the children from St. Barnabas' school; they also developed a liking for the dried "locust" which he kept in his barn for the cattle, but their cravings were entirely unofficial, as Thompson was far from open-handed.

Being a bachelor, his work was his hobby, and frivolous pursuits meant nothing to him.

One summer evening, leaning philosophically against a wall, he beheld local lads "pawsing" (kicking) a football in a field nearby. "Poor simple fools!" he observed pityingly. At home he endured the services of an unwanted (and unpaid) housekeeper who in addition to daily chores, occasionally milked the cows and performed domestic cleaning at other houses, including the "Delvers' Arms" where she received a liquid wage. Overjoyed when the housekeeper departed for a holiday with relatives, he was more than reluctant to re-admit her when she returned unexpectedly one evening after he had retired to bed. "Away wi' thee back, woman!" he called from an upper window. "Away wi' thee back!" Neighbourly intercessions eventually brought about a grumbling change of heart. He died peacefully in his bed in 1927, when neighbours attended the customary "ham tea" at the Chapel.

A familiar and useful feature of local life was the roundsmen, who on their regular journeyings always halted at recognised stopping-places to give housewives time to find their purses, go out into the street and make their purchases,

The Pot Man with his horse-drawn cart was a regular visitor until about 1950. His "pots", i.e., crockery, jugs, hardware, scouring stones, dishcloths, brushes etc, were in great demand, and part payment could be made in kind, i.e., in rags. A fresh-faced, unsmiling individual (who was once said to have killed a man - not a customer!), he tolerated no nonsense, even when his horse bolted; the author (with mixed feelings of delight and dismay!) glimpsed the cart as it thundered, rattled and clashed its way down roughly-cobbled Scotchman Road with the pot-man in hot pursuit.

Tom Hagyard of Highgate and Arthur Blakey of Park Row (bottom of Parkside Grove) served the district for many years on certain days of the week with horse-drawn carts (Mr. Blakey latterly operated a motor van). "Grey peas all hot!" were sold at 1d per pot if customers took their own mug along; enterprising children took a pint pot, but received only the customary gill (half pint) measure. The "yeast man", Mr. Mawson, later Jim Tebb from Temple Street, called weekly (or monthly in outlying areas) with a small trap pulled by a pony (Bessie) and weighed out the yeast on a small brass balance. Thomas Hook of Back Lane, retired coachman to the Vicar, sold his home-made ice cream from a handcart and announced his presence by a handbell; in later years he used a pony and cart. Handbells were progressively (?) superseded by annoying musical jingles from about 1955.

A horse-drawn, red-painted fish and chip van was often stationed in a gateway at the west end of Garter Row in the early years of the Haworth Road estate. The rag and bone man often halted outside St. Barnabas' School at lunchtime to exchange rags for balloons. His raucous, semi-unintelligible cry of "Any rags, bones?" could be heard far and wide. Dancing bears (which did not actually dance but merely shuffled from foot to foot as they stood upright) were reputed to be stabled "at t'back o't Mill", i.e., Listers, where all unknown and unexplained phenomena were thought to originate! They were not seen again after the Great War. The "tingalari" or barrel-organ, with or without monkey, was always a popular visitor. The knife and scissor grinder (pre 1955) used a pedal-operated contraption.

Established local traders continued to make house-to-house deliveries of coal, groceries, greengroceries, meat and milk. The best milk was delivered by local farmers - Alonza S. Tetley (Ashwell), Jim Greenwood (Parkside) and the Gawthorpes of Chellow. All used a 2-wheeled "float" which carried the large galvanised milk cans from which they replenished the smaller elliptical hand-held cans which they carried from house to house. With a gill or pint "measure" (a cylindrical ladle) they filled the saucer-covered jugs left on doorstep or

Alonza Greenwood of Wilsden in the splendid new milk-float of his cousin Alonza Tetley of Ashwell Farm, Heaton, about 1920. The farm lad lived in Westfield Road, Manningham.

(Courtesy of Mrs S. M. Ogden)

windowsill. The sealed, pasteurised and bottled products delivered by large retail dairies such as the Co-op or Model Milk were sarcastically derided by the farmers whose milk was fresh each morning. "Wha, they're boiled and frozzen till there's nowt left in 'em", declared noisy Jim Greenwood. Butchers made regular deliveries in Heaton until about 1975.

Following the sale of the Clockhouse estate to Bradford Grammar School by the Atkinson Jowetts in 1927 the pleasant pastures which had formerly sloped downwards to the railway were levelled for use as playing fields, so that from Keighley Road it was no longer possible to see the railway trains or the quaint singledeck trolleybuses which between 1915 and 1932 ran along Canal Road to a terminus at the foot of Frizinghall Road. Canal Road itself had been built about the turn of the century as a direct link between Bradford and Shipley, absorbing the ancient highway to Otley where it passed Dumb Mills.

Slowly Heaton was turning into a desirable residential suburb as small estates of "semis" began to spring up at random. Well built and attractive, they were soon occupied by professionals and businessmen who found them more convenient than the large terrace houses of Frizinghall and Manningham whose Victorian proportions and endless flights of stairs were losing their appeal. Spacious gardens, greater privacy and, for a few, the prospect of a motor garage proved highly popular.

Old associations were retained in new placenames such as Marriner's Drive, Garden Lane, Heaton Park Road and Leylands Avenue, but when the local Proctor family began their long and gradual programme of housebuilding, they displayed a preference for names from Lakeland and the South Coast - Brantwood, Branksome, Lynton, Durley and Alum.

The Duchy estate self-consciously reflected the "superior" character of its Harrogate namesake; the High Park and Highfield estates borrowed their names from Kays' old farm, whilst Mr. Nevill proudly applied his own surname to his little development at Heights Lane. But the whole process was piecemeal and unhurried, as the inter-war trade depressions discouraged rapid expansion; Heaton Park Drive, begun in the 1930s, did not link with Heaton Road until 1955, and the tentative extension of Haworth Road towards North Hall Farm bankrupted its builder in 1939.

The greatest single change was brought about by the City Council's decision to buy Chellow Slack and Chellow Swamp between Heights Lane and the ancient Chellow Grange farm for a Corporation housing estate. From the date of the laying of the first foundations early in 1931, progress was so rapid that a 70-year old man taking a favourite walk was seen to stand amazed on discovering a mass of houses where he had expected to see familiar fields. By 1933 a pleasant new suburb of 770 red-brick, tiled "semis" had arisen around a central playing field where old Chellow Lane reappeared as Chellow Grange Road and Lynfield and Walden Drives encircled the estate. Hathaway and Masefield Drives celebrated English literature past and present; Malham Avenue recalled a favourite Dales village while Sowden Road fittingly commemorated the Sandy Lane millowners, particularly Alderman Thomas Sowden, the Lord Mayor. Controversially, the estate was to have been named "Chellow Grange", but as the purchasers of the old farmstead, which had borne the name for centuries, had inappropriately transferred its historic title to their Victorian villa near Pearson Lane, Manningham, the Corporation had to be content with the more prosaic name of "Haworth Road".

A Corporation motor-bus service, the first in the locality, was instituted on July 20th, 1926, in the form of a circular route from Bradford via Duckworth Lane, Daisy Hill, Heights Lane and Toller Lane. When the buses began to sink into the water-bound macadam laid in Heights Lane at Sam Kay's insistence twenty years earlier, a layer of tar soon transformed it into a smooth tarmacadam highway. The bus service was later extended to Haworth Road (Lynfield Drive) and Sandy Lane, thus relieving "Sandy Loiners" of the need to trek to Allerton tram terminus or use the facilities of Briggs Bros. (later Hebble Motors) who operated to Wilsden, Harden, Bingley, Queensbury, Duckworth Lane and Bradford.

Housing development at Florida Road and lower Cottingley Road in the Allerton portion of Sandy Lane helped to swell the ranks of the primary school and the chapels, and improved the takings of the Co-op, the baker, butcher, post-office and the Victoria Hotel. But the character of the growing village was not spoiled, and even though Small Tail Bridge was now invisible beneath a sea of tarmacadam, the majestic Baptist chapel still presided over the tranquil crossroads.

In a brief and unappreciated attempt to suburbanise Heaton Woods, the Corporation Parks Department channelled a length of the stream into a series of paddling-pools whose icy waters, drawn from underground sources and overshadowed by trees, were shunned by the local children, who, more sensible than the city fathers, preferred to avoid the rigours of rheumatism. Consequently the attempted "beautification" aroused the scorn of Heaton's poet-woolman Otto Mombert, brother of local councillor Adolph F. Mombert, whose poem, "the Vandals", expressed the feelings of many.

The Vandals

When God created Heaton Woods,
    He set therein a stream –
A sweet, meandering witchery,
    As wayward as a dream.
No fairer little waterway
Whispered its secrets to the day.

And every year the miracle,
    Wrought by the Lord of Spring,
Clothed all its banks with green and blue –
    A magic carpeting;
And dainty milkmaids, white and pink,
Danced in the grasses on its brink.

Whether it tumbled on its way
    Beneath the lazy noon,
Or whether on its breast there gleamed
    The jewels of the moon,
The stream in Heaton Woods was free,
As things of beauty ought to be.

But nought is sacred in this age,
    Utilitarian;
And lovely streams are useless to
    A soulless alderman;
Or was it some dull councillor
Who asked what God made beauty for?

I know not. But from one of these
    Came, on an evil day,
Upon the stream some sons of toil,
    And hacked its curves away;
Leaving a set of paddling pools,
As fit memorial for fools.

The hyacinths are rarer now
    Than in the days of old,
And we miss the shining glory of
    The gay marsh-rnarigold.
Men might have left the fairy child
Of God, the streamlet, undefiled.

Lord of the lovely things of life,
    When wilt Thou spare us - when? -
From baneful deeds of councillors
And vandal aldermen?
When shall their impious hands be stayed
From hacking Beauty with a spade?

                O. Mombert

Although Howard Springs famous novel,"these lovers fled away" was based chiefly in Cornwall, Oxford, Manchester, London and the Dales, the author could not resist a glimpse of Heaton:-

"The dusk was setting upon the town, the lights were coming on in streets and houses, and we turned to the left and climbed higher, coming out in Heaton. There we leaned on a rough unmortared stone wall and a vast prospect rolled before us. There was still just light enough to see fold upon fold of hills melting and merging into the west".

The death of Mr. John Lee in August, 1931, removed a strong link with old Heaton. Son of Joseph Lee, the master of the pre-1871 school at Paradise, he had been a founder member of the West Bank Building Club and the first occupant of no.5, West Bank. Elected to the Local Board in 1875, his energy and dedication to detail unfortunately earned him a £44 surcharge from the District Auditor who disapproved of his action in authorising payment of a solicitor's bill sent to the Board.

Recovering from this expensive setback, he served as company secretary to Lister & Co. from 1889 to 1930, and his last residence was at "Larkfield", 67, Leylands Lane. His association with St. Barnabas' Church lasted for over seventy years; as a young man he had climbed to the top of the steeple and watched the highest stone being lifted into place.

Mr John Lee, Director and Secretary of Lister & Co. Ltd.

(Author's collection)

Neatly bearded, thin, of average height and usually to be seen in a fawn gabardine raincoat and trilby hat, he was considered aloof by the less affluent townsfolk.

During the long-remembered winter of 1933, heavy snow fell incessantly for two days, bringing traffic to a standstill and isolating Heaton Royds and Sandy Lane. The trusty trams to Frizinghall and Heaton were little affected, however, but the Haworth Road bus service was suspended for almost a week.

Typical of the philosophical thinking and lofty aspirations of the inter-war years was the remarkable "Heaton Review", produced between 1927 and 1934 by an energetic committee headed by the curate of St. Barnabas'. Appropriately entitled "A Northern Miscellany of Art and Literature", it attracted scientific, artistic and literary contributions from celebrities such as Hugh Walpole, John Galsworthy, Jacob Kramer, Gustav Holst, Augustus John, George Bernard Shaw, Dean Inge, Sir Frank Dyson, Kenneth Grahame, Ernest Sichel and Professor E.V. Appleton of future radar fame.

Local authors eulogised in lyrical terms the old Heaton sights and sounds which were slowly passing away. Picturesque Heaton Royds, in the eyes of W. E. Preston, was "a group of 17th century houses resting peacefully amidst surroundings of rich woodland and pasture, and preserving something of the atmosphere of old English life without the intrusion of the incongruous in modern architecture." Mrs. Mabel Blundell Heynemann saw Old Frizinghall as "an old-world hamlet with many attractive features . . . stone houses, low gables, wide porches, buttressed chimney stacks and mullioned windows; even the gardens create an atmosphere of bygone days with their dahlias, stocks, asters, Rose of Sharon, lavender, lad's love and rosemary bushes." Sadly, the charm of former days was diminished by the demolition of Old Castle in 1935. Originally owned by the Listers of Frizingley Hall and used by James Hargreaves for his stuffmaking business from 1779 to 1816, its modern replacement was a Workshop for the Blind approached from Paddock. Heaton, in the eyes of an anonymous businessman, remained:

Highgate in 1932. Left to right: the end of the Heaton Hall boundary wall and stables, with a police call-box resembling a sentry-box, the entrance to Heaton Lawn Tennis Club and John Lumb's garage, Garth House and the spire of Heaton Baptist Chapel.   *(Photo: the late Mr James Greenwood)*

" . . . a little dreamland where the green fields and drowsy farms of another day are fast giving place to houses   and   streets, buses and the hum of a widening city. It is . . . a memory of days when cows died or a valuable horse had to be taken to the slaughterhouse, or mornings in haytime when the hay lay on the ground all dark and wet and you woke from your troubled rest hoping to be greeted by sunshine, only to meet the rain beating on the window of the old farmhouse, and the future looked as it used to do over Stony Ridge -all black with a coming storm."

And Sir William Rothenstein:-

"T'was Heaton I knew and loved as a child . . . Most of our Sunday walks led through Heaton - its name evokes a thousand dear memories."

Past, present and future thoughts inspired W. E. Preston to contemplate "Old Clark's House", i.e., Garth House where old John Clark had dwelt not many years previously:-

"The house looks out with its age-dimmed eyes across what were once fields and wooded glades, and seeks its friends of long ago - those sturdy sycamores and oaks under whose shade the sleek cattle had lain or browsed. These old tree-friends have laughed and rocked together many a time in the riot and sweep of the north-west wind. But the eyes will now seek them in vain. If we but stay awhile and rest upon the stone seat within the recessed porch, perhaps some whisper from the past will come to us and say whose feet have worn so deep the hollows in the step before the door. Child, youth and man have come and gone, and one of them now gone we knew quite well - an aged man, grown old with years and care within its walls, who toiled amid the fields; often in our passing we have wished him well, as he has wished his neighbours too.

The first to strike the blow to lay you in the dust, old house, will not be they who love you. Who shall they be?"

The Corporation Highways Department could have told him.

By this time the Heaton tramcar service was nearing its end. For over thirty years the familiar, stately trams had rumbled and clattered up from the city centre to their tranquil terminus in the shadow of the Hall, but all over the city trolleybuses and motorbuses were replacing them. Travelling at speed along Wilmer Road had become a lively experience as they swayed and rocked on the well-worn rails, and the last car departed from the "King's Arms" at 10.51pm on April 7th, 1935.

Next day motorbuses commenced a service from Bradford via Heaton, Duckworth Lane and Lidget Green to Little Horton, although alternate vehicles terminated in Heaton at the junction of Highgate and Leylands Lane where the adverse camber caused them to tilt so ominously that within a few weeks the Heaton terminus was removed to the corner of Garden Lane. The narrow curve of Highgate outside the Hall slowed the buses to a cautious crawl if they chanced to pass at that point, but reassuringly the Corporation stated that this section of highway "was so obviously dangerous that it was no danger at all!"

Four years later, on May 6th, 1939, the Keighley Road tramcars to Saltaire, Bingley and Crossflatts made their final journeys and were superseded next day by smooth, swift, silent trolleybuses. Promises were made that the Heaton buses would be replaced by a trolleybus service through the village to a terminus at Duckworth Lane, but the activities of Adolf Hitler ensured that the plans never reached fruition.

Heaton, like all the districts round about Bradford, was a houseproud place where regular schedules of "housework" ensured that windows and exterior paintwork sparkled,

Heaton Tram Terminus, 1931, with tram 256 about to depart for Bradford Moor. Lock-up shops (centre) on the site of old Frankland Fold adjoin Freddy Smith's 'Bon Marché' sweetshop.

(Photo: Lilywhites)

pavements were "swilled" and doorsteps whitened with "donkey" (scouring) stone. Behind the pristine white net curtains the frequent lack of modern conveniences such as electricity and domestic appliances did not prevent housewives, (aided occasionally by reluctant husbands) from demonstrating the appropriate belief that "cleanliness is next to Godliness."

Each day followed its hallowed pattern. Monday was washday, when wash-tub, hot water, posser, zinc "rubbing-board", blocks of "Fairy" soap and wringing-machine, clothes-line and "flat iron" ruled supreme. On Tuesday the scents of newly-baked bread, cakes and pasties might fill the house, while Friday was a nightmare of cleaning and polishing, "to get all done afore t'weekend." Rugs and mats were shaken, linoleum and furniture polished, cast-iron fireplaces black-leaded and carpet squares, (where they existed) sprinkled with damp tealeaves to "sleck" (slake) the dust which arose when the sweeping-brush was vigorously applied. On Saturday, provisions for the weekend were bought, as shops (other than newsagents' or sweet-shops) did not open on Sundays.

On the seventh day they rested as their Maker intended - except of course for the eagerly anticipated ceremony of "Sunday dinner" with its roast meat, potatoes, vegetables and substantial pudding. The "inner man" had to be well provided for if he were to survive the rigours of the coming week! And as Gerald Brailsford recalled in 1970,

"On Sundays how different a sound vibrated on the upper air - the glorious ringing of the changes in the steeple of Heaton Church. The bells of Heaton rang out to the heavens. More than all things else it was the bells that stirred

166

in you a sense that this was your one full day of the week to yourself, veritably made for man, to do with as you wished - to attend divine worship or not, but certainly to put on your Sunday best and conduct yourself accordingly."

The quarries and the claypits were dying now, their underground treasures exhausted at last. No longer could the glow of kilns at Taffy Mires be glimpsed from Heaton Hill, and the ponderous cranes and brisk steam whistles at Dyson's delph were fading into memory. Alongside Haworth Road the deep, disused excavations remained for forty years before being filled in, and in other locations the presence of spindly, under-nourished plantations or extra-long gardens still betrays the whereabouts of former workings. Today only the Chellow quarry remains as a reminder of the once-flourishing industry. In Heaton village the tiny Highgate delph was filled about 1926 and concealed beneath a row of "lock-up" shops - Crockatts the dry-cleaners, a hairdresser's, a greengrocer's, a "lean-to" extension of Freddy Smith's shop, and, at the rear, the "King's Arms" motor garage.

Other garages were beginning to supply the requirements of Heaton's growing band of motorists - Heaton Garage in the former stables of Emm Royd, a shortlived Rossefield Garage in Dyson Street and Rossefield Motors in the former barn and mistal of Emm Lane (Cross Hill Head) Farm where Arnold Pickles maintained the luxurious chauffeur-driven limousines of the merchant and banking fraternity of Park Drive and Parsons Road.

Meanwhile the predecessors of garages - the smithies with their brawny, begrimed blacksmiths and clanging anvils - had slipped quietly into the past, the last within the township boundaries, at Haworth Road, closing when the Corporation estate was built.

A growing population needed new facilities. A bright new infants' school and adjacent public library in Haworth Road were ceremonially opened in 1931 and 1937 respectively, while at the opposite side of the road the Corporation's former Scar House Reservoir mission church - a corrugated iron structure - was bought through the good offices of Sir Anthony Gadie, who was simultaneously Chairman of the Waterworks Committee and churchwarden of St. Barnabas', the parent church. Instituted as a "conventional district" church dedicated to St. Martin in October, 1934, it served the area between Bingley Road and Stony Ridge, the Bay of Biscay and Sandy Lane areas having passed to Cottingley parish in 1921.

When White Abbey Wesleyan Chapel closed in 1932 following slum clearance in Manningham, it was replaced by a modern Haworth Road Methodist Chapel, the first in Bradford to be opened after the reunification of the various branches of Methodism. Much more spectacular, however, was the First Martyrs' Roman Catholic Church in Heights Lane, an octagonal building with a central altar and church hall beneath, designed by local architect Mr. John Langtry Langton (1899-1982) and opened in 1936.

Other amenities were promised too. At the foot of Heights Lane adjoining Garter Row the old grey cottage with its stream and apple trees was swept away about 1939 and replaced by a hoarding hopefully proclaiming it as the site of a future cinema. An even larger hoarding in Bingley Road declared the Corporation's intention of purchasing Shay Grange and building a new Belle View School on its farmland.

But the creeping shadows of war were darkening the European scene once more, and when a magnificent neo-Classical factory for W. N. Sharpe & Co., printers, arose at the summit of Bingley Road amid trim lawns, clipped yew hedges and an ornamental pond, it did so as a Government-sponsored "shadow factory" capable of producing munitions if war should come.

The sobering possibilities of enemy air raids and evacuation of the civilian population were already under discussion, obliging the headteachers of the local schools to visit the Town Hall at increasingly frequent intervals for the formulation of plans. Recalling the use of poison gas against Allied troops in the previous war, the Government prudently decided to issue gasmasks to civilians as a precaution against a surprise attack. Accordingly, local families queued in the kitchen of Heaton Hall on September 27th-30th, 1938, to receive their masks in a cardboard case, and for the next two years the equipment was kept close to hand.

This not ignoble role was the last which the old Hall performed for the people of Heaton. Plans for its replacement by a large, modern school building had been drawn up several years previously, and in the spring of 1937 the barns had been demolished, some of their well-seasoned timbers being re-used to ornament the exteriors of new "semis" in course of erection in Branksome Crescent. Next, the stately oak, elm, beech and chestnut trees were felled, and the foundation stone of the new school was laid on June 26th. Where the barns and servants' wings had stood, new classrooms arose, one of them being calculated as 53° 48 min. north and 1° 50 min. west of the meridian by the studious occupants who took possession in September, 1938.

As the new structure advanced towards completion and the Corporation began to widen and straighten Highgate, the old mansion was gradually dismantled, some of the black oak wainscot being removed to Bolling Hall museum. "The ancient Hall, stripped of its pristine

Treasures preserved: when Heaton Hall was demolished in 1939, its Adam style fireplaces were carefully removed and one can still be seen in St Bede's School. The remainder were purchased by Mr Edward Fattorini, seen here making an inspection with the Headmaster, the Rev. R. Tindall (left).

(Photo: Telegraph & Argus)

dignity, is still a noble and solid structure", the school magazine commented. "It has had many vicissitudes, . . . passing from a sedate country mansion to bustling, overcrowded school, and soon the traffic of a modern road will rush over its levelled foundation." The last school service in the Hall was held on March 27th, 1939, after which the five Adam-style fireplaces were carefully removed, one for re-installation in the new school library, and the others for acquisition by Mr. Fattorini of Empire Stores, chairman of the school governors. By midsummer all that remained of John Field's edifice – the front portico and entrance where Henry Harris and the "old folk's gathering" had been photographed seventy-one years previously – had finally vanished, and the ruthless, uncaring highway works were completed at a cost of £2,580, sweeping away almost as an afterthought the adjacent Garth House with its long mullions, central housebody open to the roof, and recessed porch. As a slight concession to sentiment, the porch joined the Hall's wainscot at Bolling Hall, where, inscribed "JG, 1681", it can still be seen. Meanwhile the 2nd/6th Duke of Wellington's West Riding Regiment (Territorial Army) had begun using the new school for drilling and recruiting in preparation for the coming conflict.

When German armies stormed into Poland on September 1st, 1939, the efficiency of the past year's preparations was amply demonstrated: before midday most of Heaton's schoolchildren had been evacuated to Embsay, Hebden Bridge and other areas which were considered safe from anticipated aerial attacks. Unlike the soldiers, however, most returned home by Christmas, as no hostile events occurred during the "phoney war" prior to the Dunkirk evacuation.

The blackout returned, with volunteer air-raid wardens in every street to ensure that no chinks of light escaped through the heavily-curtained windows. Street lamps were extinguished, vehicle headlamps were reduced to a masked beam and white paint was liberally applied to all obstructions – walls, lamp posts and pavement edges. Except when the moon was up, the ensuing darkness was more intense than anything which had been experienced since the introduction of street lighting seventy years previously.

Fuel rationing was immediately imposed. Private motoring was restricted to essential users, and the Haworth Road and Heaton bus services were curtailed, but the Keighley Road trolleybuses, energised by Bradford electricity and Yorkshire coal, were scarcely affected. Rationing of food returned also, some of it destined to last thirteen years, with 2oz. of butter per person and similar amounts of bacon, cheese and meat. Even tea was restricted, but bread supplies escaped until hostilities ceased, when "bread units" or coupons had to be issued while flour was being diverted to the starving Continent. Inferior substitutes such as coke and coal dust "briquettes" could be bought to supplement the meagre coal allowance for domestic fires, but the heat thus generated was not impressive.

Local men responded eagerly to Sir Anthony Eden's radio appeal for "Local Defence Volunteers" or "Home Guards" to defend their neighbourhoods in the face of imminent invasion threats. Charles King (the author's father and a former Lewis gunner in the 6th Battalion of the West Yorkshire Regiment, Territorial Army), recalled that,

> "We had to meet at Lilycroft School, and . . . were sorted out into platoons.
> You had to be able to march two or three miles, if I remember rightly, and also
> know how to use a rifle. I was placed in the Frizinghall platoon because I lived
> near (actually at Heaton Syke). While the Heaton platoon marched (if that was
> the correct term!) up to the 'Hare and Hounds' to 'wet their whistles', we –
> the Frizinghall platoon – marched down to Frizinghall and were told to turn

up next evening.

We duly assembled at the Grammar School. We had one rifle, a Canadian Ross .303 which had no sling, so we had to use a piece of string. Our patrol area consisted of Lister Park, the Reservoir and Heaton Hill where we had to watch for (enemy) parachutists dropping, but as we had no ammunition, we were told to keep them there until someone sped down to the Grammar School for ammo. We never gave a thought to what would have happened if they had dropped; luckily they never did. We also roamed through Heaton Woods and down to the "Britannia" (in Valley Road) for a "quick one", then back to our headquarters at the Grammar School lodge for a two-hour rest. These patrols worked on different nights, so that you did one area each night."

Soon cases of ex First World War U.S. P17 rifles were received at the local armoury in St.Bede's school, also two Browning .300 belt-fed machine-guns.

"When John Birkett and I went into Lister Park with the Ross rifle . . . the first persons to see us with it were two special constables who promptly asked us what we were doing with it in a public place. We had been warned not to tell anyone about the whole thing, but fortunately the park ranger, an ex-Coldstream guardsman, knew of us and came to our assistance.

That was the spirit of those exciting times."

The other platoon members were Arnold Pickles (garage proprietor), Ted Hudson (plumber), Fred King (landlord of the "Fountain Inn") and Jim Tebb the yeast-man. The Heaton village platoon was based on St. Bede's School.

At Chellow the Home Guard imaginatively took over the newly-built Chellow Grange Hotel, but as the beer-pumps had unfortunately not yet been installed, they had to devote their evenings to the performance of military drill and tactics in the adjacent reservoir grounds, from whence the fierce commands and colourful expletives of their instructor, Mr. Lumb (the waterworks foreman) were clearly audible at Chellow Heights Farm, to the amusement of the Gawthorpe family.

Sharpes' "shadow factory" in Bingley Road had been commandeered by G. E. C. Ltd. for the manufacture of electrical components for the "war effort", and also by the fourth local platoon - Lieut. A. B. Skelly (insurance adviser), John Pickles (chauffeur), Tom Gawthorpe (milkman), Fred Whitaker, Eric Boyden and Mr. Craven.

Recalling that tense and fiercely-loyal moment of history, Joycelyne Dickinson wrote,

"Then it was that the stars glowed more brightly in the blackout, and Christmas Eve was set in danger and peril. Some were no longer with us; others never returned. Others who survived bear scars to remind them of those dread yet splendid years. One would come out from the midnight service, often in uniform, to see the miracle of the stars over the hills and be swept by the winds which forever play around Heaton Church . . . To me it has been a fortress, in times of rejoicing and sorrow, of innocence and of sin, for those must all come to us, and not one can escape.

I have worshipped in many churches more beautiful and more impressive . . . but I have not found one which remains more closely in my heart. The hill has preserved its mystery and the church its holiness."

All over the country the church belfries had fallen silent, as their bells were needed to warn of actual invasion, and the unmusical mill hooters were banished - mercifully never to return - in case they were mistaken for air-raid warning sirens. The latter were first heard in Heaton in 1940, but initially they were false alarms, as the enemy aircraft droning overhead were believed to be more interested in far-off Liverpool with its vital ports than the areas which lay beneath their flight path.

For several nights, however, the sirens warned of real peril. Bombs on the city centre turned the night sky red, and at 10.15 pm. on August 22nd, 1940, the Home Guard platoon at their Bingley Road look-out post instinctively ducked as a hail of bombs whistled overhead. Heatonians huddling in air raid shelters or whatever part of the house they deemed the safest heard the shrill descent of the salvo followed by a loud explosion which shook houses from Haworth Road to Heaton Syke.

As the newspapers reported guardedly,

"Shortly after the noise of a plane was heard over a North-Eastern town and searchlights came into action in an attempt to spot it, residents over a wide area heard the sound of falling bombs."

Heaton's bombs fell in a line into the Red Beck, uprooting trees, hurling mud high into the air, creating 15'0" craters and disrupting the raptures of courting couples in the wood - one of the young ladies had to be carried, swooning, to nearby "Woodbrow" for succour and safety.

At Heaton Royds Mr. W. H. Gudgeon, market-gardener, heard the explosion. The paraffin lamp swayed and the cottage shook with the force of the blast, but not a single window in his greenhouses was broken. As he and his wife crouched against the stout old walls they concluded that "if that's the best the Germans can do, we can't grumble round here!"

Their neighbour Mr. Moses Smith, 78, did not hear the aircraft, but when the shockwaves blew his door open, he thought the house had been struck. As a precaution against possible unexploded bombs, the residents of the Royds were evacuated to spend the night with friends or relations.

Empty properties soon found new uses. Troops were allotted billets at "Tinakori", Belvoir Terrace and elsewhere, while their Belgian counterparts occupied no.2, Randall Place. Army lorries were parked rank upon rank in Wilmer Road, with motor-cycle despatch riders passing urgently to and fro. In Park Drive the A.T.S. settled at no.1, the Army Dental Centre at no.7 and the Inland Revenue at no.34, while "Greystones" in Parsons Road became the headquarters of the Wool Control under Sir Harry Shackleton.

Early in 1944 R.A.F. aeroplanes began unheralded rooftop-level flights over Heaton (and no doubt elsewhere!), their identification marks clearly visible to delighted boys and deafened adults as they rocketed over the chimney pots. It was realised many years later that the daring pilots had been practising to fly beneath enemy radar levels after D-Day. When the long-awaited day dawned at last, on June 6th, church bells rang once more and street lighting made a tentative reappearance, interrupted for a brief moment when one or two V1 "flying bombs" passed over Bradford Dale. When the much deadlier V2 assaults on London began, large numbers of Londoners were evacuated northwards, some being billeted in Park Drive. Innocently unaccustomed to strange accents, Heaton people assumed at first that the evacuees suffered from defective adenoids, so impenetrable was their speech to Yorkshire ears!

The return of peace in 1945 brought lighted windows, November bonfires, late buses and a return to normal life for Heaton men and women who had served in the armed

Heaton Syke in snow, 14 February 1960. The cottages on the left, built about 1856 by Thomas Thompson Hudson and William Sugden, were replaced in 1985 by the Fountain Inn car park. Heaton Road (foreground) was previously known as Cross Hill or Syke Hill.

(Copyright: author)

Snow had fallen in Heaton Road and St Bede's school playing fields (formerly Heaton Hall park) when this photograph was taken on 14 February 1960. A gas street lamp, cottages in Garden Terrace and the roofs of the buildings in Syke Road are seen on the right.

(Copyright: author)

Heaton Syke in snow, 14 February 1960. The 'Fountain Inn' and adjoining cottages in Syke Road were built by William Sugden in 1856.

(Copyright: author)

Emm Lane (formerly Cross Hill Head) Farm, seen in 1958, shortly before demolition and replacement by a motor garage. Emm Lane (right) passed behind the property, which had been converted in 1926 into two cottages and a motor repair workshop. *(Copyright: author)*

forces, the Land Army, munitions factories and other forms of war work. As soon as G.E.C. vacated Sharpes' factory the printing of high quality "Classic" greeting cards resumed. However, there was little relief from shortages for several years, and the unusually long and bitter winter of 1947 - with deep snow, prolonged frost and packed ice on the roads - tested fuel supplies to the limit, compelling many local families to resort to the cinemas as a means of conserving the last bucketful of coal.

However, by 1951 the worst was over; petrol rationing for adults and sweet coupons for children were finally abolished in 1953, when the Coronation of Queen Elizabeth II was watched on television sets (black and white) which had first appeared in Heaton homes two years earlier. The new form of entertainment drastically reduced evening excursions, and queues at the cinemas - "Elite", "Oriental", "Marlborough", "Theatre Royal", "New Victoria" and "Ritz" quietly passed away. Other old friends were passing from the scene also. The reverend vicar of St. Barnabas, Canon R. Whincup, M.C., M.A., died in 1944, and the highly esteemed headmasters of St. Barnabas and St.Bede's schools - Mr. Harold Coward and Father Tindall - took their leave.

House building resumed after having been halted in 1940. At Haworth Road the Brantwood estate crept ever-closer to Miles Rough with its reputedly bottomless pool, and on the remaining pastures of Parkside Farm, Heaton Park Drive and Branksome Crescent were completed at last, eliminating the final traces of Daddy White's Snicket and the footpath from Heaton Road to Toller Lane along the old township boundary. But official attitudes were changing; the new Town and Country Planning Act discouraged urban

Paradise and Town End 1958, when street lighting was provided by gas, traffic was light and the Baptist Players were preparing to present 'The Honey Pot' in the Sunday school.

(Copyright: author)

sprawl: "green belts" were to separate individual localities and thus preserve the identities of towns, villages and suburbs. So when Proctor Brothers applied for renewal of planning permission to transform Shay Grange into a large housing estate (the Belle Vue school scheme having been abandoned) they received a refusal and £104,500 compensation.

Heaton's "highways and byways" took on a new and lurid hue when orange-coloured sodium-vapour street lighting superseded the older forms between 1958 and 1962. Keighley Road bade a reluctant farewell to its quiet trolleybus service in 1963, and the railway, too, was in decline; the booking-office on the bridge in Frizinghall Road was demolished in November, 1956, and the station itself closed in 1965, its passengers having forsaken its empty waiting-rooms and echoing platforms for the more frequent buses.

St. Martin's Church, having outgrown the old "tin hut" with its harmonium and stifling summer temperatures, was rehoused in a dignified modern building whose dedication in October, 1955, was performed by the Assistant Bishop of Bradford. Dr. David Coggan was the first Bishop of Bradford to take up residence at "Bishopscroft" (formerly "Fieldhead" and originally built by Frederick Illingworth as the last of his three houses named "Heather Bank") when he assumed office in 1956, and after becoming Archbishop of York he

St Barnabas' Church floodlit for its centenary in October 1964.

returned to Heaton in October, 1964, for the centenary of St. Barnabas' Church. The ceremony was also attended by Michael, 6th Earl of Rosse (1906-1979) and the Countess of Rosse (1902-1992), whose Heaton estates had all passed into other hands by 1924. As distinguished as his forebears, Lord Rosse had served as a captain in the Irish Guards throughout the war and had been widely honoured - M.R.I.A., F.S.A., F.R.A.S., F.R.S.A, Vice-Chancellor of Dublin University, Chairman of the Georgian Group and the National Trust and President of Bradford Civic Society. By an earlier marriage Lady Rosse - a highly-talented connoisseur and a celebrated Society beauty in the 1920s - was the mother of Lord Snowdon, who married H.R.H. Princess Margaret in 1960.

In 1962 Heaton Baptist Church celebrated the centenary of its revival as a separate congregation, but at Frizinghall the Methodists, despite having the only place of worship in the locality, had to close their doors and demolish the church in December, 1960.

Full employment and growing affluence led to increased home comforts such as fitted carpets, refrigerators and constant hot water, though the last few outposts of domestic gas lighting and outside toilets lingered on until the end of the 1970s. Even remote Heaton Royds now enjoyed electricity and running water, although at Shay Grange Farm Ted Greenwood resolutely spurned the advance of water mains, preferring to the last the feeble flow from his old hydraulic ram in Butts Dyke. His death in 1968 broke the last and strongest link with the rural Heaton of "pleeaws" (ploughs), pewits and haycarts.

The seemingly inexhaustible supply of Heaton "characters" still continued to delight the locals. Mrs. Delia Greenwood (1872-1954) was a placid, untroubled old lady who kept her complexion clear by throwing a handful of common soda into her bathwater and lifting her backdoor from its hinges for maximum ventilation in hot weather. Living at Eden, she prescribed regular visits to Heaton Hill as a remedy for all ailments. "Gerrup on t'Hill end," she advised. "It's mah salvation!" Her advice was always philosophical. When told of an erring husband's misdeeds she observed sagely that, "If they're leet gi'en, ther's nowt yer can do wi' em!" (i.e., if they are of loose morals, you can do nothing with them).

Herbert Tetley (1897-1972) would have preferred to be a gentleman farmer, and was quite content to leave hard work to the farm hands and his aged father, Tom Tetley. Inevitably on his father's death in 1926 Ashwell Farm passed to his cousin Alonza Tetley, and he was "cut off with a (proverbial) shilling" (actually £10) which he invested in a handcart for his new career as a milkman. A small, cheerful, bandylegged individual, he was barred from each of the local hostelries in rotation. His last recorded exploit occurred in old age, when, supported by a walking stick, he gallantly insisted on escorting an even lamer (and reluctant) lady across Emm Lane. Tripped by the walking stick, both fell in a tangled heap in the middle of the road.

Heaton Post Office in Highgate was originally presided over by Charles George (1847-

1900) whose daughter Nellie married Amos Beanland in 1905. The thriving postal and greengrocery business which once supported a car, a lorry and a team of errand boys dwindled away in later years, but until his death in 1964, Amos, a gruff but ever-popular character, continued to battle valiantly with Post Office "red tape", completing his book-keeping late at night with the aid of Victorian gaslighting in unchanging surroundings which would have delighted Betjeman and Priestley.

Edwin Baines, tenant of the nearby newsagent's shop (late Freddy Smith) from 1932, was considered as living proof that "Englishmen take their pleasures sadly", indeed, a curate of St. Barnabas' was prepared to offer £1 to anyone who had seen "Eddie" smile. The author is still waiting for payment. A shy, patient man, Mr. Baines was faithful to his customers, and even in the bleakest years of wartime shortages he ensured, like Amos, that his regulars received a full share of their entitlements.

Mr Edwin ('Eddie') Baines photographed in 1977 at the newsagent's shop which he had occupied since 1932.
(Copyright: author)

It could be said that with the death of Bob Nellist in 1972 the age of "characters" had finally passed away. A jobbing gardener, Bob's distinctive garb of country clothing, brown bowler hat, sidewhiskers and luxuriant moustache gave no hint of his previous career as a Coldstream Guardsman. His love of horses ensured that he was always in demand at fetes, and he met his death in his horsedrawn trap when it collided with a car at Sandy Lane. The widespread regret which followed his hugely-attended funeral ensured his immortality: his portrait can be seen in the inn sign at the "Delvers" - his favourite "local."

Discoveries of carved stone heads in the Bradford area caused a flurry of speculation in the 1960s. One summer day in 1965 two schoolgirls found a 10-inch head in a field adjoining Heaton Woods, and an expert from the School of Scottish Studies concluded that it could be of Celtic origin. More cautiously, local archaeologists pointed out that similar heads in the Celtic style had in fact been carved as recently as ten years previously, and as the field at Heaton lay on the site of old quarry workings, pre-Victorian origins were unlikely.

In 1960 "Tinakori" in Wilmer Road was converted into a private school for adolescent pupils under the title of "Tinakori Towers," closing unexpectedly in 1985 but reopening successfully two years later in new ownership under the name of Shaw House School. Also during the 1960s Bradford Corporation transferred its Belle Vue schools from their old premises in Manningham to new buildings at Thorn Lane, Heaton. Highly esteemed for their educational excellence, the schools were eagerly sought after by generations of Bradford schoolchildren.

A new St. Barnabas' Infant and Junior School was formally opened on June 11th, 1966, at a cost of £70,000 to accommodate 280 children, and the old premises in Ashwell Road were demolished a year later. At Frizinghall the auction of nine acres of land in September, 1961, brought about the demolition of old Firth Carr farmhouse and the construction of dozens of new dwellings on a precipitous hillside, adjacent to Wellfield House and Aireville Avenue.

Cows were last seen in Heaton village in the summer of 1962 when a herd was observed ambling from a temporary pasture alongside the Cat Steps, thence by way of Highgate and Heaton Road to the Bradford markets. Happily, "beef cattle" and "milkers" can still be seen contentedly grazing at "Six Days Only" and Chellow Heights.

When this scene was photographed on 28 April 1957, Sandy Lane crossroads were so tranquil that the Bradford Corporation bus was able to pick up passengers at the junction without impeding traffic. The impressive Bethel Baptist Chapel was built in 1884.

(Copyright: author)

Chapter 21   A New Identity

On December 6th, 1968, the local press announced a new plan for the building of 400 houses on the Shay Grange farmland between Heaton Woods and Bingley Road. Warmly supported by the Corporation who foresaw a refund of the compensation paid by them to the owners, Messrs. Proctors, some years previously, as well as valuable rate income from the affluent residents of the proposed "executive" dwellings, the project entailed the suburbanisation of Heaton's chief remaining rural area.

Consternation in Heaton was widespread though unvoiced, but when the author ventured to test local feeling by reconvening the old Court Baron in May, 1969, — the first manor court to be held since the days of Joshua Field - anxious Heatonians crowded the large meeting room of the Baptist chapel. A petition and public inquiry ensued and on the rejection of the planning application by a Government Inspector, a celebratory supper was held at the new St. Barnabas' Village Hall which had arisen on the site of the old school building in 1969, following the demolition of the previous St. Barnabas' Hall in Rossefield Road.

Further sessions of the Court were held to cement the happily-rediscovered local loyalties and enthusiasm; the old Heaton Commons Inclosure Award was rescued from Babylonian exile in a Leeds library and ceremonially handed over to the Bradford Libraries in 1971, and, even more enjoyably, the ancient ceremony of "beating the bounds" was re-enacted in 1975/1976 and subsequent years. A special sitting of the Court was convened in

1 May 1969. John Stanley King, the Lord of the Manor, addresses the newly reconvened Manor Court on the heated topic of housing development at Shay Grange. Also seen (bottom left) are Mr Arnold Pickles (garage proprietor and poet) and Mrs Enid Turner, head teacher of St Barnabas' School.   *(Copyright: Telegraph & Argus)*

September, 1983, in honour of the visit of the Rt. Honble. Brendan Wilmer Parsons, 7th Earl of Rosse.

Renewed local patriotism led in 1971 to the formation of the Heaton Township Association whose ambitions to "conserve, protect and promote the amenities, atmosphere and welfare of the Township" under the inspired and energetic guidance of the late Mr. Hans Renold evoked widespread support. The long-term survival and renewal of the highly-prized local woodlands was ensured by the creation of a Heaton Woods Trust which, ably led by Messrs. A. Hepworth, D. A. Emmott, W. N. Shaw and Renold and with Lord Rosse as president not only purchased the forty acres of farmland between Ashwell Lane and the Cat Steps but also encouraged Bradford Council to improve the publicly-owned woods.

The Baptists at Heaton and Sandy Lane decided to face the challenge of changing times by replacing their hallowed but outdated Victorian chapels with buildings more attuned to modern needs. At Heaton the ground floor of the manse was transformed into a small but beautiful worship centre with plaques, stained glass and a small organ from the old chapel, whilst at Sandy Lane the religious revival in the new, stone-built chapel which arose in the midst of its historic graveyard was so compelling that within a few years the premises had to be considerably enlarged.

Mr Leonard Atkinson, shoe repairer, outside his shop at 46A, Highgate in 1974. Formerly a private residence, the premises now constitute the bar and waiting area of Clark's Restaurant, and Mr Atkinson's tools are preserved at Bradford Industrial Museum. *(Copyright: author)*

When the City and County Borough of Bradford was absorbed into a new, larger Metropolitan City on April 1st, 1974, Heaton no longer lay on the outermost boundaries, a factor which could have frustrated local hopes of a formal Green Belt. Very properly, however, the Green Belt proposed by the new local authority in 1993 embraced not only the woodlands and the valued "beauty spots" but also Heaton Reservoir grounds where the handsome sheet of water had recently been replaced by a subterranean chamber covered by new parkland through which the combined waters of the Heaton Syke and Shaw Syke were encouraged to tumble and cascade on their way to the Bradford Beck and the far-off North Sea.

As the 20th Century entered its last quarter, old certainties imperceptibly began to dissolve. New ways of thought aroused by the "Affluent Age" of the 1960s took full advantage of wider opportunities - foreign travel, motor cars, colour-television, music-playing apparatus, automatic washing machines, refrigerators, carpeted kitchens and bathrooms, double-glazed windows and central heating. Cinemas and allotment gardens had long since ceased to appeal.

The population, too, was less static. The new Bradford University with its Management

St Bede's School library was the venue for the Manor Court in 1983, when the 7th Earl of Rosse (left) and the Lord of the Manor (author) were photographed in front of one of the fireplaces from Heaton Hall.

(Copyright: Telegraph & Argus)

Centre at the old United Independent College in Emm Lane and Heaton Mount in Keighley Road brought in students as temporary dwellers, and lecturers as permanent residents. Some appreciated their new surroundings and joined in community affairs; others merely used the district as a base and rode roughshod over local pronunciations. "Toller (Lane)" began to rhyme with "collar" instead of "roller" - a far cry from the old-time "Towler" which partly rhymed with "Bowling". Some of the larger Victorian dwellings were divided into flats, and single people began to occupy cottages and "back-to-backs" which had once given shelter to large families. Property clearance at Quarry Street, Paddock, Lane side, Garter Row, Mount Pleasant and at each side of the "Fountain Inn" removed quaint dwellings as well as unfit ones, and much sought-after "sheltered accommodation" replaced a few of them.

Until the same period coloured people were almost unknown in Heaton, though a half-caste family from Manningham had attended St. Barnabas' School in the early 1940s, and once or twice a year a white-silk-turbanned gentleman had courteously hawked goods from door to door, arousing interest and curiosity as he did so. From about 1952 coloured immigrants had been attracted to Bradford by the chronic shortage of labour in its booming industries, but it was not until about 1963 that any were seen in Heaton streets. An Indian family was living in Leylands Lane by the end of the decade

Changes in property values produced startling results. Old stone-built cottages airily dismissed as "damp old holes" by those who knew them best, and valued at less than £300 in 1961, changed hands at £50,000 ten years later, albeit modernised and centrally-heated. In their new guise they attracted buyers who would otherwise have occupied more spacious but more heavily-rated modern houses.

Encouragingly, Frizinghall Station reopened in 1987 to the strains of a Jazz Band; in 1991 a Haworth Road Residents' Association was formed, and public-spirited Daniel

Sutcliffe, aged 14, set up a Brantwood Drive Neighbourhood Watch. A year later traffic lights at Sandy Lane crossroads were installed to cope with increased traffic levels. At midnight on December 31st, 1999, the new Millenium was greeted with a bonfire on Heaton Hill organised by Heaton and Manningham Council of Churches.

In recent years industrial decline, population changes, altered social values and the insistent demands of the motor car have affected Heaton as much as other parts of the city, and longstanding residents are heard to declare that "things are not what they used to be." Previous generations have uttered similar sentiments.

Looking to the unknown future we can only echo the words of the Venerable Bede as he closed his history of England more than 1,250 years ago:-

"What will be the end thereof no one can tell."

However, if the local ties so happily revived in 1969 are firmly maintained by "Heaton fowk" in coming years, the old township may yet remain a special place in which people are proud and happy to dwell. May it be so - and may they always "live as long as they like!"

THE HOME GUARD PLATOON BASED AT SHARPE'S FACTORY
Left to Right, Back Row:- no.3, Sharpes', groundsman; no.4,Mr John Gowthorpe, milkman and master of ceremonies at social functions; no.6, Mr Craven, the platoon commander,one of whose sons was killed by a hand-grenade in Bradford Moor Park: no.8, Mr Arthur Ord; no,9, Mr Fred Whitaker ; no. 10, Mr Boyden, Rossefield Road. *Front Row:-* no. 2, Mr A Barclay Skelly, insurance broker ; no.3, Mr Robinson, Heaton Park Drive ; no.4, Mr John Keighley, Sharpes' manager.
(Courtesy Mr Colin Whitaker.)

Appendix 1

HEATON SPEECH

The particular brand of Yorkshire speech formerly used in Heaton was indistinguishable from similar "talk" heard in adjoining townships within a radius of two or three miles, but as the vocabulary has almost passed out of use, an affectionate backward glance at some of the old words, pronunciations and phrases may not be out of place.

Accorn	(acorn)	from the Anglo-Saxon - ac, an oak
Agate	active	(pun - Ah'll get agate and mak a door!)
Ah were (wor)		I was
All collar-work		uphill
All fall o'foot		downhill
Bahn	(i.e., bound)	"Ah'm bahn 'ooam" (I'm going home) or "She's bahn dahn tahn" (She's going down to town)
Black as t'fireback		as black as the chimney
Brazzen	(i.e., brazen)	bold as brass, shameless (brazzen-faced)
Call (rhymes with 'pal')		literally "to pay a social call on" but actually denoting gossiping.
Call'oil		a talking-shop
Causeway		"Pavement" or "footway"
Chumping	collecting wood for "Plot" (i.e., the Guy Fawkes Plot bonfire on November 5th.)	
Claht	cloth	Clahtead - cloth-head (term of abuse)
Clem	to be hungry	(Ah'm fair clemmed; You'll noan clem)
Court Baron	the court of a baron, i.e., a free man	
Court Leet	the public court (Leet may be derived from Anglo-Saxon "leod" and German "leute", i.e., people)	
Dee	die	
Eeacre	acre	
'Eead	head	(c.f. Crossilleead - Cross Hill Head)
Fettle	to clean	(Fettle dahn - spring clean the house)
Flay	to frighten	Flaysome - frightening.
Frame	to organise oneself	(Frame thissen - pull yourself together!)"Frame" was used by the poet John Milton
Gawmless	unheeding	
Gerragate	(literally, get a-gate)	start moving; begin
Grieved	deeply disappointed	
Gurt	great, big	
Hark at, listen at		listen to
He talks as he warms		he speaks without thinking
Laike	play (as children);	also play, i.e., be on short-time work.
Lathered	"hot and bothered",	in a lather.
Leet	light	"leet gi'en" = fickle, immoral

Lig	(lay or lie down)	"Ah'm bahn to lig me dahn", "bobbin-ligger" and "Lig plenty watter on."
Madling	insane person	
Mak (or mek)		make
Master	traditionally pronounced with a short "a"	
Me	(=myself)	Ah've washed me.
Mun	must	
Nawp	knock or rap	
Nay	no, surely not?	
Nooan	(literally "none");	not
'Oil	hole or place	
Owt seems 'em		anything goes, as far as they are concerned.
Pawse	kick	
Pined	hungry	
Plaster	traditionally pronounced with a short "a"	
Plew	(or plyew)	plough

Plot, Plot Toffee (see Chumping)

Posnet	a saucepan	
Sackless	aimless	
Sam 'er 'em up an' 'ug 'em 'er		pick them up for her and carry them for her
Sen	self	(missen, thissen, herssen, hissen, theirsens)
Sitha	(literally "see thou"!)	look here!
Starved	cold	or hungry (or both!)
Stee	ladder	(Ah'm bahn for a stee)
Swill	wash; also slops for pigs	
Tab Rug	hearthrug made from odd "tabs" or selected tabs or cuttings of cloth	
Tak, tek	take	("tak 'od" = take hold)
Tan	beat, thrash	(Ah'll tan thi backside!)
Tewit	a pewit	
Tha frames lahke a pot-cat		you are disorganised
Them	they, those	e.g., them's t'biggest = those are the biggest, or them's 'em = those are they.
Thible (rhymed with "Bible")		a wooden spoon
Think on!		remember; bethink oneself.
Too ill ter rake t'fireback		unworthy even to rake the cinders in the fireplace.
Wahr	worse	(yer'd be wahr if yo' ailed owt!)
Wahr an' wusser		worse and worse.
Wahr nor nivver		worse than ever.
Wakken	wake, awake	("Liggin i'bed wakkened")
Wesh	wash	
While	until	(Ah'll wait while 'e cums")
Yond	yonder, or the person over there.	

"Calling", i.e., conversation between neighbours, especially (it must be said) the womenfolk, often produced ritual exclamations of polite surprise: "Eeh! Ay? Aw!" which could be translated as, "What a surprise! Is that so? Well, I never!"

A well-remembered dialogue took place at St.Barnabas' school some 60 years ago. "Alfred", said the teacher to the pupil whose diction was easily the worst in the class. "Say after me: 'A bit of better butter.'" Alfred did. "A bi' o' be'er bu'er!" he replied, obligingly, to the ecstatic mirth of his classmates.

SAYINGS, SUPERSTITIONS (OR WISE PRECAUTIONS?)
Do not sing or whistle Christmas carols out of season, otherwise bad luck will ensue.
Never consume food in the toilet, as it may feed the Devil!
During thunder and lightning, open the outer door and put knives and scissors away.
"Time to go to bed — we've had all we can get out of this day!"
"If I were in bed now, I wouldn't get up for a good dinner!"

Appendix 2 — The Origin of Heaton Place Names

KEY TO ABBREVIATIONS

ME	Middle English
OE	Old English
OFr	Old French
ON	Old Norse
ONb	Old Northumbrian

Place	Location	Derivation
Allans (or Annams)	Leylands	Alan's field, alongside Garden Lane
Ashwell	Heaton	OE Aesc, wella - the well by the (holy) ash tree
Ashwell Road/Lane	Heaton	Road/lane from Emm Lane past the Ash Well
Back Fold/Lane	Heaton	At the back of the village
Bairstow Street	Sandy Lane	Named by Bairstow Mortimer, farmer
Bay of Biscay	Chellow	Inspired by proverbial weather encountered on its exposed site.
Bents	Chellow	OE beonet, bentgrass
Birks	Chellow	ON birki, a birch tree
Bottom o't' Hill	Heaton	Junction of Highgate and Leylands Avenue
Boxer Lane	Chellow	Probably associated with illicit prize-fights
Brecks (Brecks)		OE brecc, a thicket, or ON brekka, a slope
Brick Kiln Field	Frizinghall	
Broom Close	Toller Lane	An enclosure where broom grows
Brow, The	Heaton	Summit of Highgate
Burnley		OE brunn, brown, and OE leah, a meadow
Buxton Lane	Frizinghall	Formerly Buckstones or Buckstalls, OE bucc, stan or stall - the stone or place of bucks
Carr Syke	Frizinghall	ON kjarr, a marsh; ON sik, a stream
Chellow Dene	Chellow	OE denu, a valley
Chellow Slack	Chellow	ON slakki, a hollow
Chellow Stile	Chellow	OE stigel, a stile
Cliffe, The	Heaton	OE cloh, a ravine, i.e. Cliffe Wood
Cliffe Gate	Heaton	Extension of Highgate from Town End to the woods
Close	(various)	OFr clos, an inclosure from the common
Cocked Hat	Chellow	Field shaped like a cocked hat
Cold Hill	Heaton	OE cald or ON kaldr, cold and exposed (the hillside west of Heaton 'town')
Cottingley Road	Sandy Lane	Modern name for Small Tail Road

Cross Hill	Heaton	ON cross, usually translated as 'lying athwart or across', i.e. Heaton Road between Heaton Syke and Heaton 'town'
Daisy Hill Lane	Chellow	Obsolete name for Heights Lane within Heaton township
Dead Lane	Chellow	OE dead – modern Stoney Ridge Avenue i.e. no longer in use
Dean Hill	Chellow	OE denu, a valley, i.e. Chellow Dene
Dean Lands	Chellow	OE land, a strip of land in the common field
Dean Orchard	Chellow	OE orceard
Delf	(various)	OE delf
Dodgroyd	Toller Lane	Familiar form of Roger, i.e. Roger's clearing
Dole	(various)	OE dal, a share or deal
Duck Sike	Stony Ridge/Shay	OE duce, ON sik, a small stream frequented by ducks
Dunsell Hill	Frizinghall	Possibly OE dune, ON skali, a hillock at the foot of the slope surmounted by huts
Emm Lane	Heaton	OE elm, an elm tree
Emm Law	Heaton	OE elm, hlaw, the hill on which elms grow
Esp Field	Heaton Royds	OE aespe, a field in which aspen trees grow, or a snake-infested field
Firth Carr	Frizinghall	Firth, a family name, and ON kjarr, a marsh
Firth Road	Heaton Syke	Named after the Firths of Heaton Syke
Footgate Close	Toller Lane	ON fotr, gata, a footpath (Daddy White's snicket)
Frankland Fold	Heaton	OE fald, an enclosure owned by the Frankland family
Frizingley Steel	Park Drive	OE stigel, a stile, i.e. the snicket from Park Drive to Frizinghall
Garden Street	Heaton	Street near Heaton Hill alongside (former) allotments
Garden Terrace	Heaton Syke	Post 1781 cottages alongside allotment gardens
Garth	(various)	ON garthr, a yard. Also a surname
Green, High and Low	Heaton Grove	OE grene, a grassy spot or village green
Harry Royds	Frizinghall	Harry's clearing
Heights	Moorside	OE hehthu, the high place
Highgate	Heaton	Formerly Town Lane (Street, Gate)
Hob Acres	Ashwell	ME hob, a hobgoblin
Hollin Field	Heights Lane	OE holegn, feld, a field with holly trees
Holt	Cross Hill	OE holt, a wood or thicket
Ings	(various)	ON eng, a meadow
Jer Lane	Heaton	Possibly Churl (OE ceorl), a peasant
Keighley Road	Frizinghall	Formerly New Road or Shipley Road

Kirkstall Hole	North Park Road	ON kirkja, a church; OE stigel, a stile; and OE/ON hol, a hollow
Lambert Fold	Heaton	Enclosure owned by the Lambert family
Lane Bottom	Heaton	Bottom of Haworth Lane (i.e. Road)
Lane Side	Frizinghall	Cottages in Frizinghall Road adjoining the railway station
Leylands	Heaton	OE laege land - fallow land
Low Fold	Heaton	Later called Stocks Yard and currently Hammond Square
Low Lane	Frizinghall	The Bradford-Otley Road, now known as Frizinghall Road
Marriners' Drive	Frizinghall	Named after the Marriners, heirs to the Listers of Frizinghall
Maylands	Park Drive	Formerly Mare Lands, the strip of land in the common field grazed by mares (or OE mare, a spectre)
Mekyll Heaton		Listed in 'Placenames of the West Riding', Oxford, 1961: Whitley - Beaumont Deeds, Huddersfield Archives - mistaken translation of Mekyll Horton (Great Horton)
Milford Place	Heaton Road	Probably mill-ford - the watersplash in Heaton Road near Lister's Mill
Mill Lane	Frizinghall	Connected Frizinghall Road and Gazeby Lane
Moorside	Daisy Hill	At the side of Heaton and Manningham Moors
Moss Croft	Frizinghall	Also callled Mosscrop, i.e. Firth Carr
New Road	Frizinghall	Keighley Road
New Row	Frizinghall	
Nog Lane	Heaton	Lane to the Nog - OE cnocc, a hilltop
Noon Nick	Stony Ridge	Cleft through which the sun shines at noon
North Sides woods	Heaton	Pastures between Back Lane and the
Paddock	Frizinghall	ME pearroc, an enclosure
Parsons Road	Heaton	A punning name relating to the Parsons family and the residence of the vicar
Pease Close		Enclosure in which peas are grown
Pewit Well	Bingley Road	Well near which pewits nest
Pighills	Park Drive	ME pightel, a small enclosure
Pit Lane	Heaton Royds	Now called Heaton Royds Lane
Pudding Pie Close	Park Drive	Pit Ing, a small enclosure frequented by magpies
Pyke (Pyche) Nook	Chellow	Small field shaped like a pike-head
Randall Place	Heaton	Randal, an ancestral name of the Field family

Ross (Rost) Rows	Heaton	Probably ON hross, rows – strips of land grazed by horses
Rossefield Road (etc.)	Heaton	Named after the Rosse and Field families; partly replaced the original Back Lane
Rough, The	Chellow	Rough, uncultivatable land later named after (James) Naylor and Miles (Gawthorpe)
Royds	–	OE rod, a clearing
Roydscliffe	Heaton	OE rodu, cloh, a ravine near the woodland clearing – the 'New Wood'
Sandy Lane	(i.e. the highway)	Obsolete name for Haworth Road from Bay of Biscay to Cottingley Road.
School Croft	Chellow, Frizinghall	Probably ON skali, OE croft, a small enclosure on which huts (shielings) stand
Searil	Heaton Royds	Possibly the sere (dry) hill
Shay	–	OE sceaga, a copse
Six Days Only	Heaton Royds	
Skep Royd	Chellow	ONb scip, OE rod, sheep clearing
Small Tail	Sandy Lane	OE taegl, a spit of land. Later called Woodhouse Grove
Small Tail Road	Sandy Lane	Cottingley Road
Spa Well	Chellow; North Hall.	Well believed to have healing qualities
Spring Gardens Road	Heaton Syke	Named after the spring or stream and the gardens which sloped towards the reservoir
Stackwell Close		Enclosure and well
Stocking	Ashwell	OE stoc, ing, a clearing from which tree stumps have not been removed
Strawberry Bank	Chellow	Bank on which wild strawberries grow; always pronounced 'Strewberry'
Stubbing	Heaton Shay	OE stub, ing, a clearing from which tree stumps have been removed
Sugar Hills	Chellow	Hills containing sweet (fertile) soil
Sun Harry Royds	Frizinghall	Possibly OE swin, swine (see Harry Royds)
Syke	(various)	ON sik, a small stream
Taffymires	Red Beck	Almost certainly toffee-mires, a sticky morass of wet clay
Tentercroft	Frizinghall	Croft where cloth is tentered (stretched)
Tewit Well	Bingley Road	ME tuwytte, a peewit
Toft		ON topt, an enclosure
Toller Lane		Lane leading to Two Laws near Oakworth
Tunstall		OE tun, stall, a farmstead
Wantna Close	Frizinghall	Origin and meaning uncertain
Weather Royd		OE wether, rod, a clearing in which wethers (sheep) graze

Whiteley (Whitley, Whetley) Lane	Heaton	The white (or wheat) field
Wilmer Drive/Road	Heaton of the Fields	Named after the Wilmer family, ancestors
Wilsden Road	Sandy Lane	Formerly Swainroyd Lane
Withins, The		OE withign, the willow copse

East front of Heaton Hall, 1883.

Bradford Libraries

Bradford Burgess Rolls and Electoral Registers
Bradford Newspapers
Bradford Parish Church Registers
Bradford Post Office Directory, 1900
Electoral Registers
Heaton and Frizinghall Church Magazine, 1899-1910
Heaton Baptist Chapel Registers
Heaton Census Returns
Heaton Commons Inclosure Award, 1781
The Heaton Review
Heaton Tithe Award, 1848
Mr George Baron's estate records
Rosse and Field family archives, the Rt. Honorable the Earl of Rosse
St Barnabas' Church minute books
St Bede's School Magazine
Trade Directories

West Yorkshire Archives, Wakefield

Heaton Local Board Records
Land Tax Records, 1703-1830
Quarter Sessions Records
Toller Lane and Bluebell Turnpike Trust Records
Vint, Hill and Killick collection
West Riding Deeds

History of Bradford by John James, 1841
History of Manningham, Heaton and Allerton by W. Cudworth, 1896